CHARLEMAGNE

CHARLEMAGNE

Roger Collins

palgrave
macmillan

Published by
PALGRAVE
Houndmills, Basingstoke, Hampshire RG21 6XS and
175 Fifth Avenue, New York, N. Y. 10010
Companies and representatives throughout the world

PALGRAVE is the new global academic imprint of
St. Martin's Press LLC Scholarly and Reference Division and
Palgrave Publishers Ltd (formerly Macmillan Press Ltd).

ISBN 10: 0-333-65054-9 hardcover
ISBN 10: 0-333-65055-7 paperback

ISBN 13: 978-0-333-65054-7 hardcover
ISBN 13: 978-0-333-65055-4 paperback

This book is printed on paper suitable for recycling and
made from fully managed and sustained forest sources.
Logging, pulping and manufacturing processes are
expected to conform to the environmental regulations
of the country of origin.

Transferred to digital printing 2001

Printed and bound in Great Britain by
CPI Antony Rowe, Chippenham and Eastbourne

For Judith

CONTENTS

PREFACE

The current lack of a monograph-length treatment of the reign of Charlemagne in print in English is rather surprising in the light of the importance long attributed to the man and to his achievements. It may be that the approach of the millennium, which brings with it the 1200th anniversary of Charles's imperial coronation in Rome on 25th December 800 will generate renewed interest in that event and in its wider contexts. If so, it will be interesting to see if quite so confident or triumphalist a tone is struck as in the 1965 celebrations at Aachen. An early twenty-first century Charlemagne may prove to be subtly different to a mid-twentieth century one.

One consequence of the lack of easily available alternative treatments has been a sense that this book should try to cover as much ground as possible, without thereby failing to have new things to say. Even so, it has seemed better to avoid a strictly chronological structure, in favour of more analytical discussion of the various areas of interest and activity that marked Charles's reign. A structural debt to Einhard's *Vita Karoli* is happily acknowledged. This also has the virtue of making it easier to see the first Frankish emperor's achievements in the light of what had gone before. All too often this reign and this monarch have been taken as a starting point, and while there are many fine contemporary treatments both of later Carolingian history and of the legacy and memory of Charlemagne across the Middle Ages and beyond, very rarely have the man and his period been examined in terms of what was owed to both his Merovingian and earlier Carolingian predecessors and their times. This does seem to be required.

It is not really possible to write a biography of Charlemagne, in the sense of a work that uncovers its subject's personal hopes, fears, aims, ambitions, phobias and foibles, and tries to explain what he thought, rather than something of what he did. The latter may give some limited clues to the former but all interpretations may prove contentious. This is equally true for all but a handful of individuals before modern times. In the case of Charlemagne, or Charles as he will normally be called here, such a view might seem slightly too pessimistic. There is, after all, the *Vita Karoli* or *Life of Charles* mentioned above. But reasons will be given at various stages in this book for not placing quite as much trust in Einhard as he might have wished us to give him. To be fair, most other Frankish historical writings of the time prove to be equally idiosyncratic, partisan and occasionally downright mendacious.

In general, what follows is as far as possible source-driven. Which is to say, it depends more upon the primary sources of evidence for the period, reference to which will be found in the notes, than upon modish or other methodologies. However, it is hoped that something of recent British, European and American scholarship will find itself reflected throughout. It may seem perverse to appear apologetic about using evidence, but these are strange times. Historians can be found muttering darkly in their prefaces about 'the tyranny of evidence' and the need to break free of its shackles. If by that they mean that they might earn better money writing fiction, they are probably right, but there is little point in thinking that what they thereby produce is history.

To make this book as comprehensible as possible, I have in general quoted original sources in translation, using several of the excellent modern versions that are listed in the bibliography. Their authors have served to render this period more accessible to students and general readers alike. Particular acknowledgement in this respect is owed to David King, whose monumental volume of translations of texts relating exclusively to the reign of Charlemagne is magisterial in its breadth and its depth and in its renderings of the far from easy language of the many literary and administrative texts that it includes. In a few cases I have made my own translation or imposed minor modification on those taken from the work of others.

I am enormously grateful to Janet Nelson, Tom Brown and David Ganz for reading through all or part of this book in typescript and for making numerous valuable comments and suggestions, and saving me from error at various points. I have also greatly benefited from generous gifts of stimulating off-prints relating to this period from many friends, not least from Jörg Jarnut and Janet Nelson. The latter kindly let me see her important article 'The Daughters of Desiderius' prior to its publication. The book was written during my time as a Fellow of the Institute of Advanced Studies at the University of Edinburgh. A more delightful context could not be imagined, and I am exceedingly indebted to the Institute's Director Peter Jones and to his Assistant Anthea Taylor for making my stay so pleasant and productive. The dedication to my wife, Judith McClure, a fellow hunter on the trail of Charlemagne, marks the greatest debt of all, and it is made not least as a reminder of Latin Vespers at Christmas time in the Palace Chapel in Aachen in its 1200th anniversary year.

LIST OF ABBREVIATIONS

ARF	*Annales Regni Francorum* (*see* Kurze)
BEC	*Bibliothèque de l'Ecole des Chartes*
Boretius	Alfred Boretius (ed.), *Pippini, Carlomanni, Caroli Magni Diplomata, MGN Diplomata*, vol. 1
CCSL	*Corpus Christianorum, series latina*
CLA	Elias Avery Lowe, *Codices Latini Antiquiores*, 11 vols and a Supplement (Oxford, 1934–71)
DA	*Deutsches Archiv für Erforschung des Mittelalters*
Dümmler	Ernst Dümmler (ed.), *Epistolae Alcuini, MGH Epp.*, vol. 4
FS	*Frühmittelalterliche Studien*
Godman and Collins	Peter Godman and Roger Collins (eds), *Charlemagne's Heir: New Perspectives on the Reign of Louis the Pious* (Oxford, 1990)
Halphen	Louis Halphen (ed.), *Eginhard, Vie de Charlemagne* (Paris, 1938)
KdG	*Karl der Große: Leben und Nachleben*, 4 vols (Düsseldorf, 1965), ed. H. Beumann *et al.*
Kurze	Friederich Kurze (ed.), *Annales regni Francorum inde ab a. 741 usque ad a. 829, qui dicuntur Annales Laurissenses maiores et Einhardi, MGH SRG*, vol. 6.
MlöG	*Mitteilungen des Instituts für österreichische Geschichtsforschung*
NA	*Neues Archiv*
NCMH	*New Cambridge Medieval History*, vol. II: *c. 700–c. 900*, ed. Rosamond McKitterick (Cambridge, 1995)
Pardessus	Jean Marie Pardessus (ed.), *Diplomata, Chartae, Epistolae, Leges Aliaque Instrumenta ad Res Gallo-Francicas Spectantia*, 2 vols (Paris, 1849)
PBA	*Proceedings of the British Academy*
PL	*Patrologia Latina*, ed. J. P. Migne

Rev.	Revised version of the *Annales Regni Francorum* (*see* Kurze)
Settimane	*Settimane di studio del Centro italiano di studi sull'alto medioevo* (Spoleto)
Wallace-Hadrill	*The Fourth Book of the Chronicle of Fredegar,* ed. J. M. Wallace-Hadrill (London, 1960)

MGH   *Monumenta Germaniae Historica*, various series:

AA	*Auctores Antiquissimi*
Capit.	*Capitularia Regum Francorum*
Conc.	*Concilia*
Diplomata	*Die Urkunden der Karolinger*
Epp.	*Epistolae*
Leges	*Leges Nationum Germanicarum*
Poetae	*Poetae Latini Medii Aevi*
SRG	*Scriptores Rerum Germanicarum in usum scholarum*
SRL	*Scriptores Rerum Langobardicarum et Italicarum*
SRM	*Scriptores Rerum Merovingicarum*
SS	*Scriptores*

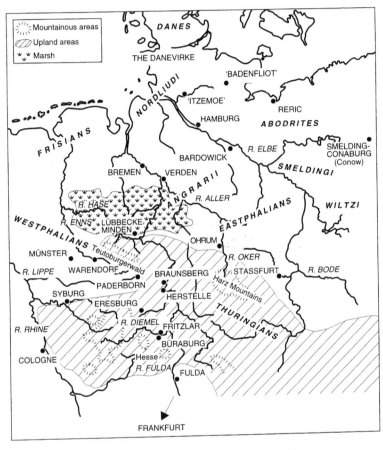

Map 1 Saxons, Danes and Slavs, 772–814

Map 2   Lombard Italy, *c*. 770

xiii

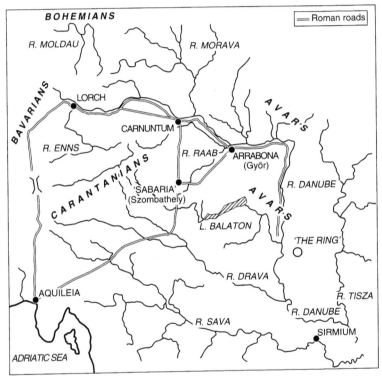

Map 3 The Avar Wars, 791–6

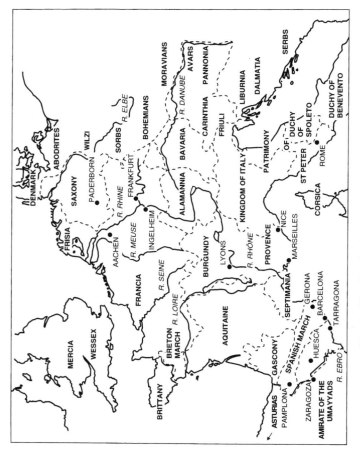

Map 4 The Carolingian Empire in 814

Based on B. W. Scholz, *Carolingian Chronicles* (Ann Arbor, MI, 1970).

XV

1

THE FRANKISH INHERITANCE

The Sources of Information

Tall, round-headed, with unusually large eyes, a short neck, a long nose and a rather protruding stomach is how Charles the Great (768–814), or Charlemagne, appeared in his later life, according to the author of the first biography of a secular ruler to be written in Europe since Late Antiquity.[1] It may not sound very flattering, and when the added observation is made from his coinage that he had a long moustache and no beard, the description may sound better suited to be that of Obélix, the tubby friend of the cartoon character Astérix, than that of 'The Father of Europe'. However, his former courtier, the lay abbot Einhard (d. 836), who wrote the *Vita Karoli* or 'Life of Charles' at some point in the second half of the 820s, a decade after his former master's death, had no intention of belittling him.[2] On the contrary, from his closely followed literary model, the 'Life of Augustus' that was written by the Roman biographer Suetonius around AD 125, Einhard had learned that the physical description of the subject of such a work, however highly admired, should be as accurate and detailed as possible, not sparing bad teeth, a wizened finger, a limp and gall-stones.[3]

Such apparent precision in matters of appearance and tastes should not be taken as a guarantee of accuracy in all other respects. Einhard's *Vita Karoli* can provide information or additional details not to be found in other sources, as for example in its account of the disaster that overtook the Frankish rear-guard at the battle of Roncesvalles in 778, but it can just as easily, and even more frequently, be shown to be erroneous or misleading on a wide range of subjects.[4] The re-creation of a historical genre that had been extinct for around half a millennium, that of the biography of a ruler, was no easy task. Einhard was feeling his way in what was effectively a new branch of literature with his only guide a work that was written 700 years before his own day, and he also had an agenda of his own to satisfy. He left only the briefest account of why he wrote what he did and in the way that he chose, and indeed in its original state his work gave no indication of its authorship.[5] However, he made it clear that his purposes did not include providing a detailed narrative of his subject's life and times.[6] His real intentions and, perhaps too, the nature or limits of his memory would dictate otherwise. But what those intentions were, like the question of exactly when he wrote, remain uncertain and matters for scholarly debate.[7] Moreover, it is a debate that concerns the troubled times of the reign of Charles's successor, the emperor Louis the Pious (814–40) rather more than it does his own. For these reasons it may be that Einhard and his *Vita Karoli* will not loom as large in this present study of his subject as might be expected.

That it is possible in part to circumvent Einhard is due not least to the substantial quantity and character of the other sources of evidence available for Frankish history in the late Merovingian and early Carolingian periods. These include administrative and legal texts and documents, as well and as much as annals, chronicles and hagiography. But any survey of the evidential base for the study of late seventh- and eighth-century Francia is bound to begin with the latter. Narrative historical sources are, obviously, of particular value in putting flesh on the past and giving vignettes of individuals and groups in their contexts, whatever may be felt about the prejudices and idiosyncrasies of their authors. For the earlier Merovingian period Gregory of Tours (d. 594) provides an almost overwhelming series of images and vistas of the society and politics of his times in his massive *Ten Books of Histories*.[8] In their way these may have served as much to distort as to illuminate modern understanding of later sixth-century Francia, but they, together with the same author's corpus of hagiographic writings, do offer a mighty resource upon which to draw in trying to understand the politics, culture, social organisation and world-view of that period.

There is nothing of comparable scale and degree of detail to take its place when attention is turned to the seventh and early eighth centuries. A compilation known as *The Chronicle of Fredegar*, which was put together some time after 660 and prior to 714, collects together a series of earlier historical texts, including a much abbreviated version of the first six books of Gregory's *Histories*, adding to them both a series of insertions and interpolations and a more substantial section of new material relating to the period 594 to 642.[9] The latter seems unfinished and the structure of the whole compilation suggests that the anonymous author left his work uncompleted. Although this work was to be significantly revised and extended in the middle of the eighth century, the chronological gap between 642, where the account of the original

'Fredegar' author ended, and 721, where the later Continuator began to add new material, was only filled by the insertion into the collection of a version of another, brief, anonymous historical text now called the *Liber Historiae Francorum* or 'Book of the History of the Franks'.[10]

This latter was composed at the monastery of Saint-Denis just north of Paris, or possibly at Soissons, around 727.[11] In the scale and the detail of its narrative and in chronological precision it is a much lesser work than that of 'Fredegar', and is one that raises more problems than it settles in such matters as the regnal dates of the Frankish rulers in the second half of the seventh century.[12] Its greatest value lies in the fact that it was written from a western Frankish or Neustrian view point and thus its account is not tinged by the propagandistic presentation of the history of the late seventh and early eighth centuries that is so marked a characteristic of later narratives written under the aegis of the new Frankish royal house of the Carolingians, which replaced the previous Merovingian dynasty in 751 and was of eastern Frankish origin.

The problem of deliberate distortion of the historical record in the interests of the Carolingian dynasty is one that appears full grown in the revised and continued version of *The Chronicle of Fredegar*, that was produced around 751 for a Count Childebrand, uncle of Pippin III (751–68), the first king of the new line. The rewriting of the history of the rise of the family remains a central feature of Frankish historiography for the rest of the eighth century and beyond, as can be seen both in the opening narrative of a compilation known as the *Annales Mettenses Priores*, thought to have been written in the convent of Chelles around 805/6, and in the introductory section of Einhard's *Vita Karoli* of the later 820s.[13] This process of historical myth-making and the re-use of already contaminated sources in later compilations adds to the difficulties of employing narrative and annalistic texts in the reconstruction of late Merovingian and early Carolingian politics and society.

Far less tendentious, though often frustratingly brief, are the various sets of annals that begin to record events in Francia on a more or less year-by-year basis from around 708 onwards. It has been thought that these originated as notes added in some monasteries to lists recording the dates, which had to be calculated for each year, for the celebration of Easter. To these annual tables scribes began adding very short notices of recent events of local or kingdom-wide significance.[14] At least one of them seems to have developed out of a calendar or record of obituaries of Irish origin.[15] When such records began to be kept, and what the relationships are between the various extant sets of annals and between them and other lost ones whose existence has been presumed remain questions that are not easy to answer.[16] A date in the 730s or 740s may be the best guess for the beginning of the process of regular annal making at one or two centres in the north-east of Francia and in the Moselle valley, possibly influenced by Irish practices.[17] These earliest sets of annals now only survive as parts of the longer and later compilations that developed in stages from them. They have received their names from a variety of sources, such as the location of a manuscript containing them (e.g. the 'Wolfenbüttel Annals' for the years 741–805), the name of an early editor (e.g. the *Annales Petaviani*, covering 708–99, called after Alexander Petau), or the general or precise location of the place in which they were thought to have been written (e.g. the *Annales Mosellani* for 703–98 and the *Annales Sancti Amandi* for 708–810 respectively).

The most important of these fuller sets of annals, not least for its detailed account of events in the reign of Charles, is the one known as the *Annales Regni Francorum* or 'Annals of the Kingdom of the Franks', though this is only a title given it by nineteenth-century scholars.[18] It begins its series of annual entries with the year 741, and in most manuscripts continues on to 829. The detailed nature of the information it contains, its sensitivity on certain issues and its lack of other clear geographical point of reference led to the suggestion being made and accepted that it was an 'official' compilation. That is to say it constituted a record made at the Carolingian court, representing the view on events of the Frankish rulers and their advisors. It was also suggested that for much of the period it covers, in particular from the early 790s up to 829, it was kept up on an annual basis, thus making of it a virtually contemporary as well as a uniquely privileged account.[19] Although these views have gone almost unchallenged for over a century, they must be said to be less convincing than is normally allowed.

One reason for suspecting that the *Annales Regni Francorum* were officially sponsored and overseen was the omission from their record of certain events, such as the conspiracy hatched against Charles in 792 by his eldest son. Likewise, certain military episodes in which the Franks were wholly or partially defeated are not to be found mentioned in these annals. The most notorious example of this is the lack of any reference to the destruction of Charles's rearguard by the Basques in 778, but there are also certain debacles on the part of some of his subordinate commanders in Saxony that are discreetly omitted. These lacunae can, however, be easily detected, thanks to the existence of a revised and partially expanded version of the *Annales Regni Francorum*, which has survived in several manuscripts.[20]

It was once thought, because of the existence of certain parallels between it and the *Vita Karoli*, that this Revised version was the work of Einhard. For linguistic and stylistic reasons this has long been recognised not to be tenable.[21] It is also possible to show that the intellectual formation of and the library resources available to the author of the Revised version in no way accord with what may known in these respects of Einhard.[22] No other attempt to identify this author has come even close to gaining acceptance. Here he will just be known as 'the Reviser'. The work itself is clearly derived from the *Annales Regni Francorum*, but apparently only extends from 741 to 801. In its entries for those years it can both expand the narrative of its model and considerably change its style and vocabulary. The Reviser was also extremely well read, and his work is interlarded with reminiscences and phrases taken from a wide range of classical authors, mostly but not exclusively historians.[23] It is a far more learned and more polished work than the *Annales* and in most respects more informative. Although it ceases to offer an alternative text on completing its entry for the year 801, most manuscripts that contain it continue without interruption with the entries for the years 802 to 829 that would also be found in the *Annales Regni Francorum*, apart from a few and very minor stylistic differences in the annals for 802 to 812.[24] It has thus been argued that the Reviser was working after 812, and quite probably after Charles's death in 814, as the king might have misliked the publication of the defeats and near disasters that had been carefully omitted by the *Annales*. On the other hand, it is assumed that it must have been completed before Einhard wrote his *Vita Karoli*, either around the year 817 or more probably in the mid to late 820s.

Such confidence is deceptive. The grounds for believing that Einhard used the Reviser's work are actually very thin. Moreover, stylistically and conceptually, and in terms of literary borrowings, there is almost complete continuity between the Reviser's work and the section of the *Annales Regni Francorum* covering the years 802 to 829.[25] In other words, the latter, rather than being a section of *Annales* tacked on to the Revised version, is more probably an integral part of the Reviser's text that also came to be borrowed as a conclusion for the *Annales*. This could mean that it was composed after 829.

The *Annales* themselves have long been seen to be a composite work, written by more than one author. (Although here for convenience reference will be made to 'the Annalist', to mean the author of the entry or section of these annals under discussion.) In particular, a break around 788 has been recognised. Recent study, however, has shown that some of the ideological slants that can be detected in the pre-787 section only make sense in the context of the events and the policies being pursued in or after 788.[26] In other words, apart from its final entry the 741 to 787/8 section is not a contemporary record, and was certainly not kept up on a year-by-year basis. A thin and ill-informed piece of patching links this text, across the divide of the years 789 to 792, to the next major section of annals, which extends only up to 801. As has been seen, the 802 to 829 portion of the text could have been composed as late as 829/30, possibly in connection with the making of the Revised version. While the details of these arguments could be pursued further, it is enough to say that there are grounds for doubting the long-established views on the compositional history of both the *Annales* and the work of the Reviser.

One reason for believing in a process of year-by-year keeping up of the former was the apparent evidence for such a practice in another major set of Frankish annals. These are the so-called *Annales Laureshamenses* or 'Lorsch Annals', named after the important monastery in the middle Rhine where it was thought that they were composed. These take the form of a continuation of an earlier set of annals, known as the *Annales Mosellani* or 'Moselle Annals' (probably compiled in Metz), whose text is followed with only minor variations up to the year 785. In its account of the years 786 to 803 the 'Lorsch Annals' becomes an original and highly informative work. One manuscript fragment containing the section of text from 794 to 803 with each yearly entry being written in a different hand seems to show that a variety of scribes were adding to the manuscript on a presumably yearly basis, making this set of annals a more or less contemporary record.[27] The palaeography of this manuscript has also shown that it was not actually written at Lorsch, but more probably to the south-east in Alamannia, which must thus be the area of composition of these annals.[28]

Another set of relatively full annals that deserves mention here has an even more chequered compositional history. This is the text known as the *Chronicle of Moissac*, named after the monastery to the north-west of Toulouse where the manuscript containing it was discovered. (Though this codex is now thought to have been written in the Catalan monastery of Ripoll.)[29] The work itself takes the form of a chronicle extending from Adam up to the year 828, but now lacking the section covering the years 716 to 770. While the act of compilation of this work may well have taken place at a later date and certainly involved the re-use of other easily identifiable texts, it is thought that this *Chronicle* incorporates a set of early annals composed in south-west Francia both in some of its entries relating to the eighth century, and particularly in its treatment of the period from 803 to 828.

While the technicalities of the problems of source criticism applied to the various Frankish annals may not always make easy reading, it is important to recognise that these sources, which present the primary level of information relating to the military, diplomatic and political activities of Charles's reign, need careful handling. None can be said to be free of doubts as to its precise compositional history, in terms of when, where and in how many stages it was compiled. On the other hand, it is only with their aid that any form of narrative account of this period can be constructed. In certain areas other kinds of evidence can be used to cross-check what the annals appear to tell us, but this is relatively infrequent.

A form of source material that has recently begun to be exploited both for its occasional insights into later seventh- and eighth-century politics and for perceptions of late Merovingian and early Carolingian society more generally is that of hagiography. The collections of saints' lives produced in Francia are far and away the most substantial of any such works written in the early medieval centuries. Those relating to the Merovingian period have been collected into seven substantial volumes, though even these do not include the full corpus of Frankish hagiographic texts.[30] Problems, however, exist in respect of the dating of many of these works. While the subjects of the *Lives* may readily be identified as bishops, monks, nuns and other holy men and women living in the Merovingian or early Carolingian periods, the date of composition of the works that record their lives and miraculous deeds needs to be argued out in each individual case. Early saints may only have had a *Vita* or 'Life' written of them in a much later period, or such a text first composed in the Merovingian period may have been heavily interpolated or entirely rewritten under the Carolingians.[31] It has been shown in the latter case that the perceptions and presuppositions of the revised work will overwhelmingly be those of the period of the re-writing rather than those of its first composition.

It can not be said that even the genuine Merovingian compositions are particularly valuable sources of information. In most cases they were composed for liturgical purposes, to provide a reading for the saint's feast day. *Lives* of episcopal saints might have thus been used publicly in the churches in which they were buried, while those of monastic saints might have enjoyed a more restricted audience within the enclosed community. The subsequent proliferation and translation, both by gift and by theft, of relics, that was a feature of the Carolingian period, explains the expansion in the genre.[32] 'New' saints were found, who needed an appropriate *Life*, or existing texts of Merovingian origin were felt to be stylistically unacceptable in later periods. Both in the earlier and the later works there is much that is highly stylised and standardised. Actual historical references are kept to a minimum, even in the case of bishops otherwise known to have been of great contemporary power and influence in secular politics, such as Leudegar of Autun and Audoen of Rouen.[33] While the dearth of other narrative texts has enhanced the value of what little can be gleaned from these works, their merits are in danger of being exaggerated.

For the period of the reigns of Pippin III and Charles hagiographic sources are relatively scanty, but they can offer some points of detail in their references to secular affairs. While a number of works concerning earlier eighth-century holy men were actually composed at this time, such as Alcuin's *Life of Willibrord*, those Lives that relate to subjects who were active under Charles were in all cases written after the latter's death in 814. They are also by and large problematic in one way or another. A *Life of Alcuin* written soon after 829 by an unnamed monk of Ferrières, of which Alcuin had once been abbot, is now considered to be more informative and reliable than used to be believed.[34] On the other hand, the lives written by Paschasius Radbertus (died c. 865) of Charles's two cousins Adalhard (d. 826) and Wala (d. 836) are very idiosyncratic and highly rhetorical. Like Paschasius, who regarded himself as their disciple, they had both held the office of abbot of Corbie. Both enjoyed periods of political favour and of disgrace under both Charles and Louis the Pious. The little hard information that Paschasius tries to convey is not easy to disentangle from its literary setting, and is far from reliable.[35]

Rather more valuable are quasi-hagiographic collections that were intended to form histories of particular bishoprics and monasteries. An Italian scholar, Paul the Deacon, who spent a few years in the 780s attached to the Frankish court, was commissioned to write such a biographical history of the bishops of Metz. This see enjoyed a special prominence, not least because it had been held in the early seventh century by a supposed ancestor of the ruling Carolingian house. Unfortunately, Paul did not make use of any of the no-doubt copious documentary records of the bishopric. On the other hand, a monastic equivalent, the 'Lives of the Holy Fathers of Fontanelle', records the incumbencies of most of the successive abbots of the monastery of Saint-Wandrille in the lower Seine valley, from its foundation up to the 830s, making considerable use of archival texts, which would not otherwise have survived.[36]

While literary sources, both historical and hagiographic, may be both scarce and sparse, documentary evidence is by early medieval standards starting to become more plentiful. While written records of a wide range of governmental and private activities were produced in very large quantities in the time of the Roman Empire, few of these have survived, particularly from the western provinces.[37] The making of written records continued to be a feature of the centuries following the end of Roman rule in western Europe, although the range of types of such documents was greatly reduced and the role of the state in both the production and the preservation of such documents declined dramatically. Amongst examples of such items preserved from this period are the wooden 'Albertini Tablets' from North Africa and a wide spectrum of texts of late sixth- and seventh-century date, ranging from school exercises to legal deeds, scratched on slate in Spain.[38] Large-format papyrus documents preserved in Ravenna are the best examples of episcopal record making and the preservation of private archives from this same period.[39]

Francia is somewhat less fortunate, though it has been shown that town archives, in which the records of private legal transactions could be deposited, survived at least into the sixth century.[40] However, ecclesiastical institutions, such as monasteries and episcopal churches, had an interest in preserving the written records of gifts, sales and confirmations of which they were the beneficiaries, and upon which they could depend if a legal challenge were ever launched against their title. Thus, some of the documents drawn up for such establishments, above all by the Merovingian kings, have been preserved. In a small but striking number of cases, mainly that of the monastery of Saint-Denis, the original deeds themselves survive.[41] More frequently such texts are now available only in the form of later copies, generally transcribed into large ledgers full of such texts, known as cartularies. With these later copies, there always exists the possibility that the documents were 'improved' in the greater interest of the church recording them, in other words they might have inauthentic interpolations inserted into them, or, indeed, the entire document could be fabricated.

While problems of the detection of forgery and the criteria for the establishing of authenticity remain crucial in the evaluation of the documentary record that survives from seventh- and eighth-century Francia, it is safe to say that a moderately substantial body of such materials is available, either in original form or as later copies.[42] The greater part of them are records of donations, though there is also an interesting body of texts recording the outcome of legal disputes over property heard before the kings.[43] A small number of wills are also extremely valuable not only in providing all too rare evidence of the nature, location and extent of an individual landowner's estates, but also in giving the possibilities in some cases of relating this to what is known from literary sources of his involvement in the political life of his day. It has been possible to draw substantial deductions of such kinds from the extant wills of bishop Bertramn of Le Mans (dating from 616) and of a Provençal nobleman called Abbo, who became an active supporter of Charles's grandfather Charles Martel in the south in the 730s.[44]

Such opportunities are, unfortunately, very rare. A will is exceptional in that it might contain information concerning an individual or a family's entire estate within the compass of a single document. Normally, however, such a picture could only be built up from an overview of the complete record collection of a landowning family. However, such private archives hardly ever survive.[45] Families die out, while institutions are better able to survive. Thus, it is in church collections that early documents and later copies have normally been preserved. Even here the vicissitudes of time have proved fatal to by far the greater proportion of such records. It is thus very difficult now to reconstruct the full extent of the holdings of land of a particular monastery or episcopal church at this time. Two monasteries, both founded in the eighth century, are exceptional in this respect. Both Fulda and St Gallen have managed to preserve relatively large numbers of early charters, recording some of the purchases, exchanges and gifts of property in which they were involved.[46] Although these do not represent the full range of the documents they once owned, enough of these have survived to give some firm impression of the extent and nature of the two monasteries' landed estates and thus the economic underpinning of their institutional existence.

Most of these documents are humble, both in terms of their physical appearance and the social level of the participants in the processes that they record. Royal charters are far grander both physically and in the potential significance of the acts recorded. In a fortunate but small number of cases names will appear in them that can be linked to the narrative histories. Unfortunately, unlike some styles of charter production, it was not thought necessary with Frankish royal documents for the king's deed to be witnessed. Witness lists can provide valuable information about the composition of a royal court, providing the names of those who were in attendance on the monarch at particular dates and in some cases recording their titles and offices. So the lack of such an element in Frankish charters is to be regretted. In the latter the king's name and usually that of an official called the *Referendarius*, who supervised the drawing up of the document, are all that are provided.[47] Even the dating is done only by reference to the ruler's regnal year. Where the inadequacies of the narrative sources has left argument open about royal chronology, the charters are thus unable to be of help. All in all, while useful deductions can be made, or at least hypotheses be advanced, on the basis of the Frankish royal and other documents, not enough has survived to provide the kind of reconstructions of family and institutional property holdings, and the impact of these on local and kingdom-wide politics, that can be undertaken in so many cases in the later medieval centuries.

Another major body of written source material of an administrative type, that is particularly distinctive of the Frankish kingdoms, especially in the Carolingian period, is the collection of texts known as Capitularies. These have aroused considerable scholarly interest, as their nature and purpose have proved less than self-evident.[48] The name, which was in contemporary use, derives from the division of the texts into separate chapters (*capitula*) or sections, and they may have derived their form from ecclesiastical legislation, particularly conciliar *acta*. Their survival has been distinctly haphazard, and some of the most important of these texts are to be found in no more than a single manuscript. Others have survived together in what appear to be deliberately made collections. Some of these divide up the contents in a systematic way, rather than keeping the individual capitularies separate. One such, composed of four sections, was formed around 806 to 808 by bishop Ghaerbald of Liège, while another was made by abbot Ansegesis of Saint-Wandrille in 827.[49] Such collections were made because the texts they contained were of immediate practical value to a working bishop or for the officers of a monastery in their daily affairs. There are references in some of the capitularies to the making of copies for keeping in the palace archives, but the fact that the emperor Louis the Pious and his advisors had to consult Ansegesis's collection in 829 would suggest that the maintenance of such central records was not always effective.

The random nature of the survival of these texts, which implies that there was probably originally a much larger number of them than are known today, and that it is possible for yet more of them to be discovered, reflects their nature.[50] Some of them are substantial documents forming what may be thought to be official records of the results of deliberations at royal and imperial assemblies. Others, however, can be rough notes made either preparatory to the final decision making process or as informal records or *aide-mémoires* for those required to implement such decisions. There are several such sets of notes for *missi*, the commissioners sent out to investigate or to transmit central government instructions to the regional authorities. In some cases it is possible to compare sets of such notes with the formal record of the assembly, and in certain instances parallel sets of notes or instructions to *missi* have survived. For example, as many as six such separate sets given to different groups of *missi* in 802 have been preserved in different manuscripts.[51]

Relatively few of these legal and administrative ordinances, or capitularies, of Charles's predecessors have survived. There are a small number of Merovingian royal decrees, mostly issued after consultations at the annual assemblies, that date from the second half of the sixth century. These were almost exclusively *edicta*, laying down new laws, adding to a growing body of royal legislation.[52] No similar texts have survived from the seventh century, though it is believed that a law code known as the *Lex Ribuaria* was promulgated in the reign of Dagobert I, prior to his establishing his son Sigebert III as king in Austrasia (i.e. at some point between 623 and 633). This is taken, by comparison with the other main Frankish law code, the *Lex Salica*, to be a codification of the legal practices of the Ripuarian or eastern Franks. Like *Lex Salica*, this is not explicitly royal legislation, though in practice it is hard to see how it could have been anything else. In both cases these codes are better seen as systematic collections of *edicta* that had come to regarded as the distinctive legal heritage of the two principal branches of the Franks. There existed a special form of capitulary text, now known as *Capitularia legibus addenda* – 'capitularies to be added to the laws' – which contained newly agreed rules and ordinances that were to be incorporated into the two Frankish codes of laws. Charles promulgated two such sets of revisions and additions in 802/3 to be added to *Lex Salica* and *Lex Ribuaria* respectively.[53] Interestingly, in a related set of instructions to *missi* they were required to present these alterations to the people of the regions or *missatica* (normally co-terminus with episcopal dioceses) to which they were sent for formal ratification, probably at the twice-yearly judicial assemblies or *mallus* that were supposed to be held in each comital district.[54] Thus, unlike the royal and imperial decisions contained in other capitularies, whose authority lay in the ruler's will, the making of changes to the two Frankish codes required at least the carrying out of a formal process of obtaining the consent of the free Frankish population at the local level.

It is not until the time of Pippin III and his brother Carloman as Mayors of the Palace that the first Carolingian capitularies laying down law in *edicta* or modifying existing legislation appear.[55] This does not mean that such items did not exist in the period between the death in 596 of Childebert II, under whom the last such Merovingian text was issued, and the 740s. It is more likely that they have not been preserved. No Merovingian collections similar to those of Ghaerbald and Ansegisis are known. Many texts of this sort will have lost their practical value when the Carolingians came to power. This limited survival, even of Carolingian texts of this kind, is less surprising than might appear, in that the procedures for the dissemination and preservation of all forms of legal and administrative texts, other than royal charters, which it was in the interests of the recipients to keep safe, were distinctly haphazard. This had, in the matter of imperial laws, also been true of the Later Roman Empire, when it was left to lawyers to make themselves aware of new legislation, rather than for the government to try to publish it widely.[56]

Other sources of evidence for this period, variable both in quantity and in value, include letters and poetry. The forming of collections of letters of *amicitia* (friendship) had been a major literary activity in Late Antiquity.[57] Such items were valued generally more for their style than for their contents, and this could lead to a certain vacuousness in the latter. Far more substantial and serious were epistolary treatises, in which a noted ecclesiastic used the form of a letter to a correspondent as the vehicle for a lengthy discourse on a theological or disciplinary topic. Both types of letter can be found in the Carolingian period. Charles set his court theologians and other favoured clerics doctrinal and other questions, to which they replied in treatises of varying length in the form of letters addressed to him. Several of these have survived, especially from the last phase of his reign. All of the leading members of the court and many others will have exchanged briefer letters, which following Roman tradition might still have been written on papyrus, as were papal epistles. The survival of such vulnerable single-sheet documents depended primarily upon their being collected and copied, either by the author or an admirer of his work, into a corpus that would be circulated in a codex. While over 300 of the letters of Alcuin, the leading clerical courtier of the middle period of Charles's reign, have been thus preserved in a series of collections of different sizes and groupings of texts, few others, including the king himself, have been so lucky. A considerable body of poetry composed at Charles's court has also survived, throwing light upon the literary tastes and skills, and some of the rivalries, of several of its leading figures, including Alcuin, Theodulf and Angilbert.[58]

To the light, however shaded and obscured, that the literary and documentary records throw on the period can be added on occasion further illumination from archaeology. The achievements of medieval archaeologists grow apace, although many sites suffered irremediably in the past when only the Roman levels were deemed to be of any serious scholarly interest. In the development of Early Medieval archaeology, attention was first directed primarily to burials. The great cemeteries, particularly in the Rhineland, of fifth- to seventh-century date provided large quantities of evidence not only for burial practices but also for the material culture, in terms of dress, adornment and other artefacts such as pottery, of Frankish society and those of other neighbouring peoples.[59] Such information, and with it the impressions that could be formed of the distribution of and frontiers between the various ethnic groups, is of great value, but gives little insight into the rituals and processes of life as opposed to those of death.

Recent study of settlements, both rural and urban, promises to redress the balance to some degree. A pioneering excavation of a late sixth- and early seventh-century Frankish village at Brebières gave some impressions of rural life in this period, making it in many respects seem even more squalid than even the most pessimistic expectations.[60] The poverty of the mud-soaked dwellings in this village and the inadequacy of the diet of its poorly endowed inhabitants may, however, not be representative. This settlement, which was abandoned early in the seventh century, probably existed only to serve a nearby royal villa, and it may well not constitute a genuine example of a village of independent cultivators. More typical and of greater evidential value may be a recently excavated village site in the western Frankish kingdom of Neustria.[61] Further such sites may well be discovered, though they are not easy to find. In some cases early village settlements will have vanished beneath later ones where there has been continuous occupation of the site.

Where this has not occurred, the complete disappearance from the surface of traces of the previous buildings makes the finding of such a settlement site exceedingly difficult, especially as it may have employed only such perishable materials as wood in its construction. However, broader regional studies, drawing on the fullest possible range of information from the archaeological record, are starting to produce more general results or even impressions that the difficulties associated with individual sites can conceal.[62]

Many of the larger settlements known to have existed in this period have so far provided no traces of themselves archaeologically. Thus, while it would be most interesting to know what late seventh- and early eighth-century Paris was like, the information is hardly forthcoming.[63] On the other hand, it is possible to know something of the location, extent and defences of early Carolingian Basle.[64] A number of towns in the south have at least provided traces of the churches and related ecclesiastical buildings, such as baptisteries and possible episcopal residences, that existed or were constructed at this time.[65] While generalisations have to be constructed around such chance and random survivals and discoveries, it seems clear that functioning towns, at least as defined by the areas within a fortified urban nucleus, in the Frankish kingdoms at this time were physically very small, and a very large percentage of their space was taken up by ecclesiastical buildings. In some cases, it is possible to speculate on the basis of literary as well as archaeological indicators that the defensible urban nucleus had contracted around a pre-existing structure that could serve as a fortification. Here, the remains of Roman amphitheatres or even theatres served particularly well.[66] However, such contraction around and into such an adapted fortress is far from being the only model. In some cases once extensive Roman towns continued to enjoy a more general occupation of most of its original intramural area, albeit with a greatly reduced population. Market gardens or small farms developed within such towns, which came to lose much of their urban character and institutions. There are thus few hard-and-fast rules, and, as in so many other ways, our ignorance remains far in excess of our knowledge of the organisation and nature of early eighth-century Frankish towns.

The same has to be said of the physical characteristics of monasteries. The existence and something of the history of many such institutions is well known and recorded in narrative and documentary sources.[67] However, all too little can be said about their physical appearance and organisation. Amongst the few exceptions that could be mentioned is Saint-Denis, outside Paris, where something of the ground-plan as rebuilt in the reign of Dagobert I (623–38/9) has been recovered.[68] For the early ninth century the evidence is considerably improved. From a handful of still-extant structures, though mostly modified in later centuries, and on the basis of some excavations rather more can be known of the physical appearance and structural organisation of a number of important monasteries of the period. These include Reichenau, Lorsch, and Fulda, as well as recently excavated San Vincenzo al Volturno in Italy. From St Gallen there has survived from around the year 820 a blue-print for a monastic lay-out, which if never executed in practice, at least gives some idea of what an ideal monastery of the time might have been intended to look like.[69]

Politics and Society in Eighth-Century Francia

From what can be gleaned from the evidence discussed above, it is possible to make some deductions about Frankish society at the beginning of the eighth century. At its apex stood the kings. From 677 until the outbreak of civil war in 715 there were no longer separate monarchs for the two main kingdoms, those of Austrasia (which was centred in the north-east and in the Rhineland) and of Neustria (between the Seine and the Loire). The latter incorporated Burgundy (in the valleys of the Saône and the Yonne), which had had a king of its own until 613. The Merovingian dynasty still enjoyed a monopoly of the royal office, but how much power in practice was wielded by the kings remains a matter of debate. Influenced by later Carolingian historiography, scholars long believed that Merovingian royal power and indeed the genetic well-being of dynasty went into a sharp decline after the death of Dagobert I in 638/9, and that what remnants of authority they still wielded were wrested from them after the battle of Tertry in 687. This view has been challenged recently, not just because of the tainted nature of the evidence upon which it is based, but because of what have been seen as proofs of the continuing exercise of royal power by some of the last Merovingians, notably Childebert III (694–711).[70] This evidence, in the form of judgements in hearings in the presence of the king given against the interests of the powerful Pippinid or Arnulfing family, ancestors of the later Carolingian kings, is by no means unambiguous, and it is also clear that there were several periods of time, extending over several years, in which the reigning Merovingian was a child, unable to exercise personal rule.[71]

From the evidence of the surviving charters and other documentary records, which normally include mention of their place of issue, it can be seen that the kings and their courts were more often than not resident in rural villas rather than towns and that they moved around between them. Gregory of Tours gives the impression that this might not have been the case or not to the same degree in the sixth century, when the kingdoms could be identified with particular towns that served as royal capitals, but the lack of comparable documentary materials from that period makes it impossible to say whether this was actually the case.[72] Unlike some of those of the Carolingians, no archaeological traces have been found of late Merovingian palace complexes, so there is no way of knowing how far they continued architectural and decorative traditions inherited from Roman rural villas. In one case in Spain an impressive fortified villa site, albeit not one that can be identified as a royal residence, has been dated to the seventh century, and gives clear proof of such continuity from Late Antiquity.[73] The same can be said of such Carolingian palaces as Ingelheim, and it would be reasonable to suspect that most Merovingian constructions would have belonged to this tradition.[74]

Of the workings of late Merovingian government little is known beyond what can be deduced from the surviving documents. It is clear from the narrative sources that under the king the principal office holder in each of the three kingdoms was the *Maior Palatii*, normally translated as the 'Mayor of the Palace'. Although the separate Burgundian Mayoralty survived the effective integration of that realm into Neustria in 623, it came to an end in the 650s. The office itself appears to be unique to the Frankish kingdoms, but its actual origins are unknown, as is the date at which it was first constituted. In practice, if not in original intention, the office could be used to give its holder considerable political and economic power and influence in times when royal authority was being weakly exercised. Not surprisingly, the title and office of Mayor seems to have been abolished when its last holder transmuted himself into the first king of the new Carolingian dynasty in 751. In the late Merovingian period rivalries between Austrasian and Neustrian Mayors served as a focus for at least the historiographical presentation of conflicts between the two kingdoms for the rest of the seventh century and the opening three decades of the eighth. Modern research, though, has tended to react against this isolation of the Mayors as the key political players, and to concentrate more on wider aristocratic factions and groupings amongst whom the holders of the Mayoral office may have been especially prominent but who also depended upon the wider backing of their noble supporters for the establishment and maintenance of their power.[75]

It is not easy to know what functions the Mayors normally carried out. They may have fulfilled various ceremonial roles in the presence of the king and certainly carried out royal judicial functions in the latter's absence or when he was too young to exercise personal authority. In such circumstances they probably also organised and led military undertakings agreed upon at the annual Assemblies. Other leading office holders included the Count of the Palace, who was responsible for the general running of the court, but in general the structure and working of the later Merovingian court remain obscure. Rather more of the organisation of the court and its hierarchy of officials in the ninth century can be recovered from the *De Ordine Palatii* ('Governance of the Palace') of archbishop Hincmar of Rheims (d. 882), which he claimed derived from an earlier treatise prepared by Charles's cousin, abbot Adalhard of Corbie (d. 826).[76] This may well record reliable details about the court personnel and practices of the latter's time, but Hincmar's reputation as an 'improver' (or forger) of texts is not savoury.[77]

From the time of the earliest accounts of the Merovingian kingdoms onwards, it seems clear that the annual Assemblies in the Spring of the leading landowners played a special role in Frankish society. Here new laws were formally proposed and agreed upon, although, as usual, we know nothing of the informal negotiations and discussions that preceded this. Nor is it clear just how 'democratic' such proceedings really were. Some stories in Gregory of Tours certainly seem to indicate that the kings had to achieve consensus rather than command it.[78] The other main function of these assemblies was to consider military objectives and to produce the armies necessary to achieve them. On this Frankish royal authority ultimately rested, whatever may be thought of traditions of sacral kingship.[79]

In the sixth-century Frankish power was extended over virtually all of the former Roman provinces of Gaul, leaving only a small enclave of the Visigothic kingdom in the region of Septimania in the extreme south-west. The expansionary drive of the Franks was thereafter checked, as far as the west and the south were concerned. Both the Visigothic kingdom in Spain and that of the Lombards in northern Italy proved resistant to further encroachments on their territories by the Frankish rulers. Only in the lands east of the Rhine, which provided an open frontier to expansion, was it possible for the Franks to extend their domination over new territories. This process of annual campaigning and territorial aggrandisement appears to have been inherent in Frankish society, and was to remain so up to the ninth century. It served as one of the principal motors of both the political life and of the economy of the Frankish kingdoms.[80] The annual assemblies of the leading men and their followers in the presence of the king seem to have been a feature of Frankish life in a way that is not apparently matched amongst the other peoples who came to dominate the parts of the former western Roman Empire. These assemblies often took place in the month of March, and have sometimes been called the 'Marchfield' (*Campus Martius*) in consequence. However, as they could also take place, according to circumstances, in April or even May, it seems more likely that the real name was 'Field of Mars' (*Campus Martis*), further testifying to the importance of the military dimension of the occasion.[81]

Something of the military machinery of the Frankish kingdom that could be brought into life each year at these assemblies can be deduced from texts of Charles's time. The accounts of his campaigns in the annals, especially in the Revised version of the *Annales Regni Francorum*, provide much useful detail on the strategy and tactics adopted by the Franks, normally with a high degree of success, in facing enemies with widely different social and military organisations and in a considerable variety of terrains, in mountains, forests and on the open steppe. Examples of these will be seen in the chapters to follow. Other, normative texts provide invaluable information, in some cases that can be corroborated archaeologically, about the structure of Frankish armies and their weapons.[82] Amongst the corpus of capitulary texts from Charles's reign is a mandate, probably issued in the Spring of 806.[83] The surviving example was that sent to an abbot Fulrad of Saint-Quentin, but is clearly one of many that will have been despatched to all major lay and ecclesiastical landholders. It orders the abbot to bring his men by a stipulated date, in this case 17 June, to the designated site of the assembly, and to ensure that they are appropriately equipped. Each horseman in the abbot's following was to have a shield, a spear, a long and a short sword, and a bow and an unspecified number of arrows. Provisions sufficient for a three-month campaign following the assembly and enough clothing to last six months were to be brought, and each unit had to be accompanied by carts, bringing a wide range of listed tools and implements. The mandate also insisted that while passing through the kingdom *en route* to the assembly, the men were not only to behave properly, but were permitted to requisition nothing more than water, firewood and grass for animal fodder from the inhabitants of the regions they traversed.

While these conditions may not have been closely adhered to in all respects in 806, let alone in earlier, more troubled periods, it is clear from this that the Frankish rulers had at their disposal a formidable and well-organised military machine, that could be relatively quickly and efficiently directed against the targets selected at the assembly, including the suppression of internal revolt and disorder. There are more details that we should like to know. While the mandate indicates with great precision the kind of armaments that the horsemen should bring, no such information is given relating to foot soldiers. Nor is it clear what kind of numbers of horsemen a magnate such as abbot Fulrad would be expected to bring. It may be assumed that some kind of ratio existed between the size or even the estimated value of estates and the military following such a lord would be required to bring to the assembly. The horsemen's equipment would be relatively expensive, and represents the kind of weaponry that would have been found only in high-status graves in the Merovingian period, when the practice of burying such items as funerary goods was still adhered to. On the other hand, another document from this period refers to the military obligations on the recently conquered Saxons as requiring every five of them to equip a sixth, to take part in this same campaign.[84] So, again, while the costs of equipping and maintaining one of abbot Fulrad's horsemen might be considerable, it may represent the contribution due from a larger number of men than the individual actually expected to turn out to accompany his lord to the assembly. There thus remains a large number of questions about the size, composition and origins of late Merovingian and Carolingian armies, to which only speculative and hypothetical answers can be given.

None of the other kingdoms of western Europe in these centuries seem so well organised or to have exercised the power that such a system gave them on so regular and in so effective a way as did the Franks. In part this may have resulted from the greater security provided by the physical frontiers of both Spain and Italy, as opposed to the very open borders of Francia, especially along its eastern side. There are indications, however, that similar obligations did exist amongst the Visigoths before the destruction of their kingdom in 711, and to a lesser degree amongst the Lombards, though the latter's state was far less centralised. However, they do not seem to have been used to anything like the same degree as in Francia. In part the obligation to military service, however organised, represented the replacement for the system of taxation that had existed under the Roman Empire, whose rulers had used it primarily to pay their armies.[85]

Despite recent arguments to the contrary, it seems that the Roman taxation system died with the Empire.[86] Indeed, even in the early fifth century, while most of the western provinces other than Britain were still under imperial rule, the system of *hospitalitas* that allotted incoming Germanic forces a fixed percentage of Roman estates may have been operated to assign tax payers to the beneficiaries of their obligations, cutting out the intermediate processes of the collecting and redistributing by the state of what was owed.[87] This, too, remains a controversial issue, but if this interpretation is correct then both the ending of the more complex Roman system of taxation and the establishment of the principle that land ownership was directly linked to the provision of military service may have resulted from the changes that took place in the first half of the fifth century. Whatever be thought of that, it does seem that under both the later Merovingians and the Carolingians state finance consisted of little more than the proceeds drawn from the exploitation of royal estates and certain customs dues.[88] The former Roman land taxes had mutated into the practice of military obligation. This explains, not least, the limited nature of the Merovingian coinage, and its exceptional lack of reference to the monarchy. While a regular 'national' coinage, in which the authority of the ruler was declared by placing of his portrait, however schematic or idealised, and his titles on the obverse, or 'heads', side of the coins, was the product of a system in which tax and other payments were collected in precious metal, which had to be seen to conform to a fixed standard of both weight and fineness, most Merovingian coinages seem to have been local products, intended for limited regional commercial purposes. The need for reference to the monarchy, which did not attempt to regulate the making of coin, was consequently reduced, and ceased entirely in the reign of Childeric II (662–75).[89]

One consequence of the disappearance of the Roman system of capitation and land taxes was the fairly rapid withering away of the administrative apparatus of the state. This in turn meant that there was little incentive to maintain the traditions and practices of secular education necessary to provide the kind of highly literate and professional bureaucracy that had been required for the running of the Roman Empire, and which continued to exist in the east, in the so-called Byzantine Empire. Frankish royal government in the later Merovingian and Carolingian periods depended upon a handful of men, probably all clerics, who served to write royal documents, though many of these may have been drawn up by their beneficiaries. The centre of this activity was the royal chapel, under the direction of the *Capellanus* or royal chaplain, whose subordinates, because of their skills in literacy and numeracy, could provide the limited scribal and record-keeping services that royal government required.[90] Royal documents were drawn up under the supervision of the *Referendarius*, whose attestation to it or that of one of his deputies would be found at the end of any charter for which he was responsible. By the later part of Charles's reign the office of *Cancellarius* or Chancellor had emerged, as that of the head of the royal writing office, which thereby became formally distinct from the chapel. A treasury would also have been required, both for the preservation and transportation of the Frankish royal treasures, accumulated over centuries and representing a tangible sense of the history of the people and its monarchy, as well as a source of real wealth, but little is known of its practical workings. Traditionally, it formed part of the royal household and was presided over by the Queen.[91]

Much of its annual income came in the form of the proceeds from the estates owned directly by the monarchy. This would have taken the form primarily of agricultural products, though it is possible that some of the local coinages of the Merovingian period were struck as a way of transmitting the proceeds of the sale of the produce of royal estates. To make use of such resources the monarchy itself became increasingly peripatetic, when not engaged in military campaigns, and the Merovingian and Carolingian kings are mainly to be found residing in a succession of rural villas. To run royal estates, relatively few of which can now be identified, would have required either a separate administrative organisation, such as that which had existed in the Late Roman period, or delegation to local officials with other responsibilities. While the Roman government had maintained two parallel finance ministries, that under the *Comes Largitionum* overseeing the general revenues from taxation and that of the *Comes Rei Privatae* administering the imperial estates, such complexity was neither possible for nor contemplated by the Franks. Supervision of the royal estates and responsibility for the revenues they generated had to be entrusted to the general regional representatives of the monarchy, the officials known as the counts.[92]

These men were royal appointees, with authority over a designated district, or 'county', whose principal duty was the provision of public justice, in the regular meeting of a court, or *mallus*, held under their presidency.[93] Such court sittings, which in larger regions might have to meet in various locations, were supposed to be held monthly, but certainly in Charles's time the lack or irregularity of meetings of the courts, as well as prejudiced or corrupt behaviour by the counts and the judges who sat with them, was a cause of frequent complaint. This was probably an even greater problem earlier in the century, when the central government was less interested in reform, and little effort was made to collect evidence of, let alone correct, such abuses.

The counts were also responsible for the maintenance of local order, and ensuring that those entitled or obliged to attend the annual assemblies and to bring armed forces for the ensuing expeditions actually did so. Their offices were in theory held at royal pleasure. In practice, however, the entrenched local political and economic power and the wider network of kinship of the men chosen for such rank made their removal hazardous. In some areas, such as that surrounding Paris, one particular family could monopolise the comital office for decades. This may be due to the entrenched strength of their position as landowners in the region, that made them the natural focus of power in it. In other cases, however, a count could be appointed who was an outsider to the district being entrusted to him, or who only had a minor landed stake in it. The surviving evidence is generally too limited to make very clear affirmations about the size and whereabouts of the estates owned by individuals or families, though some charters and wills can provide particular illumination in particular cases.

It is not easy to define the aristocracy in either the Merovingian or the Carolingian periods, despite the considerable scholarly activity devoted to the subject. As will already be clear and unlike more recent centuries, the term 'aristocracy' does not in this period refer to families holding hereditary titles. Exceptional cases apart, it was not until the later ninth century that comital and ducal offices became fully heritable. There clearly existed within Frankish society a sense of status that was quite unrelated to office.[94] That it was dependent upon wealth would seem probable, but it is possible that other factors had a part to play. It is clear that there were some families, if perhaps only a few, who were descended from Late Roman provincial aristocratic dynasties, upon whom antiquity could confer as significant a status as landed wealth. Likewise, some Frankish families that had risen to prominence under the earlier Merovingians might have origins, real or otherwise, in a distant 'heroic' past of the people that gave them a special cachet. Others clearly acquired a wealth and status under the Merovingians that predated the emergence of the Arnulfings and Pippinids, the immediate antecedents of the Carolingian royal house.[95]

Not least amongst these were the ducal houses.[96] In certain key areas, frontier districts in particular, the *Dux* or 'Duke' was a superior level of office holder to the count (*Comes*). In particular the dukes were responsible for the overall defence of the region entrusted to them, and for bringing its military resources, when commanded, to participate in royal campaigns. The Merovingian conquests east of the Rhine, especially in the time of Theuderic I (c. 511–33) and Theudebert I (533–48), had led to the subjugation of various Germanic peoples, who were placed under the authority of Frankish dukes.[97] The same happened in the south-west, where Aquitaine, and subsequently the Basque region between the Pyrenees and the Garonne, later known as Gascony, were given Frankish dukes.[98] In these cases, intentionally or not, hereditary dynasties do seem to have become established. These, despite their Frankish origins, became increasingly associated, not least through intermarriage, with the indigenous inhabitants, and in some cases subsequently came to lead them in resistance to the kings of the Franks. A case in point is Radulf who led the Thuringians in a successful revolt against the east Frankish king Sigebert III (633–56).[99] Likewise a ducal line in Aquitaine ensured the region's *de facto* independence from Frankish royal control for much of the late seventh and early eighth centuries. This was facilitated by the abrupt decline in the same period of the power of the Merovingian monarchy, a process from which the Carolingians would emerge as the principal beneficiaries.

2

THE MAKING OF THE CAROLINGIAN DYNASTY, 687–771

From Pippin I to Pippin III, 613–768

Until recently, the rise to power of the Carolingians seemed easy to explain and relatively simple to tell.[1] Few such historical certainties long survive the test of time, and what now hold sway are interpretations that are less linear and much less dictated by a sense of the inevitability of the outcome of the process. Such a change has been accompanied and in part is caused by a realisation of how effective the Carolingians were in controlling the historical record and in propagating a view of Frankish history in the seventh and early eighth centuries that was entirely favourable to their house. Few narrative sources of this period are free from this taint of *parti pris*, which also if less directly influences documentary records and much, though not all, of the ecclesiastical literature.[2] Some limited control can be exercised by use of non-Frankish sources, though these have their own problems.

The rise of the Carolingian family would previously have been described in terms of the achievements of a succession of powerful figures, who as Mayors of the Palace dominated the personalities and the policies of a series of increasingly enfeebled Merovingian kings, until finally, tiring of what had become a charade, they deposed the last of them and openly took the royal title for themselves, with the approval of the Frankish people and the assistance of the Papacy. This tale of almost unchecked Carolingian rise, with a counter-point of corresponding Merovingian decline, has at least the merits of simplicity. Moreover, it corresponds more or less with what the Carolingians thought about themselves and wished others to believe.[3] It is not entirely wrong, but is full of distortions and tendentious interpretations.

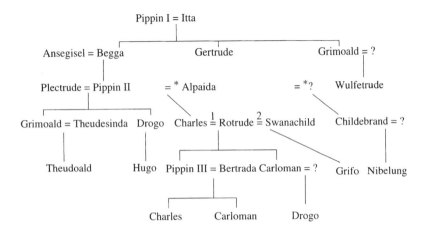

Charles's Ancestry

Despite attempts in the later Carolingian period to link the newer royal house to the old Merovingian dynasty, the earliest detectable ancestor of Charles is Pippin I (d. 639/40).[4] Pippin first appears in the *Chronicle of Fredegar* as one of the two named Austrasian leaders, the other being Arnulf of Metz, who appealed to Chlotar II in 613 to take over their kingdom from queen Brunechildis and the infant Sigebert II. It may be that the anonymous chronicler is even here exaggerating the roles of Pippin and Arnulf, in the light of their subsequent importance, as the prime beneficiary of the Neustrian king's invasion of Austrasia was a certain Rado, who was made Mayor of the Palace (613–16/17).[5] By 617/18 he had probably been succeeded by someone called Chucus, and it may not be until Chlotar II's son Dagobert I was established by his father as king in Austrasia in 623 that Pippin I finally emerged as mayor. The Fredegar chronicler anachronistically calls Arnulf bishop of Metz in 613, although he would not obtain that office until the following year, but there are no particular grounds for doubting his report that Arnulf and Pippin served as the chief advisors to Dagobert during his tenure of power in Austrasia. This lasted until 629 when he succeeded to the Neustrian kingdom and moved his court there. At that point, and hardly coincidentally, Arnulf resigned his see and retired into a life of monastic seclusion, dying at Remiremont around 640.

Doubts have been voiced about the reliability of the traditions that link Arnulf to the Pippinid and later the Carolingian family line.[6] A cult of the bishop developed in Metz, which was possibly the most important Austrasian town and diocese, and it is possible that the Carolingians found it convenient to encourage belief in their descent from such a sainted forefather. Likewise after 751, the see of Metz could expect to benefit from playing on its unique links to the new ruling house of Francia. It is notable that the evidence for the supposed marriage of a son of Arnulf to a daughter of Pippin I is to be found in what is essentially a Metz source, the *Gesta Episcoporum Mettensium* or 'Deeds of the Bishops of Metz', written by Paul the Deacon in the early 780s on the basis of information provided for him by archbishop Angilramn of Metz (d. 791).[7] Another source, possibly closer to the Carolingian house itself, is the *Annales Mettenses Priores* or 'Earlier Metz Annals', which despite their modern title were probably written c. 805/6 in the convent of Chelles, during the abbacy of Charles's sister Gisela.[8] This text merely refers to Arnulf as a close relative (*propinquus*) of the later Pippin II, rather than as his grandfather, which is what the *Gesta Episcoporum Mettensium* would have us believe.

The centre of Pippin I's landed interests, as the family's monastic patronage seems to indicate, was the central part of the valley of the Meuse. Here, following his death in 639/40, his widow Itta, also known as Iduberga, used their estates to found the convent of Nivelles over which she presided until her death in 651/2, and where she was followed as abbess by her daughter Gertrude (d. 653) and grand-daughter Wulftrude (d. 663).[9] The seventh-century hagiographic texts, above all the *Vita Sanctae Geretrudis*, that relate to Nivelles and its founding family, indicate that they encountered certain periods of difficulty after Pippin I's death.[10] The first of these may be associated with the tenure of the office of mayor by a certain Otto, and the second clearly resulted from the fall of Pippin's son Grimoald, who was almost certainly the father of abbess Wulftrude. On Pippin's death in 639/40, the mayoral office was lost to his family, going instead to Otto. However, he was murdered in 643 by Lantfrid, duke of the Alamans, at the instigation of Pippin's son Grimoald, who thereby acquired the office of mayor in Austrasia, under the nominal rule of the child king Sigebert III.[11]

On Sigebert's death in 656 Grimoald carried out a rather surprising coup, in that he had the late king's young son, Dagobert, exiled to Ireland, and placed another monarch on the throne instead, in the person of a supposed son of his own called Childebert (d. c. 662).[12] How he was able to get rid of the direct Merovingian heir and replace him with a member of his own family has long perplexed historians, and recently much more doubt has been cast on the reliability of the story, which only appears in the Neustrian *Liber Historiae Francorum* of c. 726/7. It has been suggested that Childebert might have been a genuine Merovingian, perhaps an illegitimate son of Sigebert III, and that the paternity of Grimoald was of a purely formal character.[13] He could for example have been the new king's *compater* or 'Spiritual Father'. Whatever the truth of this, his actions clearly annoyed the Neustrian court of Clovis II (639–57). Grimoald fell into the Neustrians' hands in 656/7 and was executed, eclipsing the political prominence of his family in Austrasia for two decades.

It was through a subsidiary line that they would re-emerge. Begga, the sister of both abbess Gertrude and of the unfortunate Grimoald, married a certain Ansegisel. In the subsequent Metz historiographical tradition he was the son of bishop Arnulf, and brother of another holder of the see, bishop Chlodulf (d. by 667). However, as already indicated, this is far from certain. Nothing else is known about him, other than for the fact that he was killed by a territorial rival, possibly a landowner from the middle Moselle valley called Gundewin at some point before 679.[14] It was under his son Pippin II that the fortunes of this family would dramatically revive. This was made possible not least by the latter's marriage around the year 670 to Plectrude, who was the heiress of substantial estates in the Moselle region, which seems to have contributed to the economic recovery of this branch of the descendants of Pippin I.[15]

Their political revival may have resulted from a series of coups in Neustria in the mid-670s. Following the death of Chlotar III (657–73), Ebroin, the powerful mayor of the Palace in that kingdom since c. 657, was overthrown by rivals and imprisoned in the monastery of Luxeuil in Burgundy. His candidate for the Neustrian throne, a brother of the late king called Theuderic III, was also deposed, and replaced by another of the brothers, Childeric II (c. 662–75), who had previously been ruling in Austrasia. His rule in Neustria under the aegis of an Austrasian mayor called Wulfoald proved a disaster and he was murdered in 675, allowing Ebroin to escape, eliminate his Neustrian enemies, and regain power in the name of Theuderic III. Wulfoald's failure in Neustria and subsequent death seems to have opened the way for a new leadership in Austrasia, under a duke Martin and Pippin II. Their attempt in 677 to avenge Childeric II's murder by the Neustrians failed, and following a military defeat, duke Martin surrendered on terms to Ebroin at Laon, and was promptly executed.[16]

Ebroin's own murder around 680 led to internal conflicts within Neustria, where a new mayor Waratto was overthrown by his own son, Ghislemar. Under the latter the conflict with Austrasia, where Ebroin's murderer had taken refuge, was resumed, and Pippin's forces were defeated at Namur. The death of Ghislemar and then that of his father Waratto, who had regained the mayoral office, threw Neustrian politics back into turmoil. Waratto's son-in-law Berchar became mayor, but a significant group amongst the Neustrians, led by archbishop Reolus of Rheims, made a secret approach to Pippin II for assistance. He launched a fresh Austrasian attack on Neustria, which with the aid of his Neustrian allies, resulted in the decisive defeat of Berchar at the battle of Tertry, near Saint-Quentin. The reigning Merovingian king Theuderic III (675–90/1) fell into Pippin's hands.[17]

It is difficult to recapture much detail about the ensuing period of Pippin's ascendancy, which lasted until his death in 714. But it is clear that it depended as much in Neustria as it had in Austrasia on the careful playing of factional politics. The murder of Berchar in 688, arranged by his own mother-in-law Ansfled, resolved the conflicts in that kingdom in favour of Pippin's allies, who then seem able to have rewarded themselves with the offices and no doubt some of the landed estates of those who had lost out in that conflict. Audram, one of those named as appealing to Pippin in 687, appears as Count of the Palace, the officer in charge of the daily running of the court, and a new mayor of Neustrian origin called Norbert (Nordebertus) was appointed.[18] Pippin himself played no personal role in the western court. His influence was exercised through his allies. In due course this had become so well-established that it proved possible for his family to start extending its landed interests into Neustria, and widening its sphere of influence, as for example by patronising major Neustrian monasteries such as Saint-Denis. This was achieved not least by the marriage between Pippin's son Drogo and Berchar's widow Adaltrude. This gave Drogo a large material stake in the kingdom and the traditional alliances that had supported the power of the family of Waratto.[19] One consequence of this growing Pippinid presence within Neustria was that at some point between 696 and 703 Grimoald, the second son of Pippin II, succeeded Norbert as mayor of that kingdom.[20]

Mere accidents of mortality were, however, soon to challenge this dominance. Pippin's elder son Drogo, who had held the office of Duke of Champagne, died suddenly in 708, leaving possibly four under-aged sons. Early in 714 his brother Grimoald was murdered at Liège, while *en route* to visit his ailing father.[21] Faced with a lack of legitimate, adult male heirs, Pippin was clearly influential or desperate enough to persuade or force the Neustrians to accept a child as their Mayor, in the person of his six- or seven-year-old grandson Theudoald, son of Grimoald and Theudesinda, a daughter of the Frisian king Radbod. However, it seems likely that the unprecedented step of appointing a minor to this office was deeply resented. Pippin died on 16 December 714, and by September of 715 a significant group of the Neustrian magnates were in revolt against Theudoald and his backers. They defeated those Neustrians who still supported the Pippinids in a battle near Compiègne on 26 September, and appointed one of themselves, by the name of Ragamfred, as the new mayor of the Palace. Under his leadership they invaded Austrasia via the valley of the Meuse.

In the east, the pagan Frisians under Radbod, who had been forced back under Frankish hegemony by Pippin II in the late 690s, were ready to revolt, and made a treaty with the Neustrians. At the same time Pippin's widow Plectrude was trying to secure control of the Austrasian kingdom for her grandson, the fugitive Neustrian Mayor Theudoald, by imprisoning the only surviving adult male member of the family. This was Charles, known from the ninth century onwards as 'Martellus' or 'The Hammer', a son of Pippin by a lady called Alpaida. Argument exists as to whether she was, as the Continuations of the *Chronicle of Fredegar* claim, a genuine wife of Pippin, albeit bigamously, or whether Charles was merely illegitimate.[22] As the Carolingian line sprang from him, it is not surprising that the later sources either blur the issue or describe Alpaida as Pippin's wife.

In the course of the Neustrian invasion and Frisian revolt, Charles was able to escape from custody at Cologne, where Plectrude was residing. As the only surviving adult male member of his family, whatever his origins, he seems to have been able to rally some of the Austrasians. Although the very partisan evidence tries to obfuscate this, it seems that his first moves were unsuccessful. He was defeated by the Frisians, while the Neustrians reached Cologne and forced Plectrude to surrender some of the Austrasian royal treasure, which may have included items carried off from Neustria by Pippin II after the battle of Tertry. Charles is reported as ambushing the Neustrian army on its way home, at Amblève, but whether the account of 'heavy losses' that he is supposed to have inflicted upon them should be believed is open to question. Far more clearly decisive was a battle fought at Vinchy on 21 March 717 between Charles and Ragamfred.[23] This seems to have been an outright victory for Charles, but, although he chased the Neustrians back to Paris, its main effect was to establish his undisputed authority in Austrasia. He marched on Cologne, and Plectrude was obliged to surrender the town and the rest of the royal treasure to him. Thus endowed, he was able to find a suitable Merovingian, in the person of Chlotar IV a son of Theuderic III, and set him up as the first king to reign in Austrasia since 690.

The Neustrian king, now Chilperic II who had previously been a monk by the name of Daniel, remained in the hands of Ragamfred, who bolstered his weakened military position by an alliance with the Aquitanian duke Eudo. At some point around 719/20 Charles finally invaded Neustria, and apparently took Paris and proceeded as far as Orléans without serious opposition.[24] The highly partisan Frankish accounts describe Eudo, who had become the mainstay of Neustrian resistance, fleeing before Charles just out of sheer fright. A far more likely cause of his failure to oppose the conquest of eastern Neustria was the serious military threat that he faced in the south. In 720 the vestigial Visigothic kingdom around the eastern Pyrenees, ruled by Ardo (713–20), was crushed by the Arabs, who in 721 launched their first assault on Aquitaine.[25] By this time the Austrasian king Chlotar IV had died, and faced by the Arab threat Eudo seems to have been happy to come to terms with Charles, sending him the Neustrian king Chilperic, who had taken refuge in Aquitaine, together with his royal treasure.[26]

Thus Charles gained control of the sole legitimate Merovingian king, and when he died in 721 he was able to replace him with another one in the person of Theuderic IV (721–37), a son of Dagobert III. Austrasia was already firmly in his hands, and on the death of Radbod in 719 the Frisians had been checked if not fully brought to heel. On the other hand, the rival mayor Ragamfred still controlled western Neustria, probably from a base at Angers, and the southern duchies of Aquitaine, Burgundy and Provence, as well as those to the east of the Rhine, were able to go their own way without any acknowledgement of Charles or his king.[27] While 721 may have marked a turning point in Charles's fortunes and those of his line, it was very much only the 'end of the beginning'.

In the 720s he seems primarily to have devoted his attention to restoring control over the areas across the Rhine. This may, at least in part, be due to the fact that this was an area of particular interest to and financial advantage for the Austrasian magnates, upon whom Charles depended. It also enabled him to build up his own reserves and reputation. The decade from 721 to 730 saw him undertaking campaigns against the Saxons, the Alamans, and the Bavarians.[28] That he continued to depend upon careful manipulation of aristocratic factions, and not the unchallenged personal authority that older interpretations saw him exercising, can be seen not least from his treatment of his own family. Theudoald, the former Neustrian mayor, is once found as a witness to one of Charles's few surviving charters, indicating that he could feature on occasion at the latter's court. Hugo, the son of Drogo, and thus another member of the legitimate line of the dynasty, was given considerable ecclesiastical preferment in the area of the Seine valley, coming to hold the bishoprics of Rouen, Paris and Bayeux and the abbeys of Saint-Wandrille and Jumièges.[29] These offices and the landed estates that he inherited via his father's marriage into the family of the former Neustrian mayor Waratto made him a vital figure in Charles's attempt to control eastern Neustria, all the more so while the hostile presence of Ragamfred continued to dominate the western half.[30]

It was only in 731 that Charles felt able to resume conflict in the west and try to bring Aquitaine back into subjection to the Frankish throne. The same year saw a campaign against Eudo in Aquitaine and Ragamfred's death. Real progress was made either the next year or in 733 when a powerful Arab raid was directed over the western Pyrenees and up through Gascony. Eudo's army was defeated, Poitiers sacked and Tours threatened. The Aquitanian duke was forced to appeal to Charles for help, resulting in the famous battle just north of Poitiers, in which the raiding army was defeated and its leader, the *Wali* 'Abd al-Rahman al-Gafiqi, killed. To judge by precedents from other phases of the Arab expansion, it is quite likely that their attack on Aquitaine was prompted by the knowledge of the conflict then taking place between Eudo and Charles.[31] The same is likely to have been the case with the attack on Toulouse in 721. It may also have been due to the fact that Charles was already menacing Aquitaine that he was able to bring his forces so quickly to its defence, and transform himself from its enemy into its saviour. Had he been over the Rhine or in Bavaria it is unlikely that he would have been able to react with such speed and success.

Whilst Gibbon saw the battle of Poitiers as saving Christendom, the more immediate reality was that it enabled Charles Martel to establish his control in Aquitaine.[32] Whether it was the memory of the battle or the feeling that he represented the only real defence against another Arab assault, when Eudo died in 735 Charles was able to invade Aquitaine and impose his own supporters and garrisons in the duchy with little opposition. He had to return in 736 to counter a bid by Eudo's sons to regain their father's duchy, but he does not seem to have had further trouble in the region thereafter. The same pattern of events was soon repeated in Provence. In 737 the Arabs, who had overrun the former Visigothic Septimania in 721 and were continuing to expand eastwards from Narbonne, captured Avignon. This cut the main route of trade and communications from the Mediterranean coast to the north, up the valley of the Rhône. An appeal for help to Charles led to a campaign in which Arab forces were defeated outside Narbonne, and Nimes was sacked by the Franks. As well as pushing back the Arab threat, it also made the Austrasian mayor a force to be reckoned with in the aristocratic politics of Provence. He returned with an army in 739, this time to expel the local ruler, the duke Maurontus, and to establish his own allies in positions of economic and political power in the region.[33] As Burgundy had been brought under his authority around 736, the campaign in Provence in 739 meant that Charles, now ruling as *Princeps* or Prince and without a king, had established himself and his supporters in control of most of the territory that had been under the Merovingians in their hey-day.[34] In 740 he installed one of his sons, Pippin (III), as *dux* or Duke over Burgundy and mayor of Neustria, and established the other, Carloman, as mayor in Austrasia and Alamannia.[35]

The fragility of their position was, however, to be exposed immediately after his death in 741. The various duchies on the perimeter of Francia rebelled or terminated whatever agreements they had made with Charles Martel. Pippin III and Carloman's first priorities, however, lay within Francia proper, as they clearly intended not to honour any provision that Charles Martel had made for their younger half-brother Grifo, the product of his marriage to a member of the Bavarian ducal dynasty (the 'Agilolfings') called Swanachild. The later Carolingian annals make no reference to whatever inheritance he may have received from Charles, and instead claim (mendaciously) that Grifo rebelled on his mother's advice, hoping to acquire the whole kingdom for himself.[36] A letter of archbishop Boniface of Mainz proves that Grifo was ruling legitimately in Thuringia after his father's death.[37] It thus seems probable that his half-brothers decided to eliminate him. They may have lured him from his territories, as they were able to capture him at Laon in late 741 or early 742. He was held a captive by Carloman until the latter's abdication, whilst Swanachild was relegated to the royal convent of Chelles. Another potential claimant was the former Neustrian mayor Theudoald, who belonged to the legitimate line of descent from Pippin II. One set of annals record that he was killed in 741, but gives no further details.[38]

It took far longer for the two mayors to regain their father's ascendancy over the peripheral duchies than it did for them to eliminate potential rivals within Francia.[39] A series of campaigns was initiated in 742 against the Alamans, the Bavarians and above all the Aquitanians that lasted for most of the decade. Alsace, which had been a virtually independent duchy in the hands of a family now known from the name of one of its most prominent members as the Etichonids, was deprived of its ruling house around the beginning of the decade, as was Alamannia in 746.[40] Bavaria, brought to heel in 748 only because of a succession conflict within the ruling dynasty, was able to survive as a duchy for a few more decades. There were also conflicts with the Saxons, under a leader called Theoderic.[41] Internally, too, the regime of Pippin III and Carloman may initially have been weak. In 743 they found it necessary to bring a potential candidate for the Merovingian throne out of a monastery and install him as king with the name of Childeric III.[42] No certainty exists as to his relationship to his predecessors, though it has been suggested on the basis of naming practices amongst the Merovingians that he was a son of Chilperic II (715/16–721/2).[43] He may, however, have been a far most distant relative of the previous kings than is normally allowed. As their father had been able to leave the kingship vacant after the death of Theuderic IV in 737, this need to create a new monarch was a sign that Pippin and Carloman's authority was less secure, and that a Merovingian was required to legitimise their rule.

Perhaps even more surprising was the decision, apparently announced by Carloman in 746, that he wished to lay down his office and retire into monastic life. This was not unprecedented, in that by this time a number of Anglo-Saxon kings had abdicated in order to make a pilgrimage to Rome and to die in some form of monastic life.[44] However, from the brief reports in the annals, it seems that Carloman was if anything the more active and successful of the two brothers militarily, and the problems that they faced on the frontiers of Francia were far from resolved. Moreover, Carloman had a son called Drogo, whose position needed protecting. This indeed may be the key to the issue. Pippin's elder son Charles was illegitimate, being born either in 747 or, more probably, in the Spring of 748; not till the next year did Pippin actually marry the boy's mother, Bertrada.[45] Their second son, Carloman, was born in 751. It is thus possible that whether motivated by piety or finding the system of joint rule increasingly unworkable, Carloman came to an agreement with Pippin, in the expectation that it would be his son Drogo who would eventually inherit authority in both Austrasia and Neustria. If so, the birth of Charles in 748 and his formal legitimation through Pippin's marriage in 749 would both have rendered this plan redundant and also have motivated Pippin to try to secure the full inheritance for his own off-spring.

According to the later Carolingian historiographical tradition, in 747 Carloman entrusted both Austrasia and his son Drogo to Pippin, and withdrew to Rome, where he received monastic tonsure. He founded a monastery of his own near the city, but subsequently joined the community founded by St Benedict at Monte Cassino.[46] This seems to imply that Pippin thereby legitimately became mayor of the Palace in Austrasia, as well as guardian of his nephew. However, a letter of Boniface indicates that, contrary to this, Drogo exercised the office of mayor of the Palace in Austrasia in his own name for at least a year after his father's retirement.[47] It now also seems clear that Pippin moved against him, possibly as early as 748, perhaps influenced by the recent birth of his son Charles. Drogo seems to have put up a spirited resistance to his uncle's annexation of Austrasia, a fact that the later historiography attempted with considerable success to obscure, and he seems to have remained active until 753, when finally captured and imprisoned.[48]

Drogo was not the only dissident member of the Carolingian family in conflict with Pippin in this period. The latter's half-brother Grifo, who had been captured in 741, escaped from custody in the confusion that seems to have followed Carloman's abdication in 747, and took refuge with the Saxons. His attempt in 748 to take over Bavaria, to which he had a claim through his mother, was thwarted by Pippin who invaded the duchy to install a more favourable candidate in the person of his nephew, the young Tassilo III. Pippin seems to have come to terms with Grifo, conceding him authority, though under what title is not clear, over 12 counties in Neustria. This proved short-lived, and Grifo threw in his lot with Pippin's enemy, duke Waiofar of Aquitaine (744–68).[49] In 753 Grifo was killed in a battle at Saint-Jean-de-Maurienne, *en route* for the Mont Cenis Pass into Italy, where according to the Fredegar Continuator he was intending to 'foment plots' against Pippin. Two of the latter's regional commanders, counts Theudoenus of Vienne and Frederic of the Transjura, were also killed in this battle.[50] Thus, even as late as 753 Pippin faced opposition in parts of Austrasia, in Aquitaine and in the western Alps.

It may seem surprising that he decided to make himself the first king of a new Frankish royal dynasty before he had overcome these opponents. Realisation both of the existence and of the magnitude of such continuing problems gives the lie to the older triumphalist view of the rise of the Carolingians, which saw Pippin's taking of the throne as an obvious conclusion to the supposed unification of Francia under his authority and the elimination of its external enemies.[51] That Pippin should have chosen to take the risky move of deposing the Merovingians while still engaged in trying to suppress the resistance of his half-brother and of his nephew puts his seizure of the throne in a very different light.[52] Indeed, it may be wondered if Pippin took the drastic step of deposing the last Merovingian king and substituting himself as the first ruler of a new line as a way of enhancing his status in a conflict that was still very much alive. When examined, the whole episode of Pippin's elevation is far less clear-cut than often assumed, and certainly far from being the triumphant conclusion of a clear process of the acquisition of power by a united family that had crushed all opposition to itself and gained a popular mandate from the Franks as a whole to turn itself into a royal line.

The sources are too much later in date and far too partisan to give much impression of what was really happening inside Francia, or why Pippin acted in the way he did. Some of them even suppress mention of the existence of a reigning Merovingian king at this time. Thus the author of the Continuations of the *Chronicle of Fredegar*, writing soon after 751 for Pippin's uncle, the Burgundian count Childebrand, merely stated that 'It now happened that with the consent and advice of all the Franks the most excellent Pippin submitted a proposition to the Apostolic See, and having first obtained its sanction, was made king, and Bertrada queen. In accordance with that order anciently required, he was chosen king by all the Franks, consecrated by the bishops and received homage of the great men.'[53] Later sources repeat more or less the

same story, together with additional details that should not always be taken at
face value. Thus the opening section of the *Annales Regni Francorum*, which
was probably written in the 790s, recorded that in 749 Pippin sent bishop
Burchard of Wurzburg (742–53) and Fulrad the abbot of Saint-Denis to Rome
to ask pope Zacharias if it were proper for the kings of the Franks to be
lacking in power. The pope apparently replied that it was better to give the
title of king to the man who had the power rather than to one who did not, and
in consequence 'commanded by virtue of his apostolic authority that Pippin
should be made king'.[54] The same source then reports in its entry for the year
750 that Pippin 'was elected king according to the custom of the Franks,
anointed by the hand of Archbishop Boniface of saintly memory, and raised to
the kingship by the Franks in the city of Soissons. But Childeric, who was
falsely called king, was tonsured and sent into a monastery'.[55]

Not until Einhard wrote his *Vita Karoli* in the 820s was a more extensive
justification and explanation essayed. He claimed that while Childeric III was
deposed on the orders of pope Stephen II (752–57), his dynasty had actually
lost its power long before. The real wealth and power of the kingdom were in
the hands of and exercised by the mayors of the Palace. This office Einhard
also stated was held by Pippin almost by hereditary right, having previously
been in the hands of his father and grandfather, and yet at the same time was
only conferred 'by the people' on those of outstanding wealth and distinction.[56] He also drew a deliberately satirical view of the later Merovingian
kings, presenting them as sitting enthroned with long hair and beards giving
answers to ambassadors in which they had been carefully coached by the
mayors, and travelling around the kingdom in ox carts, accompanied by a
peasant drover.[57]

While Einhard's version has long been very influential, until recently providing much of the popular level of understanding of the late Merovingians, it
is clear that it is both highly tendentious and ill-informed. It cannot be said
that the earlier Frankish sources are much better. The version of the annals is
extremely concise, while the only contemporary account, that of the
Continuator of Fredegar, is patently distorted, in trying to present Pippin's elevation as an unopposed popular choice and making no reference to the incumbent king who had to be deposed. Another very surprising silence is that of the
Liber Pontificalis, the collection of papal biographies that had been compiled
in Rome and which was normally kept up on a reign-by-reign basis. Einhard,
as previously mentioned, attributed the deposition of Childeric to the authority
of pope Stephen. This must be Stephen II, whose pontificate lasted from 752
to 757, but if so his information conflicts with the Frankish sources that place
Pippin's taking of the royal title in 750 or 751, in the time of pope Zacharias

(741–52). What is truly extraordinary, though, is that there is no mention of the event, in which the pope is said to have played a key role, in the *Lives* of either Zacharias or of Stephen II. Indeed, Stephen's biographer does not seem to have noticed that a crucial political change had occurred in Francia, as he happily assigns the title of king not only to Pippin III but also to Charles Martel. Nor is there any reference to it in the papal correspondence preserved in the *Codex Carolinus*. Compiled on Charles's order in 791, this contained copies of papal and imperial letters sent to the Frankish courts, dating back as far as 739.[58]

Another source that gives an account of Pippin's elevation is the early ninth-century Byzantine chronicle, written by Theophanes. This would seem to depend upon Frankish information, possibly from late eighth-century diplomatic exchanges between Francia and the empire. Here too what is recorded is a story referring to a pope Stephen (who again must be Stephen II), who is said to have released Pippin from his oath of obedience to the king he was about to replace. Once again, the information seems to be concerned with the subsequent diplomatic exchanges between Pippin and the pope, which led to the papal anointing of the new king in 754, and not the Frankish king-making of 751.

Indeed, so thin and contradictory is the evidence relating to this central moment in Frankish political history that, were it not for the contemporary account in the Continuations of Fredegar, there would be reasons to wonder if it ever took place. Allowing that it did, the nature of the evidence and what is known of the difficulties that Pippin was currently facing, give grounds for suspecting that the whole thing may have partaken of a distinctly 'hole in the corner' character. Indeed, it may be that Pippin felt that he needed an enhancement in his status to shore up his suppression of several of the peripheral duchies and to gain advantage over his dynastic rivals. That Soissons was chosen as the place where the ceremonies would be performed, if the Annals can be believed, is itself a little perplexing, as other ecclesiastical venues of rather greater significance existed that might have been preferred. These would have included Reims, the site of the baptism of Clovis (c. 481–c. 511), the greatest of the Merovingians and the first (certain) Christian Frankish king, as a reading of *The Chronicle of Fredegar* would have shown, and also Metz, the supposedly ancestral see of the Arnulfing–Pippinid–Carolingian line. It is possible that it was Carloman's elevation at Soissons in 768 that led the Annalist into a retrospective assumption that this must also have been his father's choice of site in 751.

On the vexed questions of whether or not Pippin III was anointed with chrism as part of the ceremonies, and whether this act was performed by the

West Saxon missionary, Archbishop Boniface of Mainz (d. 754), considerable
uncertainty must be said to exist.[59] On the one hand, it is clear that coronation,
in other words the placing of a crown on the new ruler's head, did not form
part of Frankish tradition, and would be used for the first time in the Roman
context of the coronation by the pope of Charlemagne's sons in 781. It is
equally certain that the pouring on the king's head of consecrated oil, or
unction, which had been used in the Visigothic kingdom in the later seventh
century in imitation of Biblical practices, was not previously employed by the
Franks. On the other hand, the elevation of Pippin was more than just the
enthroning of yet another Merovingian, and it may have been necessary to
find a new ritual to mark the dynastic break and to testify to the special status
of the new king and his line. If so, it remains questionable as to whence the
precedents for the use of unction for Pippin's elevation were drawn. If a
borrowing from the practices of the defunct Visigothic kingdom be deemed
unlikely, then Irish and papal origins have been suggested.[60] As, however,
there exists no evidence that any Irish king was ever anointed, the Roman
arguments win by default, as well as by their own intrinsic merits.[61] Yet it is
worth stressing that the evidence to support belief that in 751 Pippin III
received unction, either at Soissons or anywhere else, let alone by the hand of
Boniface, remains far from convincing.

Rather greater credence may be given to the claim in the annals that Pippin
III and his two sons by his wife Bertrada, Charles and Carloman, were
anointed by pope Stephen II during his visit to Francia in 754; despite the fact
that the principal contemporary Frankish source, the Continuations of the
Chronicle of Fredegar, omits any reference to it.[62] This, as previously mentioned, is the episode that was noted by both papal and Byzantine sources,
who otherwise seem entirely ignorant of the king-making of 751. The occasion for it was the papal need for assistance against military encroachment on
Rome by the Lombard king Aistulf (749–56). Through the papal vicariate
exercised by the bishops of Arles in the sixth century, Rome had come to look
to the Frankish monarchs as possible defenders of its interests against threats
that lay closer to hand in Italy. This had led, not least, to the Merovingian
Theudebert I's dramatic intervention in Italy in 539.[63] This line of policy had
also been taken up by the emperors in Constantinople, who saw the Franks, in
a part of the former Western Empire that they had no immediate prospect of
regaining as potential allies against other Germanic monarchies, notably those
of the Ostrogoths and then the Lombards in Italy, in territories that they still
hoped to control directly.[64] Although conditions in the seventh century had
limited the activities of all of these parties, the memory of such contacts sub-
sisted. In the first half of the eighth century the increasing inability of the

Byzantine governors in Italy to protect themselves, let alone the city of Rome, against Lombard expansion, and the theological division between papacy and the empire over the veneration of icons, once the latter had been condemned by the emperor Leo III (717–41), led to the popes renewing old ties with the Franks.[65]

Pippin III's invasions of Italy in 755 and 756 resulted directly from the papal involvement in the dynastic change in Francia and pope Stephen II's visit to the Frankish kingdom in 754.[66] These events created a relationship that would have long-term effects on the reign of Pippin's son Charles. He himself, however, avoided any more protracted entanglement in Italy. This was probably due to the existence of continuing problems in imposing his authority, although enhanced by the success of his Italian campaigns, on various parts of Francia. Much of the latter part of Pippin III's reign as king was taken up with his conflict with the duchy of Aquitaine. Chunoald, a son of the former duke Eudo, rebelled on the death of Charles Martel, and, despite a campaign against him by the joint mayors in 742, was able to establish himself as ruler of most of the duchy. It is possible that he was able to do so through the use of Basque mercenaries from the region south of the Garonne. So prominent a part do the Basques seem to have played in the military support for the ducal line that Frankish sources, notably the Continuations of the Fredegar Chronicle, refer to the inhabitants of the whole duchy as *Vascones* or Basques.[67] Not until 760 was Pippin able to resume the attempt to eliminate the independence of Aquitaine, now ruled by Chunoald's son Waiofar. Annual campaigns, some of which the annals indicate were very destructive and bitterly fought, from that year until 768 were required to bring this about.[68] Duke Waiofar was finally murdered by some of his own followers while trying to avoid capture by Pippin on 2 June 768.[69] While still in Aquitaine Pippin fell ill at Saintes. He managed to return via Poitiers and Tours to the great Neustrian monastery of Saint-Denis, just north of Paris, where he died on 24 September, aged 54.[70] He was buried, like his father before him, at Saint-Denis.[71]

Charles and Carloman: the Years of Joint Rule, 768–71

The brief period of joint rule between Charles and his younger brother Carloman highlights the tensions that could exist when the Frankish kingdoms were divided, even between two brothers. It could be said that Carloman's premature death on 4 December 771 was the *sine qua non* of the great period of military expansion and perhaps even of the cultural revival that would take place under the sole rule of his elder brother. According to the author of the last section of the Continuations of the *Chronicle of Fredegar*, just before his death Pippin arranged, with the agreement of the Frankish magnates attending on him, that the kingdom should be divided between his two sons, Charles and Carloman. This source also states that the former was given Austrasia, and the latter Burgundy, Provence, Septimania, Alsace and Alamannia. Recently conquered Aquitaine was to be divided between them.[72] This latter claim is implicitly denied in the historical writings produced in Charles's reign, and a dispute over their territorial inheritances may have been the first cause of friction between the two new kings. It is equally noteworthy that the Continuator of Fredegar, probably writing around 768, made no mention of Neustria. This kingdom would seem, for the first time, to have been divided, with a thin coastal strip being placed in Charles's hands.[73] This provided amongst other things an access corridor for him to Aquitaine, which would otherwise have been surrounded by Carloman's territories. The unprecedented division of Neustria, hitherto the senior kingdom, may have been the reason for the choice of two of its episcopal towns, Noyon and Soissons, which were only 40 km apart, as the locations for the simultaneous enthroning of Charles and Carloman respectively on Sunday 9 October 768.[74] Charles spent his first Christmas as king at his villa at Aachen, which later in the reign would become his principal residence.

Resistance in Aquitaine had not ended with the murder of Waiofar. Either following that event or after the death of Pippin, Chunoald II, who was probably a son of Waiofar, attempted to revive the ducal house. It was to crush this final flicker of opposition that a joint campaign by Charles and Carloman in Aquitaine was planned for 769. Charles is known to have spent the Easter of that year at Rouen, *en route* to Aquitaine. The brothers met at *Duasdives*, now known as Moncontour de Poitou, half-way between Angers and Poitiers, but there they seem to have fallen out. The narrative sources, which were all written after Carloman's death and are uniformly favourable to Charles, merely record that the younger brother then returned to his kingdom with his army. It is possible that the issue of the division of Aquitaine remained unsettled, or even that Charles had pre-empted the issue by taking over territory in the duchy that may have been assigned to his brother.

He certainly was in a position to pursue the campaign single-handedly, taking Angoulême and establishing a fortress at Veronicas on a tributary of the Dordogne. Chunoald II was unable to put up any recorded resistance, and fled across the Garonne into the Basque lands. This area south of the Garonne and around the western Pyrenees had been organised as a duchy, possibly by Charles Martel in the 730s, and was now in the hands of a duke Lupus. Under threat of war from Charles Lupus handed Chunoald and his wife over to the Franks.[75] No more is heard of the line of the former dukes of Aquitaine, and Charles made himself master of the whole of the former duchy.

The bad relations between the two Frankish kingdoms that this engendered were made worse by Italian entanglements in 770/1. The papacy had long sought to force the Lombard king Desiderius (757–74) to honour the promises made by his predecessor when faced by Pippin III's invasions of Italy in 755 and 756. This involved the return of certain towns in the Pentapolis to papal rule. Added to this a candidate for the Archbishopric of Ravenna, at the time the second most important bishopric in Italy after Rome, had gained control of his see not only against the wishes of pope Stephen III (768–72), but also with the military backing of the Lombards. Following the precedents of his name-sake, Stephen II, the pope hoped to persuade the new Frankish kings to intervene in Italy to secure papal ends. He greeted them with the honorific title of 'Patrician of the Romans', previously granted to Pippin III, and in a letter sent in the Summer of 770 urged them both to take steps to secure 'the rights of the Prince of the Apostles', warning that they would have to answer for any failure to act when brought before the judgement-seat of Christ.[76]

At this time the disagreements between the two kings over the territorial divisions in Francia had apparently been shelved if not settled, as their envoys assured the pope. However, the potential re-opening of these Italian involvements was taken, at least by Charles and his court, as an opportunity for gaining further advantage over Carloman. The latter was clearly in close touch with some of the leading members of pope Stephen's entourage, such as Christopher and his son Sergius, who in 770 were respectively the *Primicerius* and the *Secundicerius* of the notariate; in other words the head and deputy head of the papal bureaucracy. Christopher had been a councillor of Stephen II at the time of the appeal to Pippin III, and they pursued a strongly anti-Lombard policy. Their family exercised considerable power in Rome, and the previous pope, Paul (757–67), had been Christopher's brother. On the other hand, this did not necessarily endear them to the new incumbent of the papal throne.

Charles seems in his conflicts with Carloman to have enjoyed the advantage of the support of their mother, Bertrada, who although taking vows as a nun on Pippin III's death remained an active force in the politics of the Frankish courts.[77] She is reported to have held discussions with Carloman 'in the interests of peace' early in 770, perhaps bringing about the state of temporary amity, referred to in the papal letter mentioned above. However, this proved to be only part of her diplomatic activity in the course of the year. She travelled through Bavaria into Italy, and seems to have visited the Lombard court before arriving at Rome to visit the tombs of the apostles.[78] Frankish sources are laconic in the extreme on the purposes and outcome of her journey, but something of what it brought about can be deduced from ensuing papal correspondence with the Frankish kings.

Its principal achievement was a marriage alliance between Charles and one of the daughters of the Lombard king Desiderius. As the Bavarian duke Tassilo III (748–88) was already married to another of the latter's daughters, Bertrada's choice of a route to Italy through his duchy is likely to have been connected with this plan. Charles was almost certainly already married at this time, but seems to have put aside his wife Himiltrude, whom Frankish annalists would subsequently designate a concubine, in the interests of this Lombard alliance. The pope, or at least Christopher and Sergius, was horrified at the prospect of his intended protector joining forces with those regarded as Rome's main enemies, and a letter survives in which he urged both Charles and Carloman not to marry a foreign wife, and in particular not to pollute themselves by a union with one of the 'barbaric' Lombards.[79]

Whether the papal uncertainty as to which of the Frankish kings was planning a Lombard marriage was genuine or merely diplomatic is not known. In fact, the proposed alliance was clearly intended to be directed against Carloman, rather than as a *volte-face* in Franco-papal relations. Stephen III was also intended to be a beneficiary of it, as Bertrada may have explained on her pilgrimage to the city. The disputed towns that Rome had long demanded were to be handed over to the pope by Desiderius, and the Lombard-supported archbishop of Ravenna would be ousted in favour of a candidate acceptable to the papacy as part of the complex web of ties that was being devised. In Rome the only losers would be Christopher and Sergius and their supporters. Desiderius, fortified by the agreement with Charles, marched on Rome, where Christopher and Sergius tried to raise the city. However when pope Stephen made it clear that they did not enjoy his backing, by sending them a message suggesting that they should both enter a monastery, their supporters abandoned them and they were taken prisoner. Not least to save papal face, they were ordered to become monks, and in the meantime were left under guard in the basilica of St Peter's outside the city while the pope celebrated mass for king Desiderius within the walls. While this was taking place, and with whose connivance it may only be guessed, Paul the papal chamberlain removed them from St Peter's and had them blinded. Christopher died three days later, and Sergius was killed early in 772.[80]

In 771 an alliance had thus been formed that effectively encircled Carloman. Charles, the Lombard king Desiderius and pope Stephen III had been linked in ways that offered benefit to them all. Duke Tassilo of Bavaria, as brother-in-law of Charles and son-in-law of Desiderius, was clearly one of their party. Carloman's Roman allies had been killed or blinded, and the pope had been freed from the hold of the family of his predecessor.[81] However, most of the purpose, at least from Charles's point of view, was lost when Carloman died on 4 December 771. He was buried at St Remigius's cathedral in Rheims. His death was followed immediately after by that of pope Stephen III, on 24 January 772. With their removal the alliance fell apart. Charles repudiated and sent back to Italy his new Lombard wife, who is never even named in the Frankish sources. Under a new pope, Hadrian I (772–95) the policies and personnel of the last stage of Stephen III's pontificate fell out of favour and were eliminated. These included a brother of Stephen III called John, and the chamberlain Paul, who was killed at Ravenna in a way that was designed not to implicate the new pope. The bodies of Christopher and Stephen were given the equivalent of a state funeral in St Peter's.[82]

In Francia the political manoeuvrings that followed Carloman's death are almost entirely hidden from view.[83] It is recorded in the annals that the dead king's wife and two children and some of his courtiers took refuge with the Lombard king Desiderius in Italy.[84] The latter would have made little sense if the previous alliance between Charles and Desiderius was still in place, and so may be assumed to have post-dated the breach in Franco-Lombard ties. It was, therefore, some time early in 772 that this happened, and is likely to have resulted from the decision of others of the leading men of Carloman's former court that they would transfer their allegiance to Charles rather than attempt to shore up a regime operating in the name of Carloman's son Pippin. As the late king was aged only 20 at the time of his death, his offspring can have been no more than infants, and rule by his adult brother must have seemed preferable.

The *Annales Regni Francorum* record a meeting between Charles and some of those who had been prominent under Carloman. They included archbishop Wilcharius of Sens and abbot Fulrad of Saint-Denis (c.750–84).[85] Amongst the lay *optimates* only the Alamannic counts Warin (d. 774) and Adalhard (762–86) are mentioned.[86] This provides interesting evidence for the politics of that region, and it is notable in the light of this that in the Winter of 771/2 Charles chose Hildegard (758–783), daughter of count Gerold and granddaughter of the last duke of the Alamans, as his new wife. Her brother Gerold (d. 799) would become the first Carolingian Prefect of Bavaria after its subjection in 788. A major political settlement for at least some of the aristocracy of the former duchy was clearly hammered out in the aftermath of Carloman's death.[87] However, Alamannia cannot have been the only part of the latter's former kingdom in which such processes were taking place. Unfortunately, the evidence is less clear and specific in other cases. Some individuals who came to terms with Charles can at least be identified. A clear beneficiary of the change was Maginarius, who is found subscribing as *Referendarius* in the handful of surviving charters of Carloman.[88] He gained Charles's favour too, possibly through the patronage of Fulrad, whom he succeeded as abbot of Saint-Denis (784–c.792). He also came to serve as one of Charles's *missi* to Rome in 781/2 and again in 786, and in southern Italy in 788.[89]

If Einhard is to be believed, only queen Bertrada seems to have opposed Charles's breach with the Lombard kingdom and the rejection of his new wife.[90] This may have been because the policy was of her devising. She certainly brought it into being by her journey in 770, and she received diplomatic letters from Rome jointly with her son Charles. If so, this was the last time she played such a public role. She remained, honoured if inactive, until her death in 783, when she was buried alongside her husband Pippin III in Saint-Denis. However, she was not necessarily alone in opposing Charles's rejection of his Lombard wife, as his cousin Adalhard (d. 826) is said in the *Life* written of him soon after his death by Paschasius Radbertus of Corbie to have questioned the morality of the king's action. He was himself, as one of the sons of an illegitimate half-brother of Pippin III called Bernard, a potential claimant in any sharing out of the Frankish kingdoms. The career of Charles Martel gave evidence enough that any male family member could profit from troubled conditions. Whether Adalhard's opposition was motivated by moral scruple or by hope of political gain cannot be known. Although the chronology of the *Vita Adalhardi* is far from precise or its narrative entirely reliable, it seems that he took himself off to Italy soon after, and entered the monastery of Monte Cassino. This was a step previously taken by his relative Carloman, the former mayor of the Palace in Austrasia, who had thence become embroiled in Lombard diplomacy directed against Pippin III. So, Adalhard's appearance at Monte Cassino was hardly a neutral act. He was brought back to Francia by royal agents, following Charles's conquest of the Lombard kingdom in 774. However, the two cousins were apparently reconciled, and Adalhard was subsequently made abbot of Corbie.[91] By this time Charles was well advanced with the campaigns of conquest and territorial expansion that his brother's early death had facilitated, and seems to have had no fears of internal unrest within Francia.

3

THE SAXON WARS, 772–85

Charles's Saxon wars were the most protracted and most bitterly fought of the numerous campaigns of his reign. Beginning in 772 they continued, with various interruptions, until the year 804, with repercussions still being felt thereafter. The conflict with the Saxons in this period involved features such as forcible mass-conversion and large-scale deportation, together with the massacre of prisoners, that were not normal components of Frankish warfare. But even quite liberal German historians in this century have been prepared to applaud the outcome as 'one of the foundations of medieval and modern Germany'.[1] To understand the length and ferocity of these wars, it is worth looking back over earlier Frankish–Saxon relations, and forming some idea of the nature of Saxon society in this period.

The Saxons were one of a group of Germanic peoples in north-west Europe affected by the collapse of Roman power along the lower Rhine in the mid-fourth century.[2] While themselves not immediate neighbours of Rome, probably being established in the area east of the Elbe and south of the Danish peninsula, they benefited from the movement of the Salian Franks to their west across the Rhine and into the low-lying area between the river Meuse and the Channel known as Toxandria. The existence of this salient of Frankish territory within the former Rhine frontier was regularised by the agreement made by the Caesar Julian (355–60) in 358.[3] As is well known, from the early fifth century Saxons, along with Angles and Jutes from further to the east and north, migrated in increasing numbers across the Channel into the south and east of Britain. At the same time, Saxon and also Frankish sea-borne raiding affected the southern coast of the Channel, and groups of Saxons became involved in the complex struggles for dominance in the north of Gaul.[4] In 469 the future king of Italy is recorded as leading a Saxon army in the capture of Angers, on the Loire. They subsequently lost it to a mixed force of Romans and Franks.[5]

Although under Clovis (c. 481 to c. 511) the Franks came to rule over and settle most of Gaul between the Loire and the Channel, pockets of Saxon settlements in this area survived, notably in the region of Bayeux.[6]

While there may have been a major movement of Saxons both into Britain and in lesser degree into the north of what was becoming Francia, others remained east of the Rhine. In the sixth century these Saxons became subject to the Frankish monarchy of Theuderic I (c. 511–533) and his son Theudebert I (533–48), centred on Rheims, Metz and Cologne.[7] The eastern Frankish or Austrasian kingdom that was created by these rulers extended well across the Rhine and embraced a number of subject peoples, including the Thuringians and the Jutes, as well as the Saxons. Whether this represented more than a tributary relationship, perhaps following military defeat, is not clear. After the early death of Theudebert's son Theudebald (548–55), the kingdom passed into the hands of the former's uncle, Chlotar I (c. 511–561), who faced a major Saxon revolt across the Rhine.[8] In the same period we also hear of other Saxons joining the Lombard king Alboin in his invasion of northern Italy in 568, and thence raiding into Provence the following year.[9]

Frankish hegemony was maintained or restored and in 612 Saxons served along with Thuringians and others in the army of the Austrasian king Theudebert II (596–612) in his civil war with his half-brother Theuderic II (596–613) of Burgundy.[10] Up to the death of Chlotar II (584–629), the Saxons had paid a regular tribute in cattle (500 a year) and were expected to defend the north-eastern frontier against attacks by the Wends, a Slavic people. However, his son Dagobert I (d. 638/9) is said to have let them off further payments.[11] Under his son Sigibert III (633–56?) another major revolt occurred across the Rhine in 639; this time amongst the Thuringians. The defeat of the Franks in the ensuing war may have initiated the process of the collapse of Merovingian hegemony east of the Rhine, which only began to be reversed under Pippin II and Charles Martel.

The Saxons were thus well known to the Franks, and had been formally subject to them for much of the sixth and seventh centuries. This involved the payment of tribute and the occasional providing of military manpower rather than direct Frankish rule, but it did imply, in the eyes of the Franks at least, a permanently dependent relationship. Individual Saxons, such as Aighyna who was established as *Dux* over the Vascones by Dagobert I in 635, could rise to positions of importance under the Frankish kings.[12] The Saxons also seem to have had an expanding population, in that despite the export across the Channel of a significant body of manpower they were able to establish other communities in northern Francia and even play some part in the Lombard invasion of Italy. In terms of material culture they were not dissimilar to the

Franks. As can be seen from numerous grave finds, their weapons were as good, and, allowing for stylistic variations, their items of personal adornment and domestic utensils were in no way inferior to those to be found in comparable Frankish burials.[13] The principal cultural difference between the Franks and the Saxons was in religion, as the latter remained firmly pagan, at least in their homelands across the Rhine.

In the early eighth century there are reports of Saxon raids on the lands of a minor Frankish people known as the Chatuarii in 715, during the civil war between the Neustrians and the followers of the Pippinids.[14] These were obviously taken seriously enough for 'Saxonia', the land of the Saxons, to be the first target for Charles Martel after he emerged victorious from this conflict. He is recorded as invading Saxony in both 718 and 720, and planning so to do again in 729.[15] Another expedition is reported actually to have taken place in 733 or 734, and one of the sets of Minor Annals reports a final campaign in 738.[16] No details are given as to the course or outcome of these expeditions, and only one, that of 733/4, is given a more precise geographical context, that of 'Wistrigou', to be identified with the western region of Saxony. This was also the area affected by the expedition of 738.[17]

The immediate antecedents to Charles's Saxon wars may be seen in the campaigns of his uncle Carloman in 744 and his father Pippin III in 747 and 753.[18] There are clearly a number of issues involved, which are not always fully distinguished. On the one hand there were Frankish claims to hegemony over and tribute to be paid by the Saxons that stretched back as far as the sixth century. The 747 campaign was terminated by the Saxons agreeing explicitly to pay the tribute to the Franks that had been owed in the time of Chlotar, probably the 500 cows a year previously referred to, and this was raised to a higher though unspecified amount in 753. The Frankish sources consistently present the actions of the Saxons in terms of rebellion and the breaking of faith. On the other hand, there would seem to be some expansion or movement taking place amongst the Saxons. This may in part be the product of continuing growth of population in an area, the marshy lowlands north of the Lippe, that could not fully support it, or it may have been influenced by pressures from the north from the Frisians and from the east on the part of the Wends. Both of these peoples were easily persuaded to join the Franks against the Saxons in 747.[19]

As well as these longer term issues of Saxon resistance to Frankish domination and a gradual southwards movement on the part of the Saxon population, other factors could influence the conflicts between the two peoples. Thus, periods of Frankish weakness, as in the civil wars of 715 to 717, provided the Saxons with opportunities for greater freedom both from tribute and in chances to expand their territories. Similarly, Frankish dissidents might hope to take advantage of the general background of conflict to try to take refuge or to whip up a military following amongst the Saxons. Grifo, the half-brother of Carloman and Pippin III, who had failed to obtain a share of Francia in 741, took refuge with the Saxons in 747, having escaped from imprisonment in a fortress in the Ardennes.[20] This was described in the Continuations of Fredegar, which studiously avoided any mention of Grifo himself, as a case of the Saxons breaking their oath of loyalty to Pippin III.

It is clear that the main area of conflict between the Franks and the Saxons in this period lay along the river Lippe. It was here that Charles Martel had directed his campaign of 738 and this was to be the primary focus of attention throughout the opening phases of his grandson Charles's Saxon wars. References to fighting in this area and to Saxon raids on the Chatuarii suggest that they were pushing southwards into the higher ground to the south of the river. The Lippe valley had been an important line of communication and also of control of the indigenous population in the time of the emperor Augustus (27 BC to AD 14), under whom a network of forts had been built along the line of the river as far as Anreppen, 30 miles east of its confluence with the Rhine.[21] Although these Roman fortresses had long been abandoned and destroyed, the strategic significance of the region that their presence once indicated remained, and the Franks had no wish to allow further Saxon advance southwards into the territories that they themselves ruled directly to the east of the Rhine or into the area of the important settlements of the lower Rhine valley itself. By the time that Charles initiated his Saxon campaigns in 772, and despite the efforts of his predecessors, the frontier had been pushed even further south to the valley of the river Diemel, where a Saxon fortress was constructed at Eresburg. Thus, dynastic tradition, Frankish pride and a genuine military threat combined to make a definitive subjugation of the Saxons a vital goal for Charles.

Such a process involved more than a military conquest. The Saxons had been defeated or forced to come to terms and accept tributary status on numerous occasions from at least the sixth century onwards. As the Franks saw it, submissions made and oaths taken were little guarantee of continuing acceptance of their rule. In part, there may have been a recognition that such undertakings made according to Saxon custom on their weapons carried less weight while the Saxons themselves remained pagan.[22] The difference in religion between Franks and Saxons made it hard for one side to accept the sacredness of any oaths that the other might take. By the time of Carloman and Pippin III, if not that of Charles Martel, the Frankish rulers seem determined that military subjection of the Saxons had to be accompanied by their conversion to

Christianity. Thus, Carloman's campaign in 744, almost certainly along the Lippe, was followed by the baptism of Saxons he had captured, and in 747 the Saxons who surrendered to Pippin III apparently asked to receive Christian sacraments, in other words baptism.[23] A letter of pope Gregory III (730–40) to the Saxons and some items in the correspondence of Boniface that have been dated to around 738 also suggest that missionary activity and an expectation of conversion of the Saxons were closely related to Charles Martel's campaign on the Lippe in that year.[24] Although our sources are almost exclusively Frankish, it seems as if the Saxons themselves came to recognise that military defeat or political submission henceforth would involve religious conversion (even if temporary).[25] This may also explain why a, or the most significant, Saxon pagan shrine came to be established in the very frontier area where the main military conflicts were taking place.

During Pippin's reign as first king of the new Frankish royal house, difficulties with the Saxons continued, and he campaigned against them in 753 and 758. The precise causes of the 753 expedition are not explained. Frankish sources at best tend to describe motivation exclusively in terms of Saxon rebellion or their breaking of faith, and normally claim unqualified military success. The Continuations of Fredegar do both in this case, but the *Annales Regni Francorum* at least admit that archbishop Hildegar of Cologne (750-3) was killed by the Saxons.[26] Pippin is reported as reaching as far as 'Rimie', which in the annal for 785 is given a precise location at the confluence of the Weser and the Werne. This is deep within Saxon territory, and would seem to support the views that this was both a major military undertaking and essentially a successful one. The 758 campaign led to the payment of a tribute of 300 horses.[27] No more is heard of the Saxons for the next 14 years.

Not until after the death of his brother Carloman did Charles initiate his Saxon campaigns, perhaps for fear of leaving his territories open to fraternal attack while he was too deeply engaged over the Rhine. However, in 772, having held an assembly at Worms, he launched his first expedition as king of all Francia against the Saxons. Unusually, no reference is made to Saxon rebelliousness, though it is possible that they had abandoned the payment of the annual tribute while Pippin had been so much engaged in Aquitaine. This and the character of Charles's campaign may suggest that the Franks were the aggressors, and that from the very start his intentions were more far-reaching than those of his predecessors.

The 772 expedition went directly to the Saxon fortress of Eresburg on the river Diemel, which was captured, and thence to the Irminsul. This is called a shrine in the *Annales Regni Francorum*, while the later but often more reliable Revised Version merely describes it as an idol. It may have been or contained both. Because of its sacredness it was also a repository of apparently considerable treasure in gold and silver, which Charles appropriated. The complete obliteration of the site was carried out with the aid of water, which the Annalist describes as being miraculously provided.[28] While it is not wise to read too much precise detail into an account of this sort, it is possible that what was effected was the diversion of a stream or river, to bury the religious site completely. However, the Revised Version gives the story a totally different twist, stating that there was a lack of water for the army to drink, and that this problem was solved through divine benevolence. No connection is made between the newly found spring and the destruction of the *idolum* of the Irminsul. The lack of Saxon literary sources makes it impossible to say quite what the destruction of this holy place and the loss of its hoard meant to the Saxons, or indeed whether all Saxons would have felt the effects equally. However, this is the first time that a Frankish ruler is recorded as having deliberately targeted a Saxon religious site, and it may be assumed that the intention was as much to humiliate the Saxon gods as to enrich the Frankish royal fisc. As previously mentioned, though, the decision of the Saxons to locate this shrine in the crucial border area may itself have been a stage in the heightening of the conflict from one of political domination into one of supernatural confrontation between rival divinities.

The Saxons would seem to have wanted to retaliate in kind, in that in the following year, while Charles was engaged in the opening stages of his campaign in Italy, a raid was directed against the church, originally built by Boniface, at Fritzlar. The choice of this target may reflect the leading role played by Boniface's monastic foundations in previous attempts to evangalise the Saxons. Fritzlar was on the north bank of the river Eder, and a Saxon raid in this direction marked a significant threat to Frankish interests in Hesse. The attempt to burn down the church, however, seems to have failed. The Annalist gives a lengthy account of miraculous interventions, but the Reviser is both much briefer and more reserved as to the explanation for the Saxons' inability to destroy the building. Even so, this raid was bound to have repercussions, which came late in 774, after Charles had returned from Pavia, in the form of four-pronged attack on the Saxons by Frankish armies.

The Reviser obviously felt that these episodes marked a significant change in Charles's intentions, and that during his Winter residence in the royal villa of Quierzy he 'decided to attack the treacherous and treaty-breaking tribe of the Saxons and to persist in this war until they were either defeated and forced to accept the Christian religion or entirely exterminated'.[29] It may be questioned whether or not this had actually been his intention in 772, when attacking the Irminsul. He may also have recognised that Saxon intransigence made it unwise for him to absent himself from the eastern frontier in the way that he had in 773. Certainly, the next few years saw a serious effort to put his resolve of the Winter of 774/5 into practice. In 775 a large scale invasion of Saxony was led by Charles in person. He proceeded eastwards up the valley of the Ruhr, taking a Saxon fortress at Syburg, and thence to the valley of the Diemel, where he restored Eresburg, which may have been taken by the Saxons in 773. He pushed on to the Weser, effectively perambulating the whole southern frontier of the Saxons, before defeating a force that they had gathered to hold the Weser at Braunsberg. After this success he split his army into two. He continued eastwards with one detachment to the river Oker, where he received formal submissions and hostages from two of the main subdivisions of the Saxons, called the Austreleudi and the Angrarii. However, the other part of the army, which had continued northwards down the Weser into very marshy terrain, nearly came to grief in a surprise attack on their camp. This episode is concealed by the Annalist but revealed in the Revised Version. Only when Charles returned and re-united the army were the Westphalian Saxons, who were the dominant group in this border area, forced in turn to submit and give hostages.[30]

The lack of efficacy of such submissions and even the taking of hostages, whose lives would be forfeit if the agreements were broken, was demonstrated only the next year, when once more Charles had to turn his attention to Italy. In his absence, the Westphalian Saxons took and destroyed Eresburg and tried to do the same to Syburg. Once more the Annalist attributed their failure to take the Frankish-held fortress, which now housed a new church, to a miraculous aid about which the Reviser is entirely silent. He offers the more mundane, if more credible, explanation that the attackers were scattered by an unexpected sortie by the Frankish garrison. Charles's rapid return from Italy and an expedition in force to the Lippe led to a renewed Saxon submission, accompanied by the establishment of Frankish garrisons in Eresburg and in a new fortress on the Lippe. This may be the future Paderborn. It is notable that the Saxon submission was made at the 'Lippespringe', the sources of the river Lippe, which may have been a place of religious significance for the Westphalians, and that it involved their acceptance of Christian baptism. Although the Lippe now rises a few miles to the north, it is quite likely that at this period the source of the river was a series of underground springs, located and to be seen between the site of the cathedral and the Carolingian palace in Paderborn.[31] As in 744 and 747, the enforced acceptance of Christianity put the Franks and the Saxons into a common religious value system, which should have made the latter's oaths more binding, at least in Frankish eyes. If not, there was now the military power of the new or restored fortresses, which like Syburg probably housed churches as well as Frankish garrisons.

Charles returned to Saxony early in 777, to hold the Franks' annual assembly at Paderborn, his new fortress and the centre of Frankish cultural irradiation amongst the Westphalian Saxons.[32] This in itself was a significant step, holding the 'Mayfield' outside the Austrasian heartland and at the same time concentrating a major military force in southern Saxony.[33] Although this produced further submissions and mass baptism on the part of many of the Saxons, others under the leadership of a man called Widukind took refuge in the north, quite possibly with the Danish king Sigifrid.[34] The status of Widukind, who makes his first appearance in the Frankish sources at this point, is never defined in any of the annals. It is thus left to the reader to deduce that he was something of a war leader, at least amongst the Westphalians, who may have achieved his authority thanks to the special circumstances of the conflicts in which his people were engaged. It may well be, however, that once again the Frankish historical tradition is misleading, and that his real significance in Saxon society is being concealed.

As previously described, the Saxons like many of the other Germanic groups to the east of the Rhine had been under varying degrees of Frankish control for some if not all of the Merovingian period. In all other such cases that are known, ducal dynasties of almost certainly Frankish origin were imposed upon such peoples, to provide the mechanism by which such hegemony could be exercised and expressed. As has also been seen, in all such cases the imposed ducal house came to identify with its subject population and took the lead in undermining or opposing continuing Merovingian rule and in resisting the subsequent Carolingian attempts to reimpose Frankish control. It would be surprising if no such ducal house had been imposed upon the Saxons during the relatively long period that they were subject to Merovingian hegemony. There is certainly nothing in what is known of the nature and functioning of Saxon society that would make this more improbable in their case than in those of the Thuringians, Alamans and Bavarians.

In the later Carolingian period the descendants of Widukind, who would play a central if not always easily perceived role in the long period of Franco-Saxon conflict in Charles's reign, were amongst the leading members of the nobility of Saxony. In a hagiographical work the later chronicler, Sigebert of Gembloux (d. 1112) referred to the descendants of Widukind as dukes, and gave the same title to the former Saxon leader himself.[35] It may be thought that this is a *post facto* recognition of Widukind's role, and that the later standing of his family benefited from his achievements during this period. However, it is notable that in the small group of personal names used by this

kin group, those of Widukind and of Theoderic are closely and frequently
related. In this context it may be significant, therefore, that a Saxon called
Theoderic is mentioned in the *Annales Regni Francorum* as the leader of
Saxon, or at least Westphalian, opposition in Carloman and Pippin's campaigns in 743 and 744.[36] He is twice recorded as being captured, possibly on
the first occasion when the fortress of Hohenseeburg, identified with Seeburg
near Eisleben in Thuringia, was taken.[37] There are thus grounds for at least
suspecting that something of a ducal dynasty had existed in Saxony, exercising authority over some if not all of the population, in the later Merovingian
period, and that although his status was studiously concealed in the Frankish
accounts, one of its current representatives took the or a leading role in direct-
ing Saxon resistance to Charles.

Even so, with Widukind fled, it may have seemed that the display of royal
power in 777 and the establishment of Frankish forts and garrisons in key
points in the valleys of the Ruhr, the Diemel and the Lippe had effectively
cowed the Saxons and driven the irreconcilable elements into the northern
marshes, leaving the others bound to the Carolingian monarchy by ties of religion and oaths of obedience. Certainly, Charles felt confident enough to listen
to the proposals put to him at Paderborn by envoys from the local rulers in the
Ebro valley and to take himself off on his expedition into Spain in 778. That
this proved a double miscalculation is demonstrated not just by the poor
outcome of the campaign in the Ebro valley but by the scale of the Saxon
uprising that took place in 778, probably once the royal army was well on its
way to the Pyrenees.[38] The Saxons, inspired once more by Widukind, raided
the lower Rhine valley, even as far as Deutz, on the east bank of the river
opposite Cologne, and apparently burned several churches and monasteries.
They retired down the valleys of the Lahn and the Eder when faced by a force
of eastern Franks and Alamans that Charles had ordered to deal with them. A
victory over the raiders and a great slaughter of the Saxons is reported to have
taken place on the Eder near Leisa ('Lihesi'), but as with most of these battles
we only have the word of the Frankish annalists that this was such a success.
Certainly, the next two years saw major royal campaigns in Saxony, to try to
re-impose Frankish authority. That of 779 was devoted to re-subduing the
Westphalians along the Lippe and the Weser, while in 780 Charles again held
the 'Marchfield' in Saxony, at the source of the Lippe, before launching an
expedition eastwards to the Elbe. The account of this campaign in the annals
(both versions) is surprisingly brief in view of its extent and the results it
apparently achieved. Charles is said to have reached the river Oker, where 'all
the inhabitants of the Bardengau and many of the Nordleudi' received baptism
at a place called 'Orheim' (Ohrum). He thence continued eastwards to the

confluence of the Elbe and the Ohre. This was the frontier area between the Saxons and the Slavs to the east, and the expedition had thus traversed the whole of Saxony, a distance of about 400 km from its starting point on the Rhine. The two groups of Saxons said to have accepted baptism lived to the north of the Aller, and their lands were not directly in the line of Charles's march. No battles are recorded in the course of this expedition, and so it seems that the presence on the Weser and the Oker of this large Frankish army was sufficient to bring about a major, albeit temporary, submission on the part of large numbers of Saxons, even in the north. One set of minor annals also report that the success of this year's venture was such that Charles divided Saxony into a number of ecclesiastical regions, with secular and monastic clergy and bishops being appointed to preach and baptise in each.[39] The details of this scheme emerge in the capitulary he would issue, probably in 782.

The scale of the undertaking had clearly grown in the course of the 770s, and an initial raid that may have been as much in search of plunder as of humiliating the Saxon gods had had to be followed by Frankish garrisoning of southern Saxony and the undertaking of extensive military campaigns over large distances. These latter no doubt benefited from the experiences gained in the long-distance ventures into Italy and northern Spain. Although one of Charles's detachments had nearly fallen victim to the kind of tactics that had won the early Germans a spectacular victory over Rome at the Teutoberger Wald in this very region, his other armies had met little concerted resistance or had easily crushed it. Yet for all of this, the Saxon problem was as far from being solved in 780 as it had been in 772. It was, however, about to enjoy a temporary respite. Charles was able to proceed to Italy later in 780 and celebrate the Easter of 781 in Rome, without – and for the first time – a Saxon rising or raid marking his absence.

He returned to Saxony in 782, to hold an assembly at the source of the Lippe, which was attended by 'all of the Saxons except for Widukind', who had taken refuge with the Danes. Wider repercussions of Charles's 780 campaign may also had made themselves felt in the presence of envoys from the Danish king Sigifrid.[40] Although the annalists do not record what was discussed and decided upon at this gathering, it is likely that some at least of its conclusions took the form of what is known as the First Saxon Capitulary.[41] This is a small corpus of new laws to apply to the Saxons, prohibiting various practices and laying down the penalties for their infringement. It consists of 34 such clauses, divided into two sections of greater and lesser importance, and is striking testimony to the draconian way in which Frankish Christianity was being imposed upon the Saxons. Most forms of what are regarded as pagan practices or as slights on Christian rules are here declared to be punishable by death. That this should encompass murdering priests (clause 5) or setting fire to churches (clause 3) may seem reasonable by eighth-century standards, but that eating meat in Lent should also deserve the death penalty is somewhat less so (clause 4). Outside Saxony such an offence would merely incur a short period of penance.[42] Unbaptised Saxons are also liable to capital punishment, as is anyone found practising burial by cremation (clauses 8 and 7).

There is some very useful material to be found in the capitulary for the study of Saxon paganism, as some clauses condemn unacceptable Saxon practices that are taken as being distinctively pagan.[43] As well as burning the dead, whose ashes were then buried in mounds (clause 22), these will have included the burning (alive?) of those suspected of being witches and the eating of their flesh (clause 6), the making of human sacrifices (clause 9), and the offering of prayer at sacred springs and trees (clause 21). The provisions explicitly said to be of lesser importance (clauses 15 to 34) help reveal something of the way that the Church was being established in Saxon territory. Each church that was built was given a designated territory whose inhabitants had to provide a residence and a specified amount of land, together with a number of male and female slaves in proportion to the size of the population. A briefly worded clause (no. 23) seems to imply that Saxon magicians and soothsayers were to be enslaved and given to the churches, as part of their servile labour force. Ten per cent of all fines incurred within the district would be payable to the church, which was also to receive a tithe or tenth part of the movable wealth and income of the local free population of all classes (clauses 15 to 17). These provisions established, in theory at least, the economic basis for the support of each church, including the costs of its furnishing and vestments and vessels for the liturgy, and of the priests who served it. That such unprecedented impositions increased the attractiveness of Frankish rule may be doubted.

It is not possible to say how many churches were established in Saxony in the late eighth century. The endemic warfare between Franks and their various subject peoples and allies on the one hand and the Saxons on the other, which lasted until at least 804, makes it unlikely that we should envisage that the churches that were built were placed undefended in rural locations or that their clergy were left to the mercy of the local population.[44] It is more reasonable to assume that the first churches were sited within the Frankish fortresses, whose defences and garrison protected them but also provided the military power to turn the provisions of the capitulary as to the payment of tithes, fines and the allotting of lands for the church into something like reality. The Frankish church in Saxony was, thus, initially a colonial venture, whose very existence depended on the threat of force that lay behind it.

Some of the early Frankish fortresses and their churches can be detected archaeologically. One of the best examples is that of Münster, where the late eighth-century Carolingian nucleus, which was built over an earlier Saxon settlement, is still traceable, despite the subsequent growth and importance of the town from the Later Middle Ages onwards.[45] Extraordinarily, in the light of the tone of the capitulary, excavations have revealed that the creation of the ditch and bank fortifications here, probably the work of Saxon labour, was marked by a horse sacrifice.[46] The remains of a horse and of a dog were found underlying the constructions and must have been put in place at the outset of this work.[47] The dog appears to have been buried alive. This discovery might imply that pagan practices (ones used by the Franks themselves as recently as the seventh century) were here tacitly ignored or condoned.[48]

The probable immediate context of the issue of this capitulary was not very propitious, although many of its provisions would in due course come to be widely implemented in Saxony. Soon after Charles returned to Francia, a major Saxon revolt broke out under the leadership of the ever intransigent Widukind. This may have been triggered by the attempt to impose the provisions of the capitulary and/or the requirement that the Saxons provide a contingent for a proposed Frankish campaign against the Slavs. Three Frankish *missi* who were to have commanded this army turned their forces against the Saxons instead, initially co-operating with a count Theoderic, who is described as one of the king's own relatives and probably one of his recent comital appointments in Saxony. Advancing on the Saxons, who were gathering on the north side of the Süntel mountains, the East Frankish contingents under the *missi* Adalgis, Gailo and Worad are reported as having struck prematurely, without waiting for count Theoderic and his troops to join them, so as to claim all credit for the anticipated victory themselves. The result was a disaster, with most of the Franks being killed, including four counts, about twenty other nobles and the *missi* Adalgis and Gailo.[49] Not only had the promulgation of the capitulary been followed by revolt, but this had involved a Frankish military humiliation comparable to that inflicted by the Basques at Roncesvalles in 778.

Unlike the western Pyrenees, where Frankish and Carolingian interests were less involved, such a defeat in Saxony could not be left unpunished. Charles immediately returned with a large army, while Widukind took refuge with the Danes. The leading Saxons were unable to resist militarily and submitted to Charles when he summoned them, placing the blame for the revolt on the fugitive Widukind. Four thousand five hundred Saxons held to have taken part in the battle in the Süntel mountains were surrendered to the Franks and all of them were beheaded beside the river Aller, at Verden, in the course of a single day.[50] It is to the Saxons' credit that such tactics did not cow them, and by the

Spring of 783 the annalists report the existence of 'a general rebellion' in Saxony. Perhaps unwisely, though, the Saxons tried to face Charles's large and united army in open battle at Detmold, and after one defeat tried the same thing again on the river Hasse. As one of the sets of minor annals succinctly if gleefully put it: 'the lord king ... fought a battle against those who were in rebellion; and many thousands fell on the Saxons' side. And battle was joined a second time; and the Franks fought against the Saxons and enjoyed victory, with the aid of Christ's grace; and again many thousands fell on the Saxons' side, a much greater number than before.'[51]

Whatever the true number of their losses, even these defeats proved insufficient to crush the Saxons, and Charles had to return on campaign in 784 and 785. In the first of those two years his army seems to have been seriously hampered by bad weather. Having ravaged the lands of the Westphalians again, he had cut his way through to the Weser only to find progress blocked by severe flooding. This saved the northern Saxons from attack, but splitting his forces and leaving his son Charles the Younger with part of the army in Westphalia, Charles made a loop to the south-east and passing through Thuringia, re-entered Saxon territory along the Elbe and the Saale, where he destroyed the crops and burnt the settlements. Although he seems to have faced no concerted resistance, the Westphalian Saxons did try to launch an attack on the contingent left in their lands under Charles the Younger. They were apparently defeated in a cavalry battle, an interesting detail on at least one form of Saxon military tactics.

This continued defiance may have led Charles on his return from eastern Saxony to take the unprecedented step of continuing his campaigning throughout the Winter of 784/5. The intention seems, as in his expedition to the Elbe in 784, to have been one of unremitting destruction and devastation, to bring the Saxons finally to heel. As the Reviser recorded it: 'he gave the Saxons a winter of discontent indeed, as he and the *duces* whom he sent out ranged here, there and everywhere and threw everything into disorder with killings and burnings. By ravaging in this fashion throughout the whole period of the winter he inflicted immense destruction on well-nigh all the regions of the Saxons.'[52] It was enough, for both sides. Following a March- or Mayfield assembly at Paderborn, when Charles set out towards the Elbe, where he had heard that Widukind and another Saxon leader called Albio were to be found, he was able to begin negotiations with the dissidents. In consequence he was able to call off the campaign and return to Francia. Widukind and the others were promised clemency and were given hostages for their security. Charles then sent one of his court officials called Amalwin to escort them into his presence in his villa at Attigny, where in conclusion of the agreement they were baptised. Charles himself stood as godfather to Widukind, establishing the strongest formal tie between them.[53]

In the light of the extraordinary savagery of the conflict between 782 and 785, this was a remarkable resolution. Charles was clearly keen to bring Widukind into an agreement, marked by the latter's acceptance of baptism, and with it recognition of the Frankish king's authority and the making of accords backed by spiritual sanctions that both sides recognised. After the unrestricted violence of the winter of 784/5, the willingness of even the hardiest of the Saxons to submit is perhaps not surprising. What is, though, is the degree to which Charles was prepared to forgo further vengeance and even to cajole Widukind and the others around him into what was seen as a final submission. Indeed, Charles was taking a risk that became all too obvious later in 785 in bringing this about. The eastern Franks across the Rhine had borne the brunt of Saxon raids in the 770s, had provided much of the manpower for royal campaigns in Saxony and had suffered a humiliating and bloody defeat in 782 in the Süntel mountains. The latter in particular may have left a residue of unresolved blood feuds. That a conspiracy to assassinate Charles was hatched amongst the east Frankish nobility led by a count Hardrad in 785, in the aftermath of the baptism of Widukind, can hardly have been a coincidence.[54] It was detected in time and some of its leaders were blinded and others exiled, but it showed that the submission of the Saxons had been achieved at yet another cost. For the time being Saxon acceptance of Frankish rule and all that this involved in terms of the imposition of the regulations of the capitulary of 782 would last, but only briefly.

Overall, the years 772 to 785 saw a crucial change in Charles's dealings with the Saxons. Initially, he may have seen himself as doing little more than continuing the practices of his predecessors, in trying to limit Saxon encroachments on Frankish settlements east of the Rhine and making more of a reality of the traditional Merovingian claims to authority over them. Quite how soon this extended to plans for a more institutionalised conquest, with the establishment of Frankish settlements and the conversion of the Saxons becoming an integral part of the royal plan is not certain. The Reviser dates the determination to impose conversion to the year 775, but, intentionally or not, there was a religious dimension to the conflict from the start.[55] The consistency of Charles's efforts parallel those of his father in Aquitaine in the 760s, and some of his more extreme methods also had ancestral precedents. The massacre of several thousand of his leading Saxon opponents at Verden may have matched the treatment meted out to the Alamans by his uncle Carloman following his victory over them at Bad Canstatt in 745/6.[56] What was novel, however, was the winter campaigning of 784/5. Despite the severity of both the Verden massacre and the final extended harrying of Saxony, Charles did show himself to be quick to accept the submission of his opponents. He was possibly even too trusting, as events frequently proved, and in the end he faced political difficulties with the eastern Frankish nobility as a further consequence. However, in the longer term, the warfare, the fortified settlements and their churches, the capitularies and the exposure of important Saxon hostages to Frankish culture and religion would reap the desired reward, in terms of the gradual integration of the one society into the other.[57]

4

ITALY AND SPAIN, 773–801

Just as the Saxon war had represented a traditional interest of his predecessors that Charles took up early in his reign and pursued with greater determination and more far-reaching consequences, so too did the question of relations with the Lombard kingdom in Italy constitute unfinished business that he had inherited from Pippin III. Frankish–Lombard relations extended back to at least the middle of the sixth century.[1] The Lombards had been permitted by the emperor Justinian I (527–65) to establish themselves in the former Roman province of Pannonia, south of the Danube, as a means of blocking a threatened Frankish expansion into the Balkans under Theudebert I (533–48). The latter's son, Theudebald (548–55) had a Lombard wife, while the Lombard king Alboin (d. 572) who led their conquest of much of northern and central Italy in 568 was married to a Frankish princess called Chlodosuinth. She was expected to persuade her husband to convert to Christianity, and thus bring him and the Lombards under Frankish cultural and political influence.[2] Even after their Italian conquests, the Lombards had been in some danger of being subordinated to the eastern Frankish kings. The emperor Maurice (582–602) tried to encourage the Franks to intervene in Italy on the Empire's behalf, in the way that Justinian I (527–65) had engineered a Frankish attack on the Ostrogoths in Italy in 539.[3] Under the Austrasian king Childebert II (575–96) a series of Frankish expeditions were either sent against the Lombards or were threatened. These secured the Frankish kings substantial payments from Constantinople, while a submissive diplomacy on the part of the Lombard king Authari (584–90), together with payments of tribute, further enriched Childebert II and allowed him an at least nominal overlordship.[4] This and the tribute may have come to an end in the reign of the next Lombard king, Agilulf (590–616), and there seems to have been little conflict between the kingdoms thereafter. Relations were on occasion quite warm. The Lombards for much of the seventh century were ruled by the Agilolfing dynasty, that was Frankish–Bavarian in origin, while in 737 Charles Martel negotiated for military help against the Arabs in Provence from the Lombard ruler Liutprand (712–44).[5]

It was the papal pleas for military and diplomatic assistance against Aistulf (749–56), sent to Pippin III in 753, that led the Franks again to became involved in Italy. In 751 Ravenna, the administrative centre of the Byzantine exarchate, was finally captured by the Lombards. With the Empire in no position to intervene militarily and the Lombard kingdom in expansionary mood, a renewed threat to the city of Rome seemed imminent. The papacy also claimed rights over some towns and their territories that had been annexed by the Lombards in the course of their successful campaigns against the Exarchate.[6] Only Pippin was in any position to intervene militarily against Aistulf or to exercise diplomatic leverage. The papal appeals were well timed, in that the new Frankish king was only now in a position to contemplate providing such help. By this time, with Grifo dead and Drogo almost eliminated, Pippin's internal problems were greatly reduced. He may have been under some obligation to the papacy for whatever role it had actually played in the mysterious process of replacing the Merovingian dynasty in 750/1, and the story in the Continuations of Fredegar that Grifo had been killed while on his way to the Lombards could suggest that Aistulf had been aiding and abetting Pippin's enemies, or was contemplating so doing.[7]

Stephen II (752–57) was permitted to pass through the Lombard kingdom, and he and his entourage spent the winter with Pippin.[8] Aistulf clearly hoped to launch a diplomatic counter to the influence that the pope might exert over the Frankish king, and so arranged for the latter's brother Carloman, now a monk of Monte Cassino, to be sent to Francia to try to oppose Stephen II's pleas.[9] For the reasons just suggested, Pippin was probably inclined to take active steps to support the papal request, and he does not seem to have relished the political re-emergence, in whatever capacity, of his brother. Carloman was detained in Francia and kept in custody at Vienne under the supervision of Pippin's wife Bertrada until he died.[10]

As part of what had been planned and agreed to in the winter of 753/4, Pippin and his two sons Charles and Carloman received anointing at the hands of the pope. In 755, having failed to secure the required concessions from Aistulf by diplomatic means, Pippin invaded Italy, and besieged the Lombard king in Pavia. Unable to put up an effective resistance in the field but with the capital holding out, Aistulf felt it advisable to come to terms with the Franks. He promised to make the territorial concessions to Rome, took oaths and gave hostages.[11] However, with Pippin safely back over the Alps, Aistulf ignored the agreement. This led to a second Frankish campaign in 756, in the course of which Pippin took Ravenna and the surrounding region. This had been imperial territory, but Pippin rejected the request of the emperor Constantine V (741–75) that he return it to Byzantine control. Instead he gave it into the hands of the pope, to be administered from Rome. Aistulf, faced once more with Frankish military might, again promised the surrender of the towns that the pope was demanding. Pippin for his part was rewarded by the honourable if practically meaningless title of 'Patrician of the Romans', but withdrew back into Francia and avoided any further involvement in Italian affairs, despite the subsequent papal complaints over the continuing failure of Aistulf and his successor Desiderius (757–74) to fulfil the agreements made in 755 and 757.[12]

It may be that Pippin recognised that there were no results of material value to the Franks to be gained from further military ventures in Italy. He also had to face the continuing resistance of Aquitaine. As previously described, the conflicts between his sons after his death led to the Lombard kingdom becoming, briefly, a valued ally of one of them. However, the death of Carloman in December 771 put an end to Charles's marriage to Desiderius's daughter and to the Italian policy that had been created by queen Bertrada. Instead the Lombard kingdom reverted to becoming a haven for Frankish dissidents, such as Carloman's widow Gerberga and her children and Charles's cousin Adalhard. The Lombard towns and treasuries also remained tempting potential prizes for Frankish military aggression should the right opportunity arise. This came, as it had for Pippin III, in the form of a plea for help from the papacy. The papal office was now in the hands of Hadrian I (772–95), who had recently been able to purge himself of the members of the pro-Lombard clique that had supported the last phase of the regime of his predecessor, Stephen III (768–72). Faced by the loss of his allies in Rome, king Desiderius had begun threatening to take the city.

In 773 there seems to have been no Summer campaign, and Charles had already retired to the royal villa at Thionville near Metz, which he had selected for his winter quarters, when an embassy arrived from Hadrian I, requesting diplomatic and military assistance against the Lombards. Charles may have preferred the former, offering Desiderius 14,000 gold *solidi* to withdraw from the disputed towns.[13] When this was twice rejected, war was the only alternative. From an assembly of his forces at Geneva, Charles launched a two-pronged assault over the Alps, to outflank any attempt by the Lombard royal army to block the Frankish advance. Thus, Charles himself crossed by Mont Cenis, which Desiderius attempted to hold against him. But when the other Frankish army, led by Charles's maternal uncle Bernard, made an unopposed crossing of the Alps via the Great Saint Bernard Pass, the Lombard forces had to retreat before they were surrounded. Desiderius's army was clearly not strong enough to face the Franks in open battle on the plains, and so he withdrew into Pavia, to face a siege. This was the tactic previously employed by his predecessor Aistulf in 755, and it had then resulted in no more than a temporary humiliation when he had come to terms with Pippin III, who had been unable to take the city.

Whether it was due to the relative lateness of the season or because Charles's intentions went beyond those of his father, he kept up the siege of Pavia throughout the winter and then on into 774. Such an operation was inherently risky. The winter snows would have closed the main passes back over the Alps, and the siege had to be conducted from a temporary camp outside the city. For Pippin III in 755 the approach of winter and the need to return to Francia before its onset had probably been a major factor in bringing him to make a treaty with Aistulf. Charles, however, was able to maintain the siege, never an easy undertaking in medieval warfare, and keep his army in sufficient strength to prevent any break-out by the besieged. He himself went briefly to Rome to celebrate Easter of 774 with Hadrian I. It is reasonable to assume that this enabled him to discuss or lay out whatever plans he had for the Lombard kingdom before the pope. This vital first meeting seems to have established a warm personal relationship between the two of them, which lasted until Hadrian's death in 795. The continuing Frankish siege of Pavia, which must have held for nearly ten months, proved too much and Desiderius surrendered himself and the city in June, soon after Charles's return to his camp.[14] This submission, perhaps necessitated by the outbreak of disease in the city, was followed soon after by those of the other main towns of the Lombard kingdom, without further fighting.[15]

Unusually lengthy as the siege had been, the precedents of the 750s might have led Desiderius to expect that the surrender of himself and the city would result in no more than a political submission to the Frankish ruler, probably the payment of tribute and the restitution of the papal towns, together with promises and guarantees for the future. In practice, however, it was to mark the end of an independent Lombard kingdom, with Desiderius and most of his family being taken into exile in Francia and Charles having himself pro- claimed as *Rex Langobardorum*.[16] A charter of the 5 June 774 has Charles using the title by this date.[17] As the city itself is said only to have fallen in this month, the existence of this document would seem to suggest that he had already planned to take the Lombard royal title and was employing it within two or three days at most of the fall of the capital. The charter in question, which conveyed a grant to the monastery of Bobbio, only survives in a twelfth- or early thirteenth-century copy with sixteenth-century corrections, and although its authenticity has not previously been impugned, there are features in it that would imply that the text is not fully reliable.[18] At the very least it is not trustworthy enough to support the kind of deduction suggested above. The first reliable evidence of Charles's employing of the Lombard royal title comes in the form of a clearly genuine charter dated 16 July 774.

The significance and indeed the extraordinary nature of these developments have often gone unremarked, perhaps not least because of the limited treatment of them in both Frankish and papal accounts. The fact that Charles was back in Francia and issuing charters from Worms by 2 September 774 also makes what had just happened in Italy seem more casual or even normal than it really was.[19] For one powerful kingdom to eliminate another militarily was highly unusual; it was even more surprising for the king of one people to take the title and monarchical role of that of another. For Charles to have proclaimed himself *Rex Langobardorum* arbitrarily would have been a pointless gesture, all the more so if his intention was immediately to withdraw his Frankish army back over the Alps. In practice, a claimant to the Lombard monarchy required the acceptance of the dukes and of the people as well as credible military power. The lack of further resistance after the fall of Pavia and the speed of Charles's return to Francia suggest that the Annalist's brief references to 'all the Lombards' coming from 'every city of Italy' and submitting to his authority relates to just such a process. In part the *pronunciamentos* on the part of rival dukes that had constituted Lombard politics for much of the late seventh and eighth century must have established a presupposition that rightful authority was in the hands of the one powerful enough to seize it.[20] But it also seems likely that the inception of the idea of Charles's claiming the Lombard throne, together with the negotiations needed to make this acceptable, once Desiderius had surrendered, preceded the fall of Pavia in June 774. Whether the scheme was devised by Charles and/or his Frankish advisers or was of papal origin cannot be known.

The nature of the Lombard kingdom at this time, with a balance between the aspirations of regionally based dukes, none of whom commanded overwhelming military or economic resources, made it relatively easy to leave it in the state in which the Franks found it. Changes in administration and in personnel came in due course, but relatively slowly.[21] Although there is little direct evidence of any sort, it does look as if Charles confirmed the northern dukes and other officials in their posts. During the Frankish conquest of the Lombard kingdom, Charles's ally Pope Hadrian I had launched an attack on the Duchy of Spoleto, which had long been a threat to Rome and much involved in the factional conflicts that had divided the city in previous pontificates. He had been able to eliminate duke Theodicius and replace him with a more pliable successor, in the person of an exiled and popular former claimant to the ducal office.[22] Further south, though, the more powerful Lombard duchy of Benevento remained beyond Frankish or papal control. Arichis II (758–87), duke of Benevento, who was married to a daughter of Desiderius, took the title of Prince in 774 and began minting gold coins in his own name, as a sign of independence.[23] But neither he nor any of the other dukes was able to lend any support to Desiderius's eldest son and nominal co-ruler Adelchis, who had obviously avoided the siege of Pavia, and who was forced to flee Italy to take refuge with the emperor Constantine V (741–75) in Constantinople.[24]

The absence of the new King of the Lombards in Francia and Saxony almost inevitably led to conspiracy amongst the dukes, long accustomed to take advantage of any signs of royal weakness, whatever they may have thought of the notion of being ruled by a Frank.[25] The leading figure in the plot was Hrodgaud, duke of Friuli, who may have proclaimed himself king.[26] He had the support of Stabilinius, duke of Treviso, who was also his father-in-law.[27] He may also have been negotiating with his fellow dukes Hildeprand of Spoleto, Arichis of Benevento and Reginbald of Chiusi.[28] Concluding his Saxon campaign of 775, Charles had to plan for an expedition into Italy early in 776. He spent Christmas that year at a royal villa at Sélestat near Strasbourg, and entered Italy via the duchy of Friuli early the following year. The Frankish annals record hardly any details of the campaign, in the course of which Hrodgaud was killed. Stabilinius was besieged in Treviso and taken prisoner.[29] This time, Charles appointed Frankish counts to replace Lombards in the towns that he took. He is known to have been in Vicenza and then in Ivrea in June.[30] The latter stop may already have been on his way home, as he had to return rapidly to Francia to deal with a major Saxon uprising, and he made no attempt to go to Rome or to take any steps concerning the dukes of Spoleto and Benevento.

While the Italian campaign of 773/4 had proved an extraordinary success, to a degree probably quite unanticipated, it had also opened the way to new problems. Charles's conquest of the Lombard Kingdom and taking of its royal title had given him clear, if not unchallenged, authority over the territories that had been ruled by the Kings in Pavia and the duchies that surrounded it. However, this was far from encompassing the whole of Italy. Control over Benevento, if not Spoleto, was by no means guaranteed by Charles's conquest of Pavia. The standing of the city and former imperial duchy of Rome was equally problematic, if for different reasons. Papal secular authority over this region in the centre of Italy had gradually been established from the pontificate of Gregory the Great (590–604), largely due to the inability of the imperial exarchs in Ravenna to protect it from Lombard attacks. However, despite the theological friction between papacy and empire over the issue of iconoclasm, the pope was in theory a subject of the emperor, and the lands that he controlled formed part of imperial territory. On such grounds previous popes had claimed the former imperial territories of the Pentapolis and even Revenna itself when these had been overrun by the Lombards around 750. The claim to the former had been the principal cause of friction between Rome and the Lombard kingdom ever since, and Hadrian I had clearly expected it to be resolved finally in the Papacy's favour after Charles's conquest of Pavia. He was to be disappointed, as Charles seems just to have ignored the papal requests and retained the disputed territories as part of the *Regnum Italiae*.

Although what in practice may have amounted to an independent papal state had come into existence, which was able to hold its own against potentially predatory neighbours such as the duchy of Spoleto, its actual constitutional standing is far from clear. Some have thought that the Papacy had created a generally recognised autonomous political entity out of its city and related territories, functioning under the title of the *Respublica Sancti Petri*. To translate *Respublica* as 'Republic' would be misleading, as it would imply to the modern reader a fully constituted sovereign state with a clearly defined constitutional character. The term *Respublica Sancti Petri* is more likely to have been intended to signify the sum of the landed estates owned by the church of Rome, and is neither the title of an independent sovereign state nor part of a claim to constitute one. It would be fair to say that in 774 the nature of the relationship in theory and practice between the popes and the Frankish king was far from clear and would need careful working out over a lengthy period of time.

As well as the different problems constitued by Rome, the territories of the former Exarchate, and the southern Lombard duchies, there also remained the question of the continuance of small enclaves of imperial territory in the far south of Italy and above all, until it was conquered by the Arabs, in Sicily. This island also contained important papal estates under direct imperial rule. At a theoretical level, the issue of Charles's authority over regions beyond the confines of the former Lombard kingdom may not have been settled until he acquired his imperial title in the year 800. The practical problems were both more immediate and more various, but by and large the Frankish ruler's approach was highly pragmatic and generally minimalist. Which is to say, he was prepared to leave most of the structures that he found in place and only change them when forced to, as by the revolt of 776. Frankish officials and other 'carpetbaggers' did not flood into Italy, as far as the evidence of names in charters would indicate. Issues of title and authority do not seem to have been allowed to become too significant, and the achieving of real control over more distant regions such as Benevento was only pursued when his other more immediate concerns in Francia and Saxony allowed the time. Hence Charles's rapid returns from Italy in both 774 and 776. In the late 770s, even the prospect of further territorial expansion, for instance across the Pyrenees into parts of northern Spain, could seem more attractive than fuller involvement in Italy.

Over the winter of 776/7, Saxon problems were the immediate priority but, as in 773, they seemed capable of being dealt with in a single campaign. When in the spring of 777 Charles held the first assembly to take place in Saxony, at Paderborn, it was to receive the submission of the Westphalians, who had apparently been cowed by the fighting in 776. Widukind and others had fled, and it thus proved possible for Charles to think about employing the Frankish military resources in other directions. By chance, as it may have seemed, a new opportunity presented itself at that point. Envoys arrived at the Paderborn assembly from the most powerful Arab local rulers in the Ebro valley in north-ern Spain, seeking Charles's help.[31]

The interest that they had in securing Frankish aid was due to the growing threat posed by the Umayyad Amirate of Córdoba to their continuing control of the Ebro region. The Umayyad state had been established in 756, when 'Abd al-Rahman I (756–88), one of the few surviving members of a dis-possessed dynasty that had ruled the whole Arab empire up to 749, crossed into Spain from North Africa. There, with the aid of supporters of his family and other opposition groups, he raised a revolt against Yusuf ibn 'Abd al-Rahman, who, although nominally the caliph's governor of the province of Al-Andalus, had been its independent ruler since 747. While 'Abd al-Rahman had quickly been able to defeat Yusuf and to establish his regime in Córdoba, the former seat of the governors' administration, his power in practice hardly extended beyond the valley of the Guadalquivir. It took nearly twenty more years to eliminate the grip of the partisans of Yusuf on Toledo, to crush a Berber messianic movement that controlled much of the centre of the penin-sula and to put down revolts in favour of the 'Abbasids, the caliphal dynasty that had replaced the Umayyads in the East in 750.[32] It was only in 776, with the elimination of the Berber leader Shaqya, that 'Abd al-Rahman I (756–88) was first in a position to impose his authority on the north-east of the penin-sula. In the period of local disorder that had followed the overthrow of Yusuf, who had been campaigning in the Ebro valley when called south to face 'Abd al-Rahman's invasion, various regional potentates had established themselves, particularly in the principal towns of Zaragoza, Barcelona and Huesca. Faced with the gradual advance of Umayyad power, these local dynasts looked to the Frankish ruler as a possible counterweight, and thus sent the appeal that reached him at Paderborn in the spring of 777.

For Charles, an opportunity to intervene in northern Spain would, like his Saxon and Italian ventures, have had something of the character of a traditional interest. Ever since Clovis (c. 481–c. 511) had put an end to the Visigothic kingdom in Gaul at the battle of Vouillé in 507, Frankish kings had tried to eliminate the last Visigothic enclave north of the Pyrenees in Septimania, and to establish their own power south of the mountains, at least in the Ebro valley. In the sixth century there had seemed some occasional chances of success, and Frankish control may have been briefly imposed on Pamplona and the western Pyrenees until the reign of the Visigothic king Sisebut (611/12–20), but the growing strength of the southern kingdom and Frankish divisions limited the latter's interference in Spain in the seventh century.[33] The Arab conquest of most of the peninsula in 711 and their elimination of a vestigial Visigothic kingdom in Septimania in 720 played a role in bringing about the unification of Francia under Carolingian rule. The Arab and Berber attacks on Aquitaine from 720 and on Provence in the 730s weakened two regional powers otherwise hostile to the emerging dominance of Charles Martel, and their appeals for help against Arab raids gave him the opportunities to impose his own authority on the two duchies in 735 and 739. Subsequent Arab weakness, due to civil wars and conflicts with the Berbers, both in Spain and in North Africa, had given Martel's son Pippin III a real chance to extend Frankish rule in the south-west. Nimes, Agde and Béziers were surrendered to him by a local potentate of Gothic origin in 752, and in 759 he gained control of Narbonne, the former capital of Visigothic Septimania and subsequently the main Arab garrison town in the region.[34] Thus longer-term Frankish royal tradition and the exploits of his immediate predecessors would have given Charles an interest in intervening further in the area of northern Spain.

This was not in any sense a 'proto-crusade' to aid the Spanish Christians, although in later tradition that is more or less what it would become. Charles was invited to assist the Muslim rulers of a largely Christian population by those rulers themselves, and there is no contemporary evidence that he saw himself as acting to save the Spanish Christians from Islam or as appealing to the local inhabitants on such grounds.[35] The author of this section of the *Annales Regni Francorum* merely reports that Charles despatched two armies, one under his own direction which passed through Pamplona. The two forces were said to have joined together at Zaragoza, where the local rulers gave hostages. Charles and his enlarged army, which contained Lombard and

Bavarian contingents, as well as Franks, Aquitanians and Provençals, 'destroyed Pamplona, and subjugated the Spanish Basques and the people of Navarre. He then returned to Francia.'[36]

As understatement this account is masterly to the point of mendacity. It conceals a catalogue of failure and deceit, and gives a victorious gloss to a tawdry campaign that could have become a complete disaster. Fortunately, both the Reviser and Einhard were prepared to be more forthright about these events, and some further light can be shed on them with the aid of Arab sources.[37] The Frankish armies advanced via the two ends of the Pyrenees. Charles's force probably came over the pass of Roncesvalles and proceeded down the Ebro towards Zaragoza, after capturing Pamplona.[38] In the latter town a local revolt had led to the murder of the Muslim governor in 799, and it is not clear if it had retained its independence thereafter. The second Frankish army entered Spain by the eastern Pyrenees and approached Barcelona, stronghold of Sulayman al-Arabi, who was one of those who had invited Charles to intervene to support them in 777. However, the city was held against the Franks, who were then unable to take it and proceeded instead to the rendezvous with Charles at Zaragoza, another supposedly friendly stronghold. As at Barcelona, the Arab and Berber garrisons refused to admit their Frankish would-be allies, and Charles was unable to take the city by siege or by storm. Whether there had been a division over this all along or whether the scale of the Frankish intervention caused a re-thinking cannot be known, but in Zaragoza one of the two local potentates who had appealed to Charles had been murdered by his colleague, who then appears to have reneged on any undertakings made by the envoys sent to Paderborn the previous year.[39]

With both Zaragoza and Barcelona hostile and no apparent hope of taking either, or of arousing other forms of local support, the now united Frankish army retired up the Ebro valley, destroyed the fortifications of Pamplona and withdrew across the Pyrenees via the pass of Roncesvalles. Here occurred the conflict that from at least the eleventh century onwards was to be made memorable in the *Chanson de Roland*, the fictional account of the Christian hero and Frankish knight, whose final deed was to fall in mighty combat against overwhelming numbers of Muslims in this chivalric affray. The reality of the battle of 778 is more starkly preserved in the work of both the Reviser and of Einhard. Both of these report how the Basques ambushed Charles's rearguard, detached it from his main force and massacred it. The army's baggage train was also plundered. Einhard records that amongst the dead were the Seneschal Eggihard, Anshelm the Count of the Palace and Hruodland (Roland), *praefectus* of the Breton March.[40] A surviving epitaph of Eggihard gives the date of the battle as 15 August, and also confirms his importance.[41] Both he and

Anshelm were amongst the most important members of the palatine aristocracy, in personal attendance on the king. Hruodland probably held the office of count, and from Einhard's words must have controlled the frontier district with Brittany in western Neustria. The loss, which was to go un-avenged, of three such major members of the court was a considerable disgrace and blow to morale.

The Reviser, who does not name the dead, but who admits that many courtiers (*aulici*) were killed, reports that the Basques dispersed so rapidly and effectively that Charles was unable to move against them. He also faced a major uprising in Saxony. All in all the events of 778 had been unfavourable. Charles's Muslim allies had proved unfaithful, he had suffered a military humiliation in the loss of leading members of his entourage and his absence in the south had allowed large-scale Saxon plundering, in the course of which many churches had been destroyed, even well into the Rhineland. While Charles may not have lost interest entirely in the Spanish frontier area, he never returned there in person. The problems both of defending such frontier regions and of taking advantage of any opportunities that might arise for military adventure and territorial expansion, such as that apparently offered by the envoys sent to Paderborn in 777, were clearly not easily going to be dealt with by a monarchy whose centre of power and interest lay so far away.

The same difficulties had to be faced, too, in the case of Italy. By the late 770s, experience had shown that, at least until the Saxon wars were fully concluded, royal interventions in both Italy and northern Spain could only be limited. Even so, conditions in Italy seemed to be changing in Charles's favour. In 779, following one of his rare visits to Neustria, the king was met on his return to Austrasia by Hildeprand, duke of Spoleto, who came in person to bring various gifts. The Annalist, followed by the Reviser, locate this meeting at the royal villa of Verzenay, but the *Annales Mettenses Priores* and some other annals place it in the context of a Frankish assembly at Düren. The latter would have made a far more public occasion for the Lombard duke's visit and acts of submission. Little is known of the previous history of Hildeprand. During the last stages of the Frankish siege of Pavia in 774, his duchy, then held by Theodicius, had been conquered by the forces of pope Hadrian, who had then installed Hildeprand, who had been living in Rome as an exile, as duke.[42] So dependent was he on papal support that the earliest documents issued by Hildeprand employ the years of Hadrian's pontificate in their dating clause.[43] By January 776 this practice had been replaced by use of Charles's regnal years, and it may be that Hildeprand now looked to the more distant Frankish king as a counterweight to the more immediate power of Rome. In 776 he was said to have been involved in

Hrodgaud of Friuli's brief attempt to gain the Lombard throne, but this was an accusation made by pope Hadrian, whose relations with his former protégé had distinctly cooled. Hildeprand certainly took no part in the campaigning of 776, which was confined to the north. However, relations with Rome and the accusations made that year may have led to his decision to go to Francia in person in 779.

Only after two years of further campaigning against the Saxons did Charles decide to return in person to Italy, to formalise certain important dynastic changes that he planned. He left Francia late in the year in 780, spent Christmas at Pavia, and was in Rome by Easter (15 April) of 781. There he had his second son by his marriage to Hildegard and who until then had had the less well-omened name of Carloman, baptised in the new name of Pippin by the pope. This sacrament was traditionally administered on the Thursday of Easter Week.[44] Hadrian I also took the role of Pippin's 'spiritual father', an important relationship that established special ties not only with his new godson, but also with the latter's actual father, Charles. This liturgical ceremony thus had important political resonances, and it was followed by a joint anointing and crowning of both Pippin and his younger brother Louis; the former as king of the Lombards and the latter as king of the Aquitanians.[45] The *Annales Mosellani* add that the betrothal of Charles's daughter Rotrud to the very young Byzantine emperor Constantine VI (780–96) was also announced at this time.

These arrangements represented not only an attempt to settle various pressing practical problems, but also the first version of Charles's plans for his own succession. These seem to have consisted of a determination only to allow his sons by his current marriage to Hildegard a future share in the Frankish kingdoms. He already had a son called Pippin, said by Einhard to be a hunchback, from an almost certain earlier marriage to a Frankish lady called Himiltrude. To baptise the second son of his marriage to Hildegard with the same name was a clear sign that the older Pippin was being excluded, and it is likely that Charles wished to consider him as illegitimate. The only one of his sons by Hildegard not mentioned in the annal for 781 was the eldest, who was named Charles after his father. It may be assumed that he was intended to inherit the Frankish kingdoms proper and Saxony, while his brothers ruled the more recently conquered territories of Aquitaine and the Lombard realm. Such a division would have needed approval, however formal, at a Frankish assembly, and, although the major sets of annals make no mention of this, it is significant that the *Annales Sancti Amandi* report for 780 that Charles 'divided up his kingdoms between his sons' immediately prior to his departure for Italy that year.[46] In other words, grandiose as the ceremonies and constitutional arrangements made in Rome in Easter 781 may undoubtedly have been, the actual plans had been devised and approved the previous year.

Although the younger Charles was not given the title or anointed as king at this time, in practice none of the three sons were of an age to exercise any personal authority. Louis, the youngest, had only been born in 778. In the longer term, a scheme for the succession had been unveiled, but in the shorter term these arrangements also provided some way of alleviating the practical problems of administering the greatly expanded territories that Charles had acquired since 772. The establishment of permanent courts in northern Italy and in Aquitaine allowed for the better supervision of important frontiers and of officials of indigenous origin whose loyalty might not be entirely reliable. Lombard sentiment may have been appeased by having a resident king once more in Pavia rather than a distant monarch over the Alps, and there were certainly no repeats of Hrodgaud's bid for the crown.[47] Aquitaine was a rather different matter, in that there had never previously been a Kingdom of the Aquitanians. Indeed the Aquitanian ethnic identity was largely a fiction that had been fostered by the Franks.[48] While the Italian kingdom survived, that of Aquitaine lacked cohesion and fell apart under pressure in the mid-ninth century.[49] In Charles's reign, however, it served as a useful way of supervising the Pyrenean borderlands and the Aquitanian heartlands that had put up a protracted struggle on behalf of the former ducal dynasty throughout much of the middle of the eighth century. While separate courts and administrations functioned in both of the Lombard and Aquitanian kingdoms, all major decisions continued to be made by Charles. One of the merits of the new organisation was that it permitted greater military flexibility. Smaller-scale campaigns could be conducted with local resources, rather than depending on the mobilisation of the full Frankish army especially when the latter was engaged elsewhere. Thus, in 785, while Charles was committed to a full-scale campaign in Saxony, an Aquitanian army crossed the eastern Pyrenees and occupied Gerona with the support of its inhabitants. This became the first Carolingian fortress in the region and the centre of a new frontier countship.[50] In Italy the new court at Pavia and the active support of Hadrian I clearly contained any further threats from the remaining Lombard dukes until Charles was ready to return to Italy again in person.

This occurred late in 786, following the return of an expedition against the Bretons, and with an apparently decisive subjugation of Saxony having been achieved the previous year. Charles spent the Christmas of 786 in Florence, before proceeding to Rome. His intention seems from the start to have been the subjection of the *de facto* independent principality of Benevento. Arichis II attempted to make a token submission, sending his elder son with gifts to meet

Charles and ask him not to advance into Beneventan territory. But this was insufficient, and Charles continued his advance as far as Capua. Arichis was clearly unable to put up an effective military resistance, and abandoned the city of Benevento in favour of the port of Salerno, possibly preparatory to a flight into Byzantine territory if further negotiation failed. Charles, however, was prepared to accept a fuller submission, which included the surrendering of Arichis's younger son Grimoald and a few others to serve as hostages. He also sent *missi* into the principality to receive oaths from Arichis and the leading members of the population. Although the text of these has not survived, it is likely that these were oaths of allegiance similar to those that had begun to be used in Francia in the 780s.[51] The expedition achieved its objectives rapidly and with no fighting. Thus, while Charles is recorded issuing charters in Capua on 22 and 24 March, he was back in Rome by the 28th in time for Easter (8 April).[52] Although the Frankish chroniclers present the venture in the triumphalist terms of Frankish might and Beneventan capitulation, they ignore the role of one of the more significant actors in the drama, the Byzantine Empire, which still controlled Sicily and much of Apulia and Calabria, and was also host to the fugitive Lombard prince Adelchis, Desiderius's son.

Had Byzantium been prepared to support Arichis of Benevento against the Franks, a longer and more violent conflict would inevitably have ensued. However, at this time the empire was more interested in securing Frankish good-will than in initiating a war in southern Italy. The premature death of the emperor Leo IV 'the Khazar' in 780 had left the empire in the hands of an infant, Constantine VI, with power being exercised by his widow Irene. One of the latter's earliest diplomatic moves had been to secure the engagement of the child emperor to Charles's equally young daughter Rotrud in 781, but in the meantime a diplomatic bond had been forged between the Empire and the Frankish monarchy. Indeed, it was probably no coincidence that envoys from Constantinople met Charles at Capua to request that Rotrud now be sent to Byzantium. The youth of the betrothed pair meant that the wedding itself was not likely to take place until the early 790s, but Rotrud in Constantinople would serve both as a symbol of what Irene had achieved diplomatically and perhaps as a hostage.[53] It may well be that the lack of support for Arichis was a way of tacitly underlining the merits of the proposed marriage alliance.

The empress Irene, who came from Athens and did not share the Iconoclast theological views of her former husband and his dynasty, was also trying to convene an Ecumenical Council of the Church to restore the veneration of icons and undo the ecclesiastical policies of Constantine V (741–75) and Leo IV (775–80). A first attempt in 786 to hold such a council in Constantinople had had to be abandoned due to a mutiny by Iconoclasts amongst the imperial guards. A second, and successful, attempt at a conciliar gathering was made in Nicaea in 787.[54] For such a council to be ecumenical, and thus of sufficient status to overturn the decisions of the previous council of 754, required the presence at least nominal representation from the Western Church. The closeness of Frankish–papal relations in this period thus made it advisable for the empress to remain on good terms with Charles, to ensure the co-operation of Rome. So, for several reasons, Irene was not willing or in any position to support Arichis of Benevento openly against the Franks at that time, even though he entered into secret negotiations with her, offering to recognise Byzantine suzerainty in return for military assistance and the title of Patrician. It seems that Charles was subsequently told about this early in 788 by pope Hadrian, who was anxious to undermine the Franco-Beneventan rapprochement that was then taking place.[55] Rome feared the regional threat to its existing territorial interests posed by Beneventan power and also hoped to benefit materially by acquiring certain towns and their lands in the south.[56]

The secret contacts with the empire had been resumed by Arichis's widow Adelperga, following his death in 787, but a change of ruler in the principality led to a brief re-alignment of Benevento towards the Franks.[57] The Beneventan heir Grimoald was still a hostage in Charles's hand when his father Arichis died in 787, but it became clear from the reports that the king received from his *missi* that serious trouble might be expected if he were not allowed to succeed to the principality.[58] Grimoald was allowed to return to take over the principality in 788, despite warnings from pope Hadrian I that he would prove unreliable, only after he had agreed to make his subordination to the Frankish monarch clear both on his coinage and in the charters that he issued.[59] This also led to the implicit cancellation of the promised transfer to the pope of the two Beneventan towns that Hadrian had previously thought he had secured from Charles. The presence of a co-operative Grimoald in Benevento was clearly needed, as relations with Byzantium had by then soured, not least because of Charles's unwillingness to fulfil his side of the agreement over the marriage alliance. In 787, in reply to a Byzantine embassy, he refused to send his daughter Rotrud to Constantinople, and the following year Constantine VI and Irene retaliated by sending an army to Italy under John the Military Logothete and ordering Theodore the imperial governor of Sicily to join it in an attack on Benevento. However, in a battle in Calabria the Byzantines were heavily defeated and John the Logothete was killed by the forces of the new prince of Benevento and of duke Hildeprand of Spoleto.[60]

Although this was a humiliation for Irene, which may have contributed to her having to surrender supreme authority to her son in 790, it did not lead to a permanent re-alignment of Benevento towards the Franks.[61] Quite the contrary; by 791 Grimoald III was in negotiations with the Empire and had dropped all references to Charles from his coinage.[62] The Frankish chronicles become strangely silent on southern Italian affairs, and only the *Annales Guelfybertani* ('the Wolfenbüttel Annals') refer to an expedition sent to Benevento in 792 under the nominal leadership of the young king Pippin of Italy. The outcome is not mentioned, and the evidence of the coinage would indicate that Grimoald was not brought back into strict subjection to Charles. Not until the latter came to Italy in person in 800 were further moves made to bring the Beneventans to heel. The Annalist records two raiding expeditions under king Pippin being sent into the principality in 800 and in 801, but no successes are reported. In 802 the news was distinctly bad. Winigis, who had been Charles's *missus* in the Calabrian campaign of 788 and had soon after succeeded Hildeprand as duke of Spoleto, was besieged by Grimoald in the town of Lucera and forced to capitulate. This removed the principal ally of the Franks south of Rome.[63] Not until 812 would a new treaty be made with Benevento, in which Grimoald agreed to pay Charles a tribute of 25,000 gold *solidi*, as part of the wider series of agreements made with the emperor Michael I. Even so, Benevento continued for decades thereafter to be able to play off the rival claims and ambitions of the Byzantine and Frankish rulers in southern Italy.[64]

While Carolingian power in that region had gone into sharp decline after a period of initial success in the later 780s, in Spain the pattern was reversed. The 778 expedition had been an almost unqualified disaster, and Charles had not interested himself directly in military ventures across the Pyrenees thereafter. However, the establishment of a separate if subordinate Aquitanian court in 781 created the possibility of further Frankish involvement in Spain. The counts and court officers who exercised authority in the name of the infant Louis were responsible for the defence of the Pyrenean marches, but were also able to take advantage of opportunities that arose to extend Frankish power across the existing frontiers.

No riposte was made in the last years of 'Abd al-Rahman I (756–88), and the opening phase of that of his son and successor, Hisham I (788–96) was dominated by a civil war between rival claimants.[65] However, with that ending in 791, the new Frankish enclave became the first target of a raiding expedition from Córdoba in 793.[66] According to Arab sources this penetrated as far as Narbonne, and took 45,000 prisoners.[67] The premature death of Hisham I in 796 brought on another period of strife over the succession before his son al-Hakam I (796–822) could establish his unchallenged authority. It was this period that gave the Franks the opportunity for more ambitious plans for intervention across the Pyrenees. Unlike the expedition of 778, this was to involve the active participation of an indigenous Christian ally, in the form of the kingdom of the Asturias.

This small monarchy in the northern mountains had come into being as the result of a successful local revolt around 718/22, and had gradually expanded to include most of eastern Galicia and part of the Basque region on the western fringes of the Pyrenees. At the time of the Ebro expedition of 778 there is no evidence of any contact between the Franks and the Asturian kingdom, then ruled by Silo (774–83). However, for the Asturians a period of relative tranquillity on their southern frontiers had given way in the 790s to annual large-scale raids from Córdoba, the equivalent to that which was directed against the Franks in 793. In consequence of military defeat in the first of these in 791, the Asturian king Vermudo I the Deacon (788–91) had abdicated, voluntarily or otherwise, to make way for his relative Alfonso II the Chaste (791–842), son of a former king, Fruela I the Cruel (757–68).[68] It was probably the new king who initiated contact with Charles, in the light of the mounting military threat from the Arab rulers in the south, in consequence of which the new capital of Oviedo had been twice sacked.

Einhard records the existence of diplomatic exchanges between Charles and Alfonso II, in which the latter described himself as the dependent (*proprius*) of the Frankish king.[69] The only such diplomatic activity that is known took place in 797, when Alfonso sent presents to Charles, who was then based at Herestelle in Saxony. This came at the end of an important year's campaigning in Spain, in which both the Franks and the Asturians had been active, and at a time the new ruler in Córdoba was heavily engrossed in wars with his great-uncles and with other rebels in Toledo and Zaragoza. One consequence of this had been that a local potentate whom the Frankish sources call 'Sadun', but who was almost certainly named Zatun, had made himself master of Barcelona and had offered his allegiance to Charles at Aachen early in the summer of 797. In consequence, Charles ordered his son Louis of Aquitaine to launch an expedition over the Pyrenees, which led to the capture of Huesca. Charles himself led an army into Saxony, but on his return found awaiting him yet more requests for his involvement in Spanish affairs. 'Abdallah ibn 'Abd al-Rahman, who had been the principal contestant against Hisham I in 788–90 and had been forced to go into exile in North Africa, now came to Aachen to seek Frankish help against his great-nephew, al-Hakam I. In November Charles sent him off to the frontier with Louis of Aquitaine, to help him launch a bid for power in the Ebro valley.[70] The same year had also seen a major Asturian raid into Al-Andalus, in which Alfonso II's army had taken and sacked the once import-ant Roman town of Olisipo, modern Lisbon. It was some of the fruits of this success that Alfonso sent to Charles in his winter camp.[71]

The similarity to the circumstances leading to his 778 expedition may have made Charles more cautious in 797, and he certainly had on his hands a Saxon war that could not then be safely abandoned. The responses of the Franks in 797 were more measured than nearly 20 years before, and much more wary of the promises made by the Muslim rebels. The promised surrender of Barcelona never materialised, and Huesca was back in the hands of rival Arab warlords by 800. In 798 Louis launched 'Abdallah on his way, but seems not to have taken any more active part in the increasingly chaotic events in the Ebro valley that ensued. 'Abdallah rapidly fell out with his main local ally, the rebel ruler of Zaragoza, Balul ibn Marzuk, and was forced to come to terms with his nephew al-Hakam I in 801.[72] No further dealings with the Asturian kingdom are known, though there are no grounds for thinking that diplomatic contact was broken off. But when the Franks made their most important gain across the Pyrenees in the year 801, it was not with any aid from Alfonso II, who may have been in temporary exile at the time, during a short-lived usurpation.

An Aquitanian expedition led nominally by king Louis, who may have arrived at a later stage of the proceedings, finally captured Barcelona in 801, taking advantage of the still-disturbed state of the Umayyad regime in Córdoba.[73] The episode, and Louis with it, was subsequently glorified in an epic poem written around 827 by Ermold the Black, which provides much circumstantial but probably unreliable detail about the siege and the surrender of the city.[74] It was, however, a major military achievement, well timed in being so close to Louis' father's imperial coronation the previous Winter. Despite various counter attacks, Barcelona, the most important port on the northern Catalan coastline, would remain in Frankish hands thereafter, and it was made the centre of a county, which become the most important one in the 'Spanish March'. A similar, but much less well recorded, venture across the western end of the Pyrenees in 806 led to the re-taking of Pamplona, briefly held by Charles in 778, which was also integrated into the Frankish administrative system. This proved less long lived, in that a successful revolt in 824 turned the city and surrounding region into an independent Basque kingdom.[75]

Charles's dealings with Italy and Spain produce interesting comparisons and contrasts. In both cases he was following precedents from his Merovingian and Carolingian predecessors in interesting himself in military ventures south of the Alps and the Pyrenees. Similarly, in 773 and 778 he was responding in an oportunistic way to unexpected requests for his help. Neither campaign was long pre-meditated. The outcomes were very different, due to the quite contrary nature of the circumstances and of the societies in which the Franks found themselves embroiled. In the case of Spain, it is notable that Charles did not feel obliged to avenge what was a serious if brief series of reverses, both military and diplomatic. Nor did he try to achieve his objectives, as he would in Saxony, by continuous military pressure. He and his advisers clearly recognised that the Saxon wars stood much higher up the scale of priorities for a Frankish ruler whose main centres lay in Austrasia than did any adventuring south of the Pyrenees. In the same way, Charles himself showed no personal inclination to go campaigning in central and southern Italy. He achieved what he did in those regions largely vicariously, and as much through diplomacy as through warfare. The challenge to his control of the former Lombard heartlands in 776 did merit his involvement, but in general the limited nature of the changes in civil administration and its personnel, and the relatively restricted nature of his patronage of the church and of monasteries in Italy, indicate the limits of his interest in trans-Alpine affairs. It is perhaps ironic that the imperial title that he took in 800 may have been intended primarily or initially to have been a way of resolving various anomalies in his constitutional and practical position in Italy, rather than as a reflection of his achievements in Francia.

5

TASSILO III AND BAVARIA, 781–8

It is probably no coincidence that immediately after the apparent resolution in 787 of all remaining military and political problems in Italy, with the submission of duke Arichis II of Benevento and the reception of envoys from Byzantium, that Charles turned his interest towards Bavaria. This, like Italy, was a region that had attracted the interest and had required the military and diplomatic involvement of his Carolingian predecessors. Ensuring the loyalty and curbing the power of its ducal dynasty had also been interests of the Frankish kings from Merovingian times onwards.

The origins of the Bavarians, the inhabitants of the basin of the Upper Danube immediately north of the Alps, has remained a subject of scholarly debate.[1] Argument has been advanced to present them as a largely Roman population, descended from that of the former province of Rhaetia, perhaps reinforced by fugitives from Norricum. Others would prefer to see them as a basically Germanic people, equivalent to others such as the Thuringians and the Alamans who secured a significant territorial settlement but never became as powerful or extensive as the Franks. A combination of elements of both would seem probable.[2] Some scholars have also detected Slavic cultural influences, at least on the eastern area from the later sixth century onwards.[3] For present purposes, what is significant is that the Bavarians represented a distinct population established in an important area. The upper Danube basin served then as now as a corridor between the upper Rhine and Thuringia on the one hand and the northern Balkans and the Hungarian plains on the other. The frontier on the eastern side, where the lands of the Bavarians confronted the territory of the Avar confederacy, lay along the line of the river Enns, and to the south-east lived predominantly Slav populations. Important passes into Italy, such as the Brenner, are also accessible from the southern edge of Bavaria, which thus represented a significant cross-roads of communications in both north–south and east–west directions. Firmer integration of Italy into the Frankish kingdom and the security of both from Avar and Slav attacks via the Danube made the control of Bavaria particularly desirable.

The region was also of economic significance. Particularly in the eighth century, its potential as a salt-producer began to be exploited.[4] This is symbolised most directly in the way in which the old Roman settlement of *Iuvava* gained its German name of Salzburg, 'Salt-town', and in the same period also became the principal ecclesiastical centre of the eastern half of the duchy. The salt mining and trade was vital to a number of other food producing and preserving processes, and was almost certainly also a major item of exchange in economic dealings with the Avars to the east. Archaeological evidence suggests a general rise in prosperity and in the richness and diversity of the material culture of the Bavarians in the eighth century.[5] There also seems to be evidence of a growth in the size of the population, which began to affect their relations with their neighbours.[6] This period saw Bavarian expansion southeastwards, bringing the Slavic Carnantanians under their control in the in the 740s and then, following a revolt, even more firmly in 772.[7]

Like the Germanic peoples east of the Rhine, such as the Thuringians and Alamans, the Bavarians had been brought under Frankish hegemony early in the Merovingian period. They had been placed under the authority of a *dux* of Frankish origin by the mid-sixth century. The late eighth-century Lombard historian Paul the Deacon gives the title of king to Garipald, the first member of this ducal family to be recorded, but there is no other evidence to confirm this status.[8] He married Walderada, daughter of the Lombard king Wacho (c. 510–40), who had previously been the wife of the Frankish king Theudebald (548–55). Tassilo I, who is most likely to have been their son, is said to have been made king of the Bavarians around 593 by the Frankish monarch Childebert II (584–96), but Paul only gives him the title of duke when recording his death around 610.[9] Although the early history of this dynasty, known as the Agilolfings, is poorly recorded, it is clear that they were regarded as amongst the most prestigious of Frankish families, and had interests well beyond Bavaria.[10] A member of the family living in Austrasia was murdered on the orders of Dagobert I (623–38/9) because he was 'proud and insolent'. His son, not surprisingly, later supported the revolt of the Thuringian duke Radulf against Sigibert III.[11]

The Agilolfings' descent from the daughter of king Wacho seems to have made them particularly significant for later Lombard rulers who lacked this royal pedigree. The family's status was enhanced by the marriage in 589 of the Agilolfing Theodelinda (d. 627), sister of Tassilo I, to the Lombard king Authari (584–90). On his death without heirs the following year, the seizure of the throne by Agilulf (590–616) duke of Turin was formalised by his marriage to his predecessor's widow.[12] Although their son Adaloald (616–26) was in due course deposed, his sister married the next two kings and was the mother of another, and the king after that, Aripert I (653–61), was the son of Theodelinda's brother Gundoald. Even when this dynasty lost the throne in 712, the Agilolfing connection continued to be highly valued. Thus, the powerful new Lombard king Liutprand (712–44) soon married the daughter of duke Theodo of Bavaria (died c. 717).[13] These matrimonial ties could also work in both directions. Thus the wife of the last Agilolfing duke, Tassilo III (748–88) was daughter of the Lombard king Desiderius (757–74) and thus brother-in-law of the exiled claimant Adelchis. These close and continuing ties with the Lombard kingdom made the Bavarian dukes particularly significant in respect of Frankish involvements in Italy, and might have been expected to make them more sympathetic to Lombard than to Carolingian interests. However, their relationships were by no means one-sided, nor was the ducal dynasty unchallenged in its own lands.

The initial relationship with the Frankish monarchy meant that the Agilolfings always remained theoretically subordinate to the Merovingians and then their Carolingian successors, and at the very least had to remain sensitive to the fluctuations in the power of their overlords. There were also other, lesser but still powerful landowning families in Bavaria. Some of these, like the Agilolfings themselves, were of ultimately Frankish origin, and others were very much aware of how the Frankish monarchy could be used to serve as a counterweight to the authority of their ducal overlords.[14] Ultimately, it may have been the willingness of some of the other noble houses in Bavaria to co-operate with Charles that brought about the elimination of the Agilolfing dynasty in 788. The ensuing partition of the duchy into a series of smaller counties gave far more scope to the local ambitions of such aristocratic families than had the single over-arching dukedom of the preceding period. It has been argued that the Bavarian aristocracy to the west of the river Inn were predominantly pro-Frankish, while the dukes drew their main support from the area east of this line.[15] This has perhaps proved too hard and fast a divide, as the patterns of land holding and kinship were more complex and noble estates more widely distributed than this suggestion implies, but it may represent a general impression of the political realities of the mid to late eighth century in Bavaria.[16]

Other influential interests that may not have been entirely well disposed towards the Agilolfings included those of the Church, or at least some of its bishops. It was the ducal dynasty, particularly in the person of duke Theodo (d. 717), who in 716 was the first of his line to make a pilgrimage to Rome, that

had been particularly active in building up the ecclesiastical structures of
Bavaria, and in promoting missionary activity both within its borders and then
beyond them into the Slav lands of Carantania.[17] Dioceses were established at
Regensburg, Freising and Salzburg, and a series of monasteries were founded,
often under ducal patronage, that served to extend the landed possessions and
the organisational structures of the Church into important frontier areas.[18] Not
least active in this respect was duke Tassilo III, who founded the monasteries
of San Candido (or Innichen) in 769 and Kremsmünster in 778.[19] Frankish
attempts to become involved in these processes, as in Boniface's efforts at
diocesan reorganisation in the 740s, seem to have been resisted, but the
Bavarian episcopate itself could not be indifferent to the growth of interest in
reform in the western Church at this period, and thus increased its contacts with
Francia. At the same time, for both ideological and economic reasons, it may
have come increasingly to favour the authority of the more distant Frankish
kings over that of the ducal dynasty.[20] The rise of conflicts between the two in
the course of the eighth century certainly gave increasing opportunities for both
secular and ecclesiastical magnates in Bavaria to decide in which direction they
should align themselves.[21] As in the case of the lesser aristocracy, it is worth
stressing that the evidence is ambiguous, and that the possible anti-Agilolfing
sentiments amongst the episcopate should not be over-emphasised.[22]

The Agilolfing family emerges rather more clearly than it had in previous
periods in the sources relating to the earlier eighth century, when, like the
other dukes east of the Rhine, they seem to have secured a *de facto* freedom
from rule by the Frankish kings. This was something that the Pippinid or
Carolingian Mayors of the Palace sought to reverse. Charles Martel is
recorded as having campaigned in Bavaria in 725.[23] A second campaign
followed in 728.[24] The very brief sets of Minor Annals do not report either the
aims or the outcomes of these two expeditions. The Continuations of the
Chronicle of Fredegar, which although nearly contemporary are often chronologically vague and misleading, record a single campaign in which Charles,
passing through the lands of the Alamans and the Suabians, reached the
Danube. Having 'subdued the region', he is then reported to have returned
with much treasure, together with a lady called Beletrude and her niece
Swanachild.[25] Just how much reliance should be placed on the unsupported
claims of this source is a matter for debate. The Agilolfings certainly retained
their territorial authority, which is more than the ducal houses in Aquitaine
and Provence would be permitted in the 730s. On the other hand, the fact that
Charles Martel did not return to Bavaria after 728 would suggest that he had
secured some recognition of his wider authority. This was symbolised by his
subsequent marriage to Swanachild.

As previously discussed, the succession to Charles Martel's power by his two elder sons was by no means easy or rapid. Those who had been oppressed or had suffered under Charles's regime were quick to try to reassert themselves. It took several years of fighting for Pippin III and Carloman to regain most of what their father had once held. Bavaria, as much as Aquitaine, was probably a case in point. Their own sister, Chiltrude, fled to Bavaria in 741 and there married its duke Odilo.[26] The new Mayors launched a campaign against him in 743 but no report is given of its outcome, which in the light of the normally triumphalist tone of the Annals would suggest that it met with little success.[27] The even less objective Continuations of the *Chronicle of Fredegar* claim a victory in a battle on the river Lech but admit to heavy Frankish casualties and an immediate return home.[28] What may have been the first opportunity for the Carolingians really to impose themselves effectively on Bavaria and its ducal house came when duke Odilo died on 18 January 748. By this time Grifo, the son of Charles and Swanachild, was once more a player in this complex game, having escaped from captivity and taken refuge with the Saxons in 747. He seized control of the duchy with the aid of a Bavarian count called Suidger, dispossessing Odilo and Chiltrudis's infant son Tassilo. The latter and his supporters could only turn to Pippin III for help. This took the form of an expedition that captured Grifo, and re-installed Tassilo '*per suum beneficium*'.[29]

That Tassilo was thereby made to accept the superior authority of his uncle, Pippin, and had been placed under obligations to assist him militarily, is demonstrated by the extraordinary account of these events given by the Continuations of the *Chronicle of Fredegar*, which refer to this whole episode as a Bavarian revolt against the authority of Pippin III.[30] According to this account, written only three years later in 751, the Bavarians then became so terrified at Pippin's approach that they fled across the river Inn and 'sent envoys with many presents and submitted to his authority, taking oaths and giving hostages that they would never become rebels again'. Even for this source this is an amazing travesty of the truth, but on the other hand represents very clearly what Pippin and his closest followers may have felt had been achieved. In 756 Tassilo was summoned by Pippin to take part in his second Lombard campaign, and marched with him to Pavia.[31] The following year he was apparently summoned to a Frankish assembly held at Compiègne, where he was required to 'commend himself into vassalage' and to swear 'innumerable oaths'. He 'promised fealty to king Pippin and to his sons Charles and Carloman, behaving honestly and faithfully, in accordance with the law and as a vassal should to his lords.'[32] The oaths were taken on the bodies of Saints Denis, Rusticus, Eleutherius, Germanus and Martin, representing a surprising array of the saints venerated in northern Francia, whose relics would have had to be brought to Compiègne specially for the purpose and from locations as far away as Paris and Tours.

It is perhaps not surprising that this detailed narrative, heavily underlining the nature and the seriousness of the oaths taken to Pippin and his young sons, has recently and rightly been called in question as a strictly contemporary record.[33] It is quite out of keeping with the rest of the Annalist's brevity and style in the treatment of the events of this period, and at the same time corresponds suspiciously closely with arguments and claims that would be made in the late 780s. Indeed, the whole character and conception of the oaths supposedly taken by Tassilo at this time appear anachronistic in the context in which this description is placed. It may be doubted whether the event here described ever took place. No mention is made of it in the final (and now rather more reliable) section of the Continuations of the *Chronicle of Fredegar*, covering the years 751 to 768. The heavily propagandistic nature of this work would have made the inclusion of such information very likely, as can be seen from the treatment of the events in Bavaria in 748.

The doubts that can be felt about the reliability of the Annalist's account of the 757 oaths, and possibly of their very existence, casts suspicion on his subsequent references to duke Tassilo and his obligations to Pippin III and then to Charles. If hindsight was dictating the narrative for 757, then it is bound to have influenced other sections. Caution is needed in trying to estimate just what did happen in subsequent years. In the next reference to Tassilo in the *Annales Regni Francorum*, the oaths are brought up again. In 763 Pippin launched his fourth Aquitanian campaign, initiating it with an assembly held at Nevers on the upper Loire. There, we are told 'Tassilo brushed aside his oaths and all his promises and sneaked away on a wicked pretext, disregarding all the good things which King Pippin his uncle, had done for him. Taking himself off, with lying excuses, he went to Bavaria and never again wanted to see the king face to face.'[34] Again, the final phrase here indicates hindsight. That Tassilo and Pippin would never meet again could only be affirmed after the latter's death in 768. That Tassilo took no part in the 763 campaign is not improbable, but whether we should accept the Annalist's gloss on his motives and on the character of the reason why he did not accompany his uncle into Aquitaine is another matter. This all sounds much more like a subsequent raking up of accusations that could be made against the duke. Certainly Pippin is not recorded as taking any action against his Bavarian nephew during the last five years of his life.

The Annalist indicates that Bavarian contingents continued to fight in the Carolingians' wars.[35] Also, in the difficult period of joint rule between Charles and Carloman, when in 770 what may have been intended as an alliance against the latter was being put together, their mother queen Bertrada is reported as passing through Bavaria on her way to Italy. Although nothing more is said, at the very least it may be suspected that she sought to enlist Tassilo's support for the league that was being formed against Carloman. If so, it is not known which if either party he actually favoured, but as the son-in-law of the Lombard king Desiderius he might have been expected to support the latter's rapprochement with Charles.[36] Although hagiography is not always easy to use as a source for precise historical details, a reference in Eigil's *Life of Sturm* indicates that good relations were established between Tassilo and Charles early in the latter's sole reign. Sturm (d. 779), the first abbot of Fulda, served as an envoy from the king to the Bavarian duke probably just before the outbreak of the first Saxon war, in other words in 772/3, if the implications of the *Life* be accepted.[37] Little as we know in general of the internal events in the Bavarian duchy at this time, there are also some indications that ducal power was expanding in this period. One set of annals records a victory by Tassilo over the Carantanians, in the south-west of modern Austria, in 772.[38] For this he was hailed by an Irish cleric living in Bavaria as a new Constantine. He was also active in promoting conversion to Christianity amongst the recently conquered Slavs.[39] His foundation of the monastery of San Candido or Innichen in 769, situated on the line of the old Roman road from Augsburg to Aquileia, was specifically intended to facilitate the evangelising of the Slovenes, another of the Slav groups on the frontiers of Bavaria.[40]

781 appears to mark a change in relations between Charles and his cousin Tassilo, but it is possible that some of the reporting is again influenced by hindsight. In some of the minor annals there may be found a simple record that Charles held the annual assembly at Worms that year, and that Tassilo came and presented gifts to the king.[41] However, the *Annales Regni Francorum*, followed here by both the Reviser and the compiler of the *Annales Mettenses Priores*, have a fuller and more complex tale to tell. According to this tradition, following Charles's visit to Rome in 781 and the baptism there of his sons Pippin and Louis, the king and pope Hadrian I agreed that ambassadors should be sent to Tassilo 'to remind him of his previous oaths, and not to do anything other than what he had long previously promised under oath to the lord king Pippin, to the great king Charles and to the Franks.' The envoys are named; two bishops, Formosus and Damasus, were appointed by the pope, while Eberhard the Magister Pincernarum (or Chief Butler) and a deacon called Richulf served as Charles's appointees. Tassilo apparently then agreed to come to the assembly at Worms to which he was summoned, in return for 12 hostages being given for his safety. At the assembly he in turn is said to

have pledged 12 hostages of his own for his future good conduct. These were subsequently delivered to the royal villa of Quierzy by bishop Sindbert of Regensburg.[42]

The giving of the names of the envoys inspires some confidence in this narrative, but its dependence on hindsight is once more revealed by the Annalist's parting comment that Tassilo 'did not long remain in the faithfulness that he had pledged'.[43] References to the previous oaths and the gloss put on Tassilo's motives may indeed be suspect, but the basic procedures outlined, as with the personnel involved, are probably more reliable. Charles clearly wanted Tassilo at his assembly at Worms, and exchanges of hostages are likely then to have been arranged to achieve this. At the very least, for Charles to give hostages for Tassilo's safety would imply that the latter's relationship was not that of a master to a vassal.[44] This was a recognition of the high standing and independence of the Bavarian duke, who clearly did not normally have to attend the annual assembly. Why Charles wanted him particularly to appear in 781 is never explained, but it may be a reflection of the recent establishment of the sub-kingdoms in Italy and Aquitaine. Bavaria was of military and political significance as far as the former was concerned, and the assembly was itself the first occasion on which the Frankish aristocracy as a whole came together after the crowning of the new child kings. There are, thus, reasonably obvious motives for Charles wanting Tassilo's presence. The very hostile interpretation put upon the episode by the author of the *Annales Regni Francorum* does not have to correspond exactly with the contemporary realities of 781, and may yet again be a reflection of what was to happen later in the decade. However, the hostage exchange must be seen as testimony to the degree of independence of Frankish royal authority that the Bavarian duchy could still enjoy. This was something that Charles would soon be in a position to extinguish.

Whether Tassilo and his duchy's anomalous status was itself felt to be a provocation, or whether Charles felt that he needed to exert more direct control over Bavaria, it was to be in 787 that he first found an opportunity to act. When celebrating Easter in 787 at Rome, following the submission of Benevento, Charles and Hadrian I received envoys from Tassilo, in the persons of bishop Arn of Salzburg and abbot Hunric of Mondsee. They apparently requested the pope to act as peacemaker between the king and the duke. We are given no information as to the causes or consequences of any conflict between the two in the preceding years. However, the Annalist states that the king was keen to make a peace and the pope to broker it. The Bavarian envoys, though, said that they could not make any such agreement on their own authority.[45]

Although this might have seemed reasonable enough, it gave rise to an outburst from the pope, who is said to have recognised that they were lying and prevaricating. He immediately threatened to impose an anathema on the duke and his supporters if the oaths taken to Pippin and Charles were not fulfilled, and warned that if this were not done Charles and his army would be free from any danger of sin whatever burnings and killing they might care to inflict on the duke's territories. All responsibility would lie with Tassilo and his supporters.[46] This, it might be thought, is the logic of terrorism: the victim is made responsible for his own sufferings. It might also be wondered whether this episode had not been deliberately stage managed to achieve the precise result that it did. It is inconceivable that Charles would ever have permitted Frankish *missi* to make any form of treaty in his name without his consent and consultation. Requiring the Bavarian envoys so to do, for which they were most unlikely to have had any authority, provided the opportunity for the papal outburst and sanctioning of the use of any degree of violence. There are no indications given that there had been any previous attempt at negotiations, nor anything beyond Hadrian's feelings to justify his claim that the ambassadors, both clerics of high status, were shifty liars. Indeed, it is worth noting that the senior of the two, bishop Arn of Salzburg, who was a Bavarian and formerly a deacon of the see of Freising, had also been a denizen of Charles's court and had been made abbot of Saint-Amand by 782.[47] It seems improbable that he would be a committed partisan of the duke in any conflict with the king.

It is notable that the annals for 787, and to a slightly lesser extent for 788, are disproportionately long in comparison to those that both precede and succeed them. The lengthy account of the papal intervention and threats is one reason for this, and the degree of detail exceeds that normally to be found in the annual entries. This episode was, therefore, considered to be particularly significant by the compiler of the annals and deserving fuller than usual reporting. Above all it provided a justification for what was to come, the overthrow of the Bavarian duke and the ending of his dynasty. That no hostile military act is ever recorded of Tassilo against Charles and that no more obvious *casus belli* was provided in contemporary sources, makes these papal pronouncements and the repeated reference back to oaths supposedly taken in 757 specially important in the justification of the king's actions.

Returning to Francia, Charles called an assembly in Worms, where he apparently explained to the bishops and nobles what had been achieved in Italy and 'what had been done concerning Tassilo', in other words the papal anathema and justification for a campaign. *Missi* were then sent to order Tassilo to come to the assembly 'in order that all should be fulfilled according to the order of the Apostolic (pope) and as was only just … that he should be obedient and faithful to the lord king Charles and to his sons and to the Franks'. As no mention is made of any negotiation over hostages, this was probably not offered, and Tassilo, whose sense of insecurity must have been considerably greater than in 781, refused to come. This provided a final excuse for action. As the Annalist, here continuing this lengthy apologia for the king, put it 'Then the lord king Charles, together with the Franks, seeing the justice of his cause, prepared a campaign.'[48]

This was to take the form of a three-pronged assault on Bavaria. Charles and the Frankish forces advanced from Worms to the river Lech, near Augsburg. A second army, made up of eastern Franks, Saxons and Thuringians, was to assemble on the Danube at Pförring between Ingolstadt and Regensburg, while a third force from Italy, initially under the nominal command of the child king Pippin, proceeded via Trento to Bolzano. Bavaria was thus threatened simultaneously from the north, the south and the west. Tassilo submitted without resistance, and coming to meet Charles 'returned the dukedom that had been given to him by the lord king Pippin (III) and acknowledged himself to have sinned in all things and to have acted evilly'.[49] He then took an oath of vassalage to the king and surrendered 13 hostages, including his son Theodo, and was permitted to leave. The Reviser adds that Charles took oaths from the Bavarians and pardoned Tassilo. How extensive the oath taking was is not known. It may have been confined to the leading men of the duchy. The pardon, though, was to prove a temporary affair.

In 788 Charles held an assembly at Ingelheim, where he had spent the Christmas of 787. Hither came Tassilo, whose status after his 'return' of the duchy is uncertain, as was required of a royal vassal. In theory the slate had been wiped clean by the royal pardon of 787, but new accusations were forthcoming. Unnamed Bavarians accused him of conspiring with the Avars beyond the frontiers of the duchy and of uttering treasonable statements against the king. This was all said to have occurred after the submission made the previous year, and to have been prompted particularly by Tassilo's wife Liutperga, the daughter of Desiderius. Once more, the Annalist goes into surprising amounts of detail in recording the charges against Tassilo, who is said to have 'ordered his *homines* to make mental reservations when they were swearing oaths and to swear deceitfully; what is more, he confessed to having said that even if he had ten sons he would rather lose every one of them than accept that the agreements should remain as they were or allow what he had sworn to stand'.[50] To all of this Tassilo is said to have confessed, though the Reviser weakens this assertion on the part of the Annalist by stating instead that the duke did not attempt to deny the accusation. But he also adds that the charge concerning the conspiracy by the Avars was proved by what was to happen later in the year.[51]

As the assembled lay and clerical notables were not to know what was going to occur on the eastern frontiers of Bavaria in a few months time, this can hardly have been the cause of their sentencing Tassilo to death. Nor can his apparent inability to deny the charges brought against him be taken entirely at face value. The *Annales Nazariani*, although nothing like so detailed in the account as the *Annales Regni Francorum*, have some interesting information to offer as to the precise ordering of these events. They indicate that Tassilo came to Ingelheim as commanded. 'Following this' Charles 'sent his legates into Bavaria in search of the wife and children of the aforementioned duke. They carried out the king's orders conscientiously and effectively and brought all of these, together with their treasures and household, extremely numerous, to the ... king. When this had been done, the duke was arrested by the Franks; his weapons were taken away and he was brought before the king.'[52] In other words, as well as already having Tassilo's son Theodo in his hands, Charles arranged for the seizure of all of the other members of the duke's family before levelling charges against him. In the circumstances is it surprising that he 'was unable to deny' them? The outcome of these proceedings can hardly have been in doubt.

The sentence of death was not carried out. It was hardly necessary, as the king had now secured what he sought, the elimination of the Bavarian duchy. 'Moved by mercy', Charles had Tassilo tonsured as a monk.[53] He was despatched to the monastery of Jumièges (in what would become Normandy). His sons Theodo and Theodebert suffered a similar fate, though it is not known where they were sent, and his Lombard wife was exiled. The ducal line thus was terminated. Other Bavarians were also banished from the former duchy, which was promptly broken up into a number of countships, under the direction of a *Praefectus* or 'Prefect'. The first incumbent of this office was Charles's brother-in-law, the Alamannic noble, Gerold (d. 799).[54] Later in 788 Charles took an army into Bavaria, as far as Regensburg, where he received the submission of the people, who were also required to hand over hostages for their future good behaviour. Only the *Lorsch Annals* and the conciliar *acta* record Tassilo's final appearance, at the Council of Frankfurt in 794. Although the main purposes of this great ecclesiastical assembly were concerned with the theological problems of Adoptionism and the restoration of the veneration of icons in the Byzantine Empire, Tassilo was apparently brought to Frankfurt from Jumièges, and was there 'reconciled with the lord king, renouncing and handing over to the lord king all the rights which he had in Bavaria.'[55] As this was already have supposed to have occurred in 787, it must be assumed that

Charles felt it useful to have his position in Bavaria further buttressed by requiring the former duke to make an even more public renunciation in this impressive gathering, attended by bishops from Italy and probably from Britain as well as from Francia. Tassilo then returned to permanent obscurity in his monastery.

In eliminating Tassilo and his dynasty, however ruthlessly, Charles brought to a successful conclusion a line of policy that had been pursued over many decades by his father, uncle and grandfather. This was the removal of the quasi-independent ducal houses, all of Merovingian origin, that controlled the major ethnic groupings on the periphery of Francia. Charles's methods were as brutal and as cynical as those of all his predecessors. It is particularly notable how the Carolingian besmirching of the reputations of the ducal dynasties is fully reflected in contemporary Frankish historical writing, be it in the Continuations of the *Chronicle of Fredegar*, the *Annales Regni Francorum* or the numerous other sets of lesser annals. It is rather more surprising to see how widely this highly partisan and even mendacious historiography has been accepted at face value by several generations of modern scholars.

6

CONFLICT ON THE STEPPES:
THE AVARS, 788–99

Although the accusation levelled against Duke Tassilo III of Bavaria in 787/8, that he was plotting with the Avars against Charles and the Franks, was made by the Annalist and was later to be repeated with even greater verve by Einhard, who blurs the precise chronology of his predecessors to make the Avar alliance precede the campaign of 787, it is far from proven.[1] Such charges of conspiracy with enemies from beyond the frontiers had also been made against the quasi-independent dukes of Aquitaine and of Provence in the 730s, when Charles's grandfather Charles Martel had been trying to get rid of them. In their cases it was the Arabs who filled the role of pagan allies. It is possible to show that the charge levelled against duke Eudo of Aquitaine was entirely false and that against duke Maurontus of Provence almost certainly so.[2] As in the case of the Aquitanians in 732 or 733, so with the Bavarians in 788, it is highly surprising to find that they themselves were the first target for attack by their supposed allies. An Avar raid on Bavaria was launched in 788, which was driven back by the local forces prior to Charles's arrival at Regensburg.[3] It is probably more sensible to consider the intermittent war that followed between the Franks and Avars more in terms of the wider context of frontier relations than as the unexpected outcome of a supposed plot with a deposed Bavarian duke.

The Avars were one of a succession of primarily nomadic peoples who rose to dominance in the area of the plains north of the Danube following the first arrival there of the Huns in the late fourth century.[4] The first appearances of the Avars in western sources date to the mid-sixth century, though they had been known to the Byzantines for rather longer. Dominance along the middle Danube had been disputed between three Germanic peoples, the

89

Gepids, the Heruls and the Lombards. According to literary texts, it was the last of these who allied themselves with the Avars to try to break the power of the Gepids. The Avar response is said to have been far more effective than the Lombards anticipated, in that the Gepids were eliminated and their territories were occupied by the victors.[5] The presence of these new and powerful neighbours was, according to Lombard tradition, the reason that they in turn abandoned their lands around the upper Danube and invaded Italy in 568. Whatever the truth of the details of these tales, archaeological evidence seems to confirm their general outline. Early Avar burials dating to the second half of the sixth century have been located both in the valley of the Tisza and also in the areas to the north and east of Lake Balaton. In the former context they are located in a region that is also rich in Gepid cemeteries and in the latter these finds are clearly on the edge of what had been a Lombard cultural area.[6]

As members of a non-literate society, the Avars have left no written record of themselves, and, apart from what can be deduced archaeologically, it is only from the accounts of their neighbours that anything can be known of their history.[7] Scholarly argument exists as to the possible origins not just of the Avars but of other nomadic confederacies from the time of the Huns onwards in developments taking place on the other side of Asia, on the north-western frontiers of China. For some historians successive waves of peoples displaced from the latter area, partly due to military successes on the part of some of the Chinese dynasties and partly due to local rivalries and conflicts between nomad confederacies on the frontiers of China, are thought to have made their way across Asia to reappear on the eastern fringes of Europe. Thus, the Huns have been identified with the Hsiung Nu, who were dislodged from a dominant position on the frontiers of China by the Han dynasty in the first century AD.[8] By a similar line of argument the Avars have been seen as a continuation in the West of the eastern nomad confederacy of the Jou-Jan, that had periodically menaced the northern frontier of China in the time of the T'o-pa Wei dynasty.[9] The Jou-Jan had finally been eliminated by the Turks. However, it has to be said that the identification of the Huns with the Hsiung Nu is far from convincing and has been powerfully challenged.[10] The notion that a confederacy in defeat could transfer itself successfully over a distance of several thousand miles and during a period lasting over centuries, from the edge of the Gobi to the plains of Hungary, is by no means self-evident. From what is known of the history of such nomad groupings, it is their fragility and fissiparousness that is more marked than their cohesiveness and longevity. These are characteristics of their society that also emerge from the study of the Avars in the time of their dealings with Charles. It may be better to seek for the origins of the Huns and of the Avars in a western Asian rather than a far eastern context.[11]

The period of greatest Avar power was probably the first decades of the seventh century, when from their settlements around and to the north of the Danube they came to exercise a hegemony over many of the Slavic peoples both in that area and in the Balkans. This culminated in a bid to capture Constantinople in 626. Although the city was subjected to an extended siege, the lack of the necessary military technology on the part of the Avars and their Slav dependents together with continuing Byzantine naval dominance led to the failure of the attempt.[12] By the time of the emperor Constantine IV (668–85), Avar power along the lower Danube had been replaced by that of another nomad confederacy, the Bulgars.[13] The latter seem by this time to have defeated the Avars, who were thereafter confined to a more westerly sphere of influence. This remained centred on the areas around the Tisza and Lake Balaton. In the south Avar settlement extended beyond the Danube to the valley of the Sava, while its western edge probably reached from the latter river up to the lower valley of the Morava. There remained a small *cordon sanitaire* of minor Slav peoples between the principal area of Avar occupation and the territories of the Bavarians.

In several respects the conduct of the Avars resembled that of the Huns in the first half of the fifth century.[14] Although both were to all appearances powerful military forces, able to inflict defeats on more sophisticated, sedentary neighbours and oblige them to pay annual or other tributes, neither confederacy ever seems to have tried to conquer the territories of the empires on whom they preyed. It was the Slavs under Avar hegemony who settled in increasing numbers in the Balkans, while their masters remained predominantly to the north of the Danube, as had the Huns before them. Similarly, both Avars and Huns had, like most nomadic pastoralists, a considerable dependence upon the agricultural economies of their southern neighbours, but they appear to have tried to trade with them while keeping them culturally at a distance.[15] In the 440s the Huns had created a depopulated and devastated zone along the Danube to serve as a clearly demarcated frontier area between themselves and the Roman Empire, and had tried to restrict trading contacts to specific locations. The Avars achieved something similar by their establishing of regions of subject Slav peoples around the edges of their khaganate.[16]

However, the subjection of some of these Slavs, notably the Carantanians, by the Bavarians from about 742 onwards brought these two peoples into closer contact. While Carolingian propagandists made out that Tassilo and the Avars were allies, what little is known of the preceding 40 years would suggest that the gradual eastwards expansion of Bavarian power and influence, not least through Christian missions, had been a cause of friction between them and the Avars.[17] Although little is known of the details of the inner workings of such steppe societies as that of the Avars, from parallels with the better known Huns, it is very reasonable to believe that they were relatively well informed, if only in general ways, of what was happening beyond their own territories. Thus, the replacement of Bavarian ducal rule by that of the more powerful Frankish king in 787/8 may well have seemed a serious threat. They were possibly aware of Frankish expansion through Saxony into the Slav lands further north.

The effects of these changes along their western frontiers, and the growth of the power of the Bulgar confederacy to the east, seems to have thrown the Avars into what for want of a better word could be called a state of crisis. Unfortunately, we have little more than Frankish sources to rely on for our understanding of the ensuing events, and these chroniclers, naturally enough, tended to interpret them exclusively in military terms, and as yet another triumph for the Franks and their ruler. While the outcome was, in terms of treasure gained and prestige won, a remarkable achievement for Charles, it may not have been obtained in quite the simple way that the Frankish annalists describe.

The first conflicts between the Avars and the Franks took place in 788, in the aftermath of Tassilo's condemnation at Ingelheim. The author of the *Annales Regni Francorum* is not particularly well informed on these events, recording three battles, all of which, unsurprisingly, are seen as Frankish victories. One took place in Italy, probably in the duchy of Friuli, and the other two in Bavaria. Only the first of the Bavarian battles is precisely located, *in campo Ibose*,[18] taken to be on the river Ybbs, on what was then the eastern edge of Bavaria. The Reviser specifies that the second attack on Bavaria was in revenge for this defeat and the failure of the raid on Italy. In the same year conflict had broken out in southern Italy between the Byzantines and the Lombard dukes of Spoleto and Benevento, the former of whom had submitted himself and his duchy to Charles in 779 and the latter in 787.[19] Frankish forces were sent to assist them, and the whole campaign was apparently directed by a trusted *missus* called Winigis, who was himself made duke of Spoleto the following year. Although Byzantine sources do not confirm this, it is just possible that imperial diplomacy had also been at work amongst the Avars, and that their involvement on the frontiers of northern Italy in 788 was also, at least in part, inspired from Constantinople.[20] It is much more likely that the threat of greater Frankish involvement in Bavaria and the temporary power vacuum there resulting from Tassilo's downfall seemed to provide opportunities for raiding the temporarily weakened duchy. In no sense, though, are there solid grounds for believing that these Avar raids were something that Tassilo and his Lombard wife had instigated while facing the summons to meet Charles at Ingelheim.

Whether or not the Frankish (and Bavarian and Lombard) reactions to these raids were as decisive as the Annalist claims, two years of peace ensued between the Franks and the Avars. It was not until 791 that Charles, who had spent most of the intervening period in Worms, proposed military action against the Avars.[21] The Annalist's words seem to imply that there had been various diplomatic exchanges in the meantime, and this is made explicit by the Reviser. The principal issue appears to have been the frontier between Frankish and Avar territory, probably meaning the increasingly contentious eastern edge of Bavaria. The failure of these exchanges of envoys led to Charles proposing a campaign against the Avars at the assembly called at Regensburg, to avenge what were described as injuries inflicted upon 'the Christian people'.[22]

It is conceivable, as with the Saxons, that the conflict was exacerbated by the religious division between the Franks and the Avars, and that the missionary activities that had been sponsored by the Bavarian dukes and by the Frankish rulers amongst the Slavs, whom the Avars regarded as their subjects, were a particular cause of offence and of cultural friction. It is possible too that Avar raiding had also been directed against Christian sites, which would in any case have been the most obvious targets for such attacks.[23] Charles certainly made the ensuing expedition explicitly Christian in character. On reaching the river Enns the army spent three days (5–7 September) in penitential litanies, fasting and prayer and in performing of the liturgy, prior to entering Avar territory.[24] In one of the very few of his letters to have survived, Charles described these three days of litanies to his wife Fastrada.[25] According to this, the bishops accompanying the expedition decreed that, unless exempted on grounds of age or illness, everyone should abstain from meat and wine during the three day period. Delightfully, Charles also told Fastrada that it was possible to buy a daily exemption from the prohibition on wine, at a rate varying according to social class. Special masses were said and each cleric had to recite 50 psalms, while there was expected to be general almsgiving. It also seems from the lacunose final section of the letter that the queen and others not taking part in the expedition were required to carry out a similar three day fast for victory during the course of it.

The entry of the army into Avar territory no earlier than the second week in September 791, as confirmed by this letter, seems surprisingly late in the year, and certainly testifies to the degree of planning and preparation that had gone into the venture.[26] This seems to suggest a degree of healthy respect for their

logistics

opponents, which the outcome may not have justified, but the previous reputation of the Avars was formidable. The Frankish assault was two-pronged. One
division of the army, led by Charles, proceeded along the southern bank of the
Danube, while another one which included Saxon and Frisian contingents,
under the command of Count Theoderic (d. 793) and the Chamberlain
Meginfred (d. 800/1), followed the northern edge of the river.[27] A fleet, which
brought the baggage, maintained communications between the two. Both
detachments met local resistance in the form of earthworks and other defences
along the river banks and at the confluence of the Danube with some of its
tributaries, but there was no large-scale opposition, and certainly no pitched
battles. The annalists report that the various defences were taken and that the
Frankish forces were able to ravage the lands they passed through with
impunity, but in comparison with the Saxon campaigns there is something
of an air of anti-climax about this expedition, all the more so in the light of
the high degree of spiritual and temporal preparation that had been put into it.
A halt was finally called where the river Rába flows into the Danube about

Want
home

240 km east of the Enns. Charles led his detachment back to Regensburg via
the valley of the Rába, while Theoderic and Meginfred were ordered to take
their Saxon and Frisian contingents home via the intervening lands of the
Bohemian Slavs.[28] The only Frankish loss of any significance reported by the
annalists was that of about 90 per cent of the expedition's horses, caused by
the outbreak of a virulent equine disease.[29] In its way this expedition was a
major triumph of organisation and an enormous boost for Frankish morale and
prestige, but it had hardly penetrated the areas that can be shown archaeologically to have been the centres of Avar settlement and culture. Even so, the
Avar response must seem surprisingly limited in the light of their previous
military reputation.[30]

   The following year saw no renewal of hostilities, although Charles had a
floating pontoon bridge specially constructed for use on the Danube; no doubt
to facilitate communication between two parts of an army on opposite banks
of the river if an expedition similar to that of 791 were to be repeated.[31] In 793
such an operation appears to have been planned, but the army of northern
levies under the command of Theoderic was set upon and destroyed by the
Saxons on the river Weser, forcing Charles to abandon his scheme, while
trying to conceal knowledge of this disaster from the Avars.[32] It is testimony
to the spread of news over wide areas that the Arabs launched a very successful raid across the Pyrenees into Frankish Septimania this same year, because
they had heard that Charles was going to be embroiled in an Avar campaign.[33]
Renewal of war against the Saxons took up Frankish military efforts in 794
and 795.

In the course of his expedition into Saxony in 795, when Charles was on the Elbe, he received envoys from 'one of the leaders of the Huns (i.e. the Avars) known as the Tudun'.[34] The latter, who is never named other than by his title, apparently offered to come in person before Charles and to accept baptism as a Christian. In other words he was proposing a political submission to the Frankish ruler; this became a reality at Aachen in 796. Something of the background to this, apparently unexpected, development is explained by the annalist's references to a civil war that had broken out amongst the Avars. The Khagan and the 'Jugur' are said to have been fighting each other, and both then to have been killed by their own people. Taking advantage of this conflict, Eric duke of Friuli, the Frankish appointee to this important Lombard frontier march, had sent an expedition under a Slav leader called Wonomir to raid the *Hringum* or 'Ring' in 796.[35] This was also called 'the Field' by the Lombards, and appears to have been the main royal residence of the Avars.[36] Here considerable treasure, consisting of many generations worth of loot and tribute, was found and carried off, firstly to Aachen and thence for some of it to Rome, as a gift from Charles to the new pope, Leo III. In the light of this extraordinary opportunity a second expedition was launched the same year, under the command of king Pippin of Italy, to complete the removal of the Avar treasures and the total destruction of the Ring.[37] The Reviser also mentions the Tudun's submission and the baptism of himself and his followers, but adds that he subsequently broke his oath to Charles and came to an unhappy end.[38] What this was and when it occurred are not specified.

All of this information is depressingly cryptic, in that it constitutes virtually the only evidence for the collapse of Avar military and political predominance in the middle Danube and Hungarian plains. Frankish military involvement was relatively slight, and despite Charles's obvious concern and the elaborate and rather ponderous nature of the campaign of 791, little by way of a large-scale confrontation between Franks and Avars ever occurred. The Franks were to be the primary beneficiaries, not least in being able to carry off, apparently unhindered, the Avar royal treasure, accumulated over centuries. It is perhaps particularly surprising that after duke Eric and Wonomir's expedition, the remainder of it was still in the same place when Pippin came for it later in the year. This might seem to argue a considerable degree of demoralisation amongst the Avars and an almost total collapse of central authority.

One indicator of what had been happening is the behaviour of the Tudun. Nothing like the quantity and quality of information on the politics and inner working of steppe nomad societies that is available for eastern Asia exists for the west, but the one can be used, with care, to help illuminate the other. The office and title of Tudun, whose function in Avar society is not described in

Frankish sources, is also known from Chinese texts relating to the Turkish empires that existed in the seventh and eighth centuries. Amongst them the office was that of a regional governor over subject peoples.[39] That this may also have been the case amongst the Avars in the west is suggested by the 811 entry in the *Annales Regni Francorum*. This is the last Frankish mention of a Tudun, probably not the same man as the one who submitted to Charles in 796, who is here listed as being amongst *primores ac duces* (nobles and leaders) of the Slavs living along the Danube.[40] While the previous Frankish references to this title make its holder out to be an Avar, this one locates it firmly within a Slav context, perhaps suggesting the kind of viceregal role over a subject population that can be more clearly documented in the Chinese accounts of the Turkic Tuduns.

If it be true that the Tudun was an Avar official ruling over a subject population, then it seems very likely that the Avar empire was in full decline by 795. For in that year Charles received the offer of submission from someone bearing this title. The Tudun referred to in the 795 annal was thus offering to transfer authority over a Slav population, formerly subject to the Avars, to the Frankish monarch. In other words, the Franks appear to have been the beneficiaries of an internal collapse on the part of Avar society. Had they, though, had any role in precipitating that collapse? The problem is, inevitably, one of evidence. Clearly, dramatic events had taken place within the Avar polity between the time of the raids of 788 and the Frankish looting of the Ring in 796. The limited response of the Avars to the great expedition of 791 may have been part of the same process, though it may be that they had merely been waiting to lure the Franks away from the banks of the Danube into terrain more favourable to their own style of warfare.[41] Even if the Avars had been functioning effectively in 791, within the next five years their empire had broken up and elements of the subject population and some of their own leaders were making offers of submission to the Frankish king.

The 791 expedition was indeed the first large-scale venture into Avar territory by a hostile power, and the failure to check it may have lost the khagan some of his prestige. This in turn may have prompted a challenge from one of his subordinates, the mysterious Jugur of the annal of 796. Such an internal conflict in Avar society could also have been precipitated by a succession dispute within the ruling kin group. The very limited nature of the evidence on the inner workings of Avar society from any period means that we do not know how the succession to the khaganate operated. In the much better documented case of the First Turkish Empire, which destroyed the Jou-Jan khaganate in the 550s, problems of the transfer of power within the ruling dynasty nearly proved fatal on several occasions.[42] Rules of succession were ambiguous, and led to

Khagan also baptised.

violent disputes. At the same time the existence of subordinate khaganates and an elaborate hierarchy of regional potentates, including several Tuduns, meant that rival claimants to the main khaganate had to bargain for their support. This led to periods of great internal instability and division within the Turkish Empire. From what can be seen of the details of its history in the final decade of the eighth century and the opening one of the ninth, and on the basis of comparisons that can be made with similar cultures, it is hard not to suspect that Avar society and those of its subordinate Slav populations were already in some form of internal crisis by the time of Charles's great Danube expedition of 791. The rise of Frankish power in the late 780s may have contributed to this, but Charles's actual Avar campaigns would seem only to have been the final gust of wind that brought down an already decayed structure.

In the short term the collapse of the Avar empire brought enormous benefits to Charles and the Franks, way beyond the removal of a military threat along one frontier area. The wealth acquired in the form of the Avar treasures may have enormously enhanced royal financial resources, making possible the expensive diplomatic gifts that are reported being distributed in the later 790s, and probably also underwriting major construction projects, such as the additions to the palace complex at Aachen. Prestige was certainly gained, and not just in the west.[43] Before their decline the Avars were known and feared in Byzantium and even further east. To be able to claim responsibility for their final defeat offered a considerable enhancement of the Frankish ruler's wider reputation. However, for all of these benefits, there were clearly new dangers and difficulties resulting from the dramatic changes in the balance of power in the westernmost edge of the steppe.

It is obvious from what followed that Charles did not, as in Italy or Saxony, see the collapse of the Avar empire as an opportunity for the territorial expansion of his own. While there may have been minor adjustments in the once disputed frontier areas, no attempt was made to establish direct Frankish rule out in the steppe or in the former Avar territories south of the Danube. An almost permanent cultural frontier was thus created.[44] Even so, Frankish interests required a measure of influence to be exerted in the region beyond that frontier and for some degree of stability to be regained. The collapse of the Avar hegemony created a vacuum, and various Slav former subject populations were now free to carve out their own territories and to engage in intense regional rivalries. What remained of the Avars themselves seemed to have been squeezed in the course of these processes into a much more limited territory on the western edges of their former empire.[45]

The Frankish annalists provide virtually the only written evidence of any value for these developments, which were taking place at some distance from where they themselves were working, and relatively little precision may be expected from their accounts in terms of geographical locations and other points of detail concerning areas beyond the bounds of Frankish territories. Archaeology might have been expected to be of help in establishing the boundaries between different cultural regions, and to some extent this it can do. However, the material finds are not ethnospecific, nor can their chronology be as precisely established as might be desired.[46] That is to say only broad chronological bands can be devised, and the items of material culture in themselves do not indicate which historically documented population may have produced them. These evidential problems have come to the fore in this region in particular in recent years thanks to a controversy over the geographical location of the heartlands of a ninth-century Slav kingdom, eventually destroyed by the Magyars, known as Great Moravia. The historical evidence has proved capable of being interpreted as indicating that this was based in the valley of the Morava (in the modern Czech Republic and Slovakia), or on the Hungarian Alföld, or between the Danube and the Sava in the north of Serbia.[47] While distinct material cultures may also be identified in these areas, none of these can by itself be shown to be that of the Great Moravian kingdom, and the attribution has to be argued almost entirely in terms of the far from reliable literary sources.

The current debate over the location of the heartlands of 'Great Moravia' has to take account of the period under consideration here, in that it was the movements of population in the former Avar empire during the last phase of Charles's reign that led to the emergence of this Slav kingdom. The Frankish annalists, accustomed to seeing most of their kingdom's neighbours in terms of definable ethnic groups or as having clearly delineated political institutions, probably misled themselves and subsequent generations by continuing to think of the Avars as a united and homogeneous people. What they have to record might suggest otherwise. In 799 Charles's brother-in-law, Gerold, who had been placed in charge of Bavaria, was defeated and killed by an Avar force.[48] As there is no reference to avenging him, despite his having been the brother of the late queen Hildegard, and this was never made an issue in subsequent diplomatic dealings with Avar rulers, it may be that this was an isolated episode, and not the great treaty breaking that the Annalist thought. In 803 the – or possibly more correctly *a* – Tudun, also described as Prince of the Pannonians, submitted to Charles at Regensburg. He was apparently accompanied by a mixed Avar and Slav following.[49] In 805 the principal Avar potentate, the khagan, who had previously converted to Christianity and had received the baptismal name of Theodore, also came to Charles and asked that he and his people should be assigned territory between *Sabaria* (modern

Szombathely in Hungary) and *Carnuntum*, as they could no longer live on the lands they had previously been given, because of 'infestation' by Slavs. Charles consented, and it may be assumed that this move took place, although the khagan died the same year. *Carnuntum* (modern Petronell) was a Roman fortress on the Danube, about 30 km east of Vienna, where Licinius I (309–24) had been proclaimed emperor.[50] This territorial adjustment would seem to locate the main Avar group, that still remained loyal to the khagan, in a relatively small area south of the Danube and on the extreme western edge of the Hungarian plains. They there served as a buffer between the open plains to the east and the route via the valley of the Danube into Bavaria.[51]

The khagan Theodore's unnamed successor sent a leading Avar noble to seek Charles's consent to his taking over this office, or at least that is how the Franks saw it. The Annalist clearly found it difficult to distinguish between the various Avar groupings and their leaders, and seems to have perpetuated confusion for his readers by calling the khagan who died in 805 'the Capcan', while giving his successor the title of 'the Cagan'. Both would seem to be Franco-Latinisations of one or more spoken forms of the title 'khagan'.[52] This problem with nomenclature may not be the Annalist's fault, as another quite independent source uses the two different titles. This is the set of minor annals known as the 'Annals of Saint Emmeram', which also record that the new khagan was baptised on the river Fischa, and took the baptismal name of Abraham in this same year.[53] This it may be assumed was a condition of or prelude to Charles's recognition of him as khagan. This same period saw attempts being made to establish Christianity more generally amongst the Avars, through missionary ventures directed from 796 onwards by Arn of Salzburg (d. 821). In consequence of these, his see was raised to the status of an archbishopric by Leo III in 797, at Charles's request.[54]

Conflicts between the Avars and the Slavs clearly continued beyond 805. In 811 the Annalist reports that, amongst other ventures, Charles sent an army into 'Pannonia' to put an end to the disputes between the Avars and the Slavs.[55] When he himself returned to Aachen in November, after his inspection of the coastal defences, an Avar ruler called the *Canizauci*, a Tudun and various Slav leaders were awaiting him, having been sent by the commanders of the army that he had despatched to the Danube earlier in the year.[56] Quite what was then discussed and what may have been achieved is not known, as the Annalist leaves this episode without further discussion. Nothing more is heard of the Avars living around the Danube until 822, when they sent presents and envoys to Louis the Pious.[57] This, surprisingly, is their last appearance in history.

The Slavs with whom the Avars are found fighting around the years 805 to 811, and who may eventually have eliminated them entirely, were probably coming from further to the south. Another Slav confederacy was already established to the north-west of the Avar's much reduced territories. These were the Bohemians.[58] Their land first appears in the Reviser's account of Charles's Avar campaign of 791, in which his commanders Theoderic and Meganfrid are ordered to take the Saxon and Frisian levies home from the Danube via Bohemia. For reasons that are not explained, Charles sent an army under his son Charles the younger against the Bohemians, which ravaged their territory from one end to the other and killed their leader, Lecho. A second raid, with forces drawn from Burgundy, Alamannia and Bavaria, was also carried out in 806.[59] It would seem tempting to associate these campaigns with the difficulties of which the Avars were complaining to Charles in 805. However, as the Annalist was aware of and referred more than once to the distinct ethnic identity of the *Beheimi* or Bohemians, it would be surprising that he did not indicate that it was they of whom the Avars were complaining. The very compressed account of these events in the entry for 805 in the *Chronicle of Moissac* might also be taken to imply that the Bohemian campaigns were connected with the current problems with the Danes and the Slavs north of the Elbe.[60]

The term used by the Annalist in describing the khagan's request, 'an infestation of Slavs', would suggest that the already reduced Avar lands were being overrun by Slav migrants, rather than that they were being driven off them by the superior forces of some Slav ruler. Some form of northwards migration out of the western Balkans would seem to be indicated.[61] That such a movement was taking place would seem to be corroborated by recent developments in that area. Firstly, the Byzantine empire was, for the first time since the reign of Maurice (582–602) making significant gains in trying to re-establish control over parts of its former territory in the region. A substantial area, stretching from the Tanzus river, south of the Balkan mountains, to the lower valley of the Strymon on the Aegean coast, had been brought back under imperial rule during the reigns of Constantine VI and Irene. This was exceeded by a rapid westwards advance across the Balkans and into northern Greece that took place under Nicephorus I (802–11). This included the reoccupation of Serdica in 807. These gains proved short-lived, in that Nicephorus's campaign against the Bulgars in the eastern Balkans in 811 turned from initial success into a total disaster.[62] However, both the phases of Byzantine expansion in the years 780 to 811 and the ensuing Bulgar counter-attack that took them to the gates of Constantinople in 813 put considerable pressure on the Slav populations of the central and western Balkans, and probably explain the northwards movement of elements of the latter into the Danube–Sava areas and beyond, into the former Avar territories. Out of these a variety of new ethnic and political entities would emerge, of which the Great Moravian kingdom would initially be the most significant, that would present difficulties and opportunities for successive East Frankish Carolingian and then Ottonian rulers. These developments were only in their earliest stages when Charles died in January 814.

7

REFORM AND RENEWAL, 789–99

It could well be argued that Charles's military conquests, some of which proved short lived, were of far less significance for the future development of European civilisation than the parallel attempt to match the physical expansion of the Frankish empire with a programme of intellectual and spiritual reform and revival. In the course of this a vital impetus was given to both ideals and institutions of learning that continued to be felt throughout most areas of western Europe long after the Carolingian dynasty had ceased to rule.[1] While these longer-term developments can not be followed here beyond the confines of Charles's reign, their importance gives the latter its greatest claim to fame, and some of the processes, institutions and ideas involved will more than repay examination, however brief.

It has long been recognised that Charles's recruitment of scholars and ecclesiastics from non-Frankish lands was an essential part of this process, not least because the resources and abilities they brought to the task were apparently not to be found in Francia at this time. It should also be noted that most of the underlying ideals that they promoted had not been intrinsic to Francia in the Merovingian period. They came principally from a papal tradition of reform, associated particularly with Gregory the Great (590–604), which was transmitted and given added zest not least in the writings and lives of a number of distinguished Anglo-Saxon clerics, of whom the greatest was Bede (d. 735).[2] This current of ideas began to make itself particularly felt in Francia thanks to the activities of Boniface (d. 754) and his disciples. To succeed, though, in their self-appointed evangelising and reforming tasks, the latter required the active support and patronage of the rulers of Francia. This meant in practice the Carolingian mayors and kings, who for a variety of reasons found what the reformers offered to be of political and cultural advantage. From the time of Charles's uncle Carloman onwards the resulting alliance shaped more and more features not just of the structure and functioning of the Church but also of the practical and ideological underpinning of secular government in Francia. It gave Charles's regime many of its distinctive characteristics, and provided the foundation for developments, as previously mentioned, that would long outlast the rule of his dynasty.

The Frankish Church had in the early and mid-seventh century been able to produce a distinguished body of clerics who served as both secular and ecclesiastical administrators, and in some cases played central roles in the rather tangled politics of the royal courts. It has to be admitted, though, that it is hard to establish anything of these men's intellectual accomplishments from the brief and bland accounts to be found in the remains of Merovingian hagiography.[3] Only the existence of the letter collection of bishop Desiderius of Cahors gives some indication of the survival of Late Antique epistolary traditions in the Gallic Church of his day.[4] The important and wide-ranging change in script in the time of Charles made manuscripts in earlier forms of handwriting seem both more difficult to read and less worthy of preservation. Thus, only a relatively restricted body of codices of Merovingian date have survived, and they may be far from representative. The works contained in them are certainly not negligible and can give some impression of the nature and extent of learning in this period, but this evidence is far less substantial for the seventh and early eighth centuries than it is for the sixth.[5]

Whatever the merits of the episcopate of the time of Dagobert I (623–38/9), by the early eighth century the Frankish Church had in the eyes of papal and Anglo-Saxon reformers become highly secularised. Its bishops were great land-owning magnates, and some, those in the Rhineland in particular, were notorious for their involvement in warfare and for their promotion of the material interests of their own families and off-spring. The practice of holding of diocesan or larger synods to discuss and regulate doctrinal and disciplinary matters, of which records have been preserved for most of the Merovingian period, seems to have ceased. The last such meeting that is known was held in the diocese of Autun some time between 692 and 696.[6] While it is important not to take the rhetoric of reformers of any period as an objective presentation of reality of the abuses they claim to be opposing, it has to be said that the Frankish episcopate of the first half of the eighth century has left little positive evidence of itself to weigh the scales against the accusations levelled at it by Boniface and his allies.[7] On the other hand, the interest in monastic foundation and the patronage of monasteries by members of the Frankish aristocracy is a marked feature of both the seventh and eighth centuries, and this may help to explain why ideas of spiritual regeneration in Francia seem to have aroused not only ecclesiastical but also lay interest.[8]

It has been suggested that the reign of Pippin III saw the beginnings of a process of intellectual renewal and the revival of the Frankish Church that would really come into full growth under his son.[9] However, this view has attracted little support, and depends on very limited and ambiguous evidence.[10] Even so, while the real achievements in these areas belong in the later period, there are indications that some sense of the need for reform was being felt in Francia by at least the mid-eighth century. The mayor of the Palace Carloman's patronage of Boniface and his Anglo-Saxon missionary ventures east of the Rhine might in part be put down to the need to integrate these areas into Frankish rule culturally as well as politically, but this is not a sufficient explanation in itself for some of the aspirations that were expressed and for the ideas for reform that were considered at this time. It is in the decisions of a number of assemblies presided over by the Carolingian mayors of the Palace and kings that the evidence for these intentions, whatever may be thought about the attempts to put them into practice, may be found.

What is notable in general about the capitulary legislation of both Charles and his father Pippin III is that the contents embrace what might normally be regarded as separate secular and ecclesiastical spheres of legislation. In the Merovingian period the royal law making that has survived, in the form of a series of late sixth-century capitularies as well as the two basic Frankish law codes, is almost entirely secular in character.[11] The few references to matters concerning the Church are mainly devoted to setting wergilds and to the protection of various categories of cleric. On the other hand, there were relatively frequent ecclesiastical councils, ranging from diocesan synods to larger-scale gatherings of bishops from all of the Frankish kingdoms. These do not seem to have played the role of similar councils in the seventh-century Visigothic kingdom in combining both political and ecclesiastical matters in their agendas.[12] The Frankish episcopal synods were predominantly concerned with the doctrinal and disciplinary concerns of the Church, and the Frankish kings do not appear to have attended such meetings. The existence of such parallel legislative bodies as the synods and the annual royal assemblies kept canon and secular law distinct. However, under the Carolingians the royal assemblies came to be the principal occasions on which regulations affecting the Frankish Church were formulated and given authority.

This process can be seen in action as early as the time of Carloman, the brother of Pippin III. The text of a gathering of clerics and nobles, held on 21 April 742, has been preserved.[13] Unusually, in the light of later practice, the names of the bishops present have been recorded, and Boniface, by then archbishop of Mainz, is first amongst them. He is also described as the *Missus* of St Peter, in other words the agent of the papacy. This gathering is normally seen as an episcopal synod, inspired and directed by Boniface, to try to introduce ecclesiastical reforms, some of which derived from the practices of the Anglo-Saxon Church.[14] However, the presence of Carloman is made clear from the outset, as is the consent of *optimates meos* ('my nobles'), referring to the presence and agreement of the secular aristocracy that would have been present at the ordinary annual assembly which was normally held at this time of year. What is significant is that such an assembly is being used as the venue for an episcopal synod. Lay and ecclesiastical issues were probably separately debated, as would happen under Charles, but the final legislation is issued by the ruler and with the consent of the secular and clerical magnates. The mechanisms seen in place here served for the rest of the century and for the opening years of the next one, until Charles's successor Louis the Pious divorced episcopal synods from secular assemblies.

The first of the acts of the assembly was the establishment of Boniface's archiepiscopal authority over his suffragan bishops. It is thought that he was trying to re-introduce into Francia the clear organisation of the Church into archbishoprics with subordinate bishoprics, that had been a marked feature of the Anglo-Saxon Church since Gregory the Great had laid down regulations for its structuring in 601.[15] An equivalent organisation around a number of key metropolitan bishoprics had been a feature of the Gallic episcopate from its earliest days, but this had decayed in eastern Francia in the late Merovingian period. Some sees, especially in the north-east where urban decline was particularly marked, were administered from monasteries rather than being based in towns. Although this was an acceptable practice in parts of Ireland and in Bernicia, the northern component of the kingdom of Northumbria, it was contrary to the traditions of the rest of the western Church.[16] Rival claims to jurisdiction also remained a problem, as with arguments over which sees were under the authority of Arles and which under Vienne, a problem that would face Charles and his bishops at the Council of Frankfurt in 794.[17] Other clauses of the 742 assembly concern the proper observation of canonical rules on the subjection of priests to the authority of a bishop, the actions to be taken against pagan practices, a prohibition on clerics bearing arms, and attempts to eliminate fornication and other vices amongst the clergy. The prevalence of such abuses was said to be due to the laxity of earlier rulers, here implying the Merovingians.

In essence the programme laid out in the seven clauses of the *acta* of this assembly remained the goal of subsequent generations of Carolingian monarchs and their ecclesiastical advisors, although their success in practice proved initially limited and always variable. Carloman held a second such assembly in 743, and his brother Pippin presided over at least one such gathering of lay and ecclesiastical notables during his tenure of the office of mayor of the Palace. This latter assembly met at Soissons on 2 March 744. In its *acta* similar phraseology was employed to that used in Carloman's 742 council, principally concerning the need to restore 'The law of God' and ecclesiastical discipline, which had been allowed to become neglected in the preceding period. Pippin used the occasion to re-impose a hierarchical structure on the Church, under the presidency of two new archbishops, Abel of Rheims and Ardobert of Sens. A heretic called Aldebert, judged before a panel of 23 bishops, was here condemned, and the oratories and *cruciculas* (small preaching crosses) that he had had built as popular places of prayer were to be burnt and destroyed.[18] Monks and nuns were ordered to remain in their monasteries and not wander at will. Clerics in general were instructed to avoid fornication, the wearing of lay clothing, and going hunting with dogs. As under Carloman, it was decreed, if not executed in practice, that episcopal synods should be held annually.

The prime influence on these assemblies of the early 740s was almost certainly that of Boniface, but even after his death in 754 orders for the improvement of the organisation and of the moral character of the Frankish Church continued to be issued from such meetings of lay and clerical notables under the presidency of Pippin, who had now become king. Thus an assembly in 754/5 concerned itself with issuing a law against incest and trying to establish a procedure whereby the regional counts would ensure that diocesan clergy held annual meetings with the archdeacon. Failure to attend was to be penalised by a fine of 60 *solidi*. Similarly, regulations concerning tolls also were made to include exemptions for pilgrims, and the last clause of the *acta* decreed that justice should be done for laymen and clerics alike. Procedures were decreed to ensure that those denied justice by local officials should be able to bring their cases to the king's court.[19] An even more extensive and elaborate set of regulations were issued by an assembly that met at the palace of Verne in 755. These dealt with matters such as the location of baptisteries and the holding of episcopal synods twice-yearly, but also with the protection of widows and orphans, a theme that continues to appear throughout the capitulary legislation of Charles.[20] Likewise, at the very end of his reign it seems that Pippin III and his advisors were concerned both with the material restoration of the Church in Aquitaine after nearly two decades of warfare and with ensuring that monastic life in Francia generally was conducted on a regular basis, essentially following the *Rule of Benedict*.[21] It is notable, too, that the requirement that heads of monastic houses, both male and female, should live under regular discipline was then also extended to bishops.

One of the most influential members of the Frankish Church in the time of Pippin III was bishop Chrodegang of Metz, who died in 766.[22] Born around

712 of an aristocratic family in the area of Liège, he was a referendary at the court of Charles Martel prior to his appointment to the see of Metz in about 742. One of his brothers was to be the first abbot of Lorsch, founded by a relative of theirs, and he himself established the monastery of Gorze in 748. He was responsible for producing a set of rules of life for the secular clergy of his cathedral, in which the influence of the practices of the Roman Church and also of the *Rule of Benedict* was highly marked.[23] It is very probable that his influence lay behind the ideal of the episcopate living under some form of quasi-monastic discipline in their households. An ecclesiastical assembly was held at Attigny under his presidency probably either in 760 or 762.[24] All that survives of this are the list of names of the bishops and abbots present, who agreed to say 30 masses on the death of any one of their number. It is probable that this represents only a little of what was discussed, and also that this synod was associated with a general 'Marchfield' assembly, of which there is no other record.[25]

All of these subjects to be found in the *acta* or *capitula* of Carloman and Pippin's assemblies and the general aspiration behind them that there should be a thorough-going reform of ecclesiastical discipline feature prominently in the far more substantial legislation of the next reign. While the scale and intensity of the efforts made, together with the degree of success achieved, increased markedly under Charles, it is worth noting that he had inherited many of his objectives from the reigns of his father and uncle. It proved equally possible to find not only foreigners such as Boniface, but also members of the Frankish episcopate itself, like Chrodegang, who were both aware of the need for reform and willing to work closely with the secular rulers to encourage them to promote it.

The decline, at least in evidential terms, in legislative activity that marks most of the final decade of Pippin's reign continued into that of his sons. No capitularies of Carloman are known. Apart from a undated confirmation of his father's brief Aquitanian ordinances of 768, Charles's only known capitulary predating 779 is one issued in Italy in 776, dealing exclusively with Italian matters.[26] A Frankish document once assigned to the opening of the reign, and possibly to the year 769, has been shown to be a forgery, probably composed around 847 to 852, when it was included in the capitulary collection of 'Benedict the Levite'.[27] In its preamble Charles is made to call himself 'the devoted helper and defender of Holy Church', and the very first clause, which is a repetition of the earlier prohibition on clerics bearing arms, is described as being issued at the urging of the Apostolic See; both of these features are quite anachronistic in the context of c. 770. The contents of this spurious capitulary are made up largely of regulations from Carloman's capitulary of 742.

Problems of the limited nature of the dissemination and of the preservation of
capitulary texts may explain the lack of such documents from the earliest part
of Charles's reign, but it was also a period of considerable activity in other
areas. A decade of warfare would intervene between his accession and the
promulgation of his first known Frankish capitulary, which, in comparison
with those of his predecessors, marked major developments in reform ideology and practice.

   The capitulary of Herstal of March 779, named after the palace in which
Charles is then known to have been residing, contains 23 clauses, the first
seven of which deal with primarily ecclesiastical affairs, mainly of a disciplinary kind. More than any of the preceding such records, it is clear from this
that the assemblies considered both secular and religious questions. The latter,
as here, are given first place in the ensuing report of the decisions, but in some
gatherings the secular legislation can be of greater weight. It seems that the lay
and ecclesiastical participants initially held separate sessions before uniting for
joint meetings, and that in some cases the bishops and the monastic representatives further sub-divided themselves to discuss their own particular interests.
From the evidence of this document, considerable attention was given at
Herstal to problems of local order, especially robbery, inside Francia.[28] This
may be a further reflection of the particular difficulties resulting from the failed
Spanish campaign and the Saxon uprising of 778. Stern measures were to be
taken, including the instruction that those accused of such offences but who
were living in areas of private jurisdiction should nevertheless be handed over
to the comital court for trial. Likewise, it seems to have been agreed that the
counts could resort to summary measures in dealing with these malefactors.
The bishops present accepted that killing and maiming such men would not be
sinful as long as there was no personal malice involved. Thus, summary execu-
tions and mutilation by the counts was permissible in dealing with brigands as
long as this was not just an excuse for self-interest or revenge.

   While problems of theft and banditry clearly took up much of the delibera-
tion of secular issues, other partly related matters of local order were also discussed and new regulations were issued. Sanctuary rules were also defined
more severely. Those taking refuge in a Church would not thereby be
reprieved nor was it permissible to feed them, though by implication no
attempt should be made to evict them forcibly. The forming of private bands
of armed followers was here forbidden, as was the making of any form of oath
of association. The forming of fraternities for charitable purposes and for fire-
watches was permitted, but in no case could an oath be used in the initiation of
members. This is a particularly interesting, if at first sight rather arcane,
decree, as it prefigures an issue that became increasingly prominent later in

Charles's reign, the use of the oath as a means of securing the political allegiance of the subject to his ruler. Here, at a relatively early stage in the reign,
it seems to have been recognised that other sworn associations, in which oaths
would have been taken on Gospel books and/or relics and thus be sacred in
character, could cut across what should have been the clear lines of obligation
between subject and monarch. This is but one way in which the Herstal capitulary, which also re-confirmed the applicability of the decrees issued by all of
Pippin III's assemblies, marks the appearance of major themes in the ideology
as well as the practice of government under Charles. It is important, though, to
recognise that, as in the decision concerning summary justice for brigands, the
actual apparatus of enforcement of the law remained limited and probably
over-stretched.

By the time that the long list of new rules and instructions, known as the
Admonitio Generalis, was promulgated at Aachen, probably on 23 of March
789, Charles and his advisors had begun to use a much more sophisticated terminology than that found in his earlier capitularies. He is described as *rector*
as well as king of the Franks. This is a term much used by pope Gregory the
Great (590–604), and it probably under Gregorian influence that it began to be
used in such contexts as this. Although often taken to refer to those, such as
bishops, with formal authority, Gregory himself used the word to embrace all
those exercising any form of spiritual responsibility. Thus, an abbot could be
described as a *rector*, but this meaning did not require the existence of formal,
institutional authority. A preacher was a *rector* because he was leading his
hearers towards spiritual improvement.[29] It was, in Gregory's eyes, a word
implying not so much hierarchical status as a heavy responsibility for the
spiritual progress of those in the *rector*'s care. While Charles may not have
been aware of the full range of meaning with which Gregory had invested the
term, its appearance in the preamble to the *Admonitio* implies that the king
was presenting himself as having a special duty towards his subjects, and a
responsibility for their welfare that went beyond the temporal.

The nature of the *Admonitio* furthers this impression. There is a lengthy preamble, which starts by outlining the need for continuous praise (in the form of
worship) and for the performance of good works, both to give thanks to God
for the benefits he had already bestowed on the kingdom of the Franks and to
ensure its continued preservation. Charles is here explicitly addressing the
ecclesiastical hierarchy of the kingdom, the 'brightest luminaries of the
world', whom he instructs to 'strive with vigilant care and sedulous admoni-
tion to lead the people of God to the pastures of eternal life' and to 'bear the
erring sheep back inside the walls of the ecclesiastical fortress on the shoulders of good example and exhortation, lest the wolf who lies in wait should

find someone transgressing the sanctions of the canons or infringing the teachings of the fathers of the universal councils ... and devour him'.[30] He com-
pares his role to that of king Josiah (II kings 22–3), who 'strove to recall the
kingdom which God had given him to the worship of the true God'.

What he was doing in practice was distributing across his territories, via
missi who were sent to the bishops and leading abbots of the realm, a
codification of 82 ecclesiastical laws most of which had been excerpted from
the acts of a range of councils dating from the fourth to sixth centuries. For the
greater part, though not exclusively, they were drawn from the proceedings of
the first four ecumenical councils, which were held to have special authority as
they had been attended by representatives from all of the major Churches of
Christendom. Collections of complete texts of such conciliar *acta* of both the
ecumenical councils and of some of the sets of local synods had been made in
Africa, Spain and in Gaul in the Merovingian period. Amongst the most
influential in the West was the seventh-century *Hispana* collection, first
formed by Isidore of Seville (d. 636) and re-issued in an expanded version by
Julian of Toledo (d. 690), containing the proceedings of the African, Spanish
and Gallic councils as well as the ecumenical ones and a collection of papal
letters.[31] The *Admonitio* was principally a small series of extracts, given in
précis form, from such a collection; in this case one of Roman origin known
as the *Dionysio-Hadriana*, which had been given to Charles by pope Hadrian I
in 774. It was intended to serve as a core text containing what were regarded
as the most important of such regulations. To make it even more precisely
applicable, each item was prefaced by a statement as to which section of the
ecclesiastical community – bishops, priests, monks and nuns, or the entire
body – it particularly applied.[32]

The content of the *Admonitio* was for the most part not original, other than
for its final section. What was particularly striking, though, was that its compilation was the work of a secular ruler issuing a selection of canonical legislation as if it were royal law, and explicitly claiming responsibility for the moral
and spiritual welfare of his realm. The material was organised chronologically
rather than analytically, in that items taken from the same council were placed
together and in the order in which the councils were held, rather than all of the
regulations of special concern to bishops or to priests being grouped together.
The decrees chosen for inclusion are of very uneven weight, though their contemporary significance may have been greater than we can now appreciate.
Thus, the prohibition on the invention or use of names of unauthorised
archangels (number 16), taken from the mid-fourth-century Council of
Laodicaea, may have had a resonance in late eighth-century Francia that
eludes us.

There is a change in both the sizes and the character of the enactments after Clause 59. The concluding regulations are not drawn from earlier canons but represent new injunctions, which are delivered in a fuller and more verbose fashion. Some, urging the observance of the canons, the honouring of parents, and the need for peace and harmony between Christians, may seem rather platitudinous or represent more of a pious wish than an enforceable legal injunction. Others, such as the one (number 65) forbidding the performance of religious rites beside streams or trees or on sacred stones, are much more specific and of clearly legal character. All of these rules contained in the final chapters of the *Admonitio* are justified by quotation of biblical texts. Some of the chapters seem to demand major changes to established social *mores*, for example the prohibition (number 67) of killings for vengeance, which would imply the outlawing of the practices of bloodfeud. A new moral purpose is seen to be underlying the judicial functions of the state, and judges are instructed to fast while hearing and resolving disputes (number 63).

The majority of the regulations are ecclesiastical in character, and range from very specific prohibitions on what must be taken as being contemporary practices now regarded as unsuitable to more generalised exhortations. Amongst the former may be included a prohibition on abbesses making blessings with their hands on men's heads and another on naked men wandering about in chains on the pretext of fulfilling a self-imposed penance (numbers 76 and 79). Similarly, tree felling and gardening are forbidden on Sundays, as much as hunting and the holding of judicial assemblies (number 81). The most general command, which also serves to tie the whole text together, comes in the final chapter (number 82), which urges the *rectores* of the Churches, here almost certainly meaning just the bishops, to make sure that the priests they appoint only teach that which conforms with the rules of the canons of the councils and the text of the Scriptures. What that preaching should consist of is then outlined. This, briefly, consists of the doctrines of the Trinity, the Incarnation, the Resurrection and of Judgement. The latter is treated in some detail, as ultimately it is the sanction upon which all of the foregoing has to be made to rest. Thus, the preachers have to explain how Christ will come again 'in divine majesty to judge all men according to their proper deserts', and how 'the wicked, for their sins, will be despatched to eternal fire with the devil and the righteous to eternal life with Christ and the holy angels'. Quoting from Galatians (V: 19–21), the sins that lead to this eternal punishment are then listed: 'fornication, uncleanness, lasciviousness, idolatry, sorceries, feuds, contentions, jealousies, animosities, wrath, strife, dissensions, heresies, factions, malice, killings, drunkenness, revellings and suchlike'.[33]

Overall, this document, for all of the generalised nature of some of its aspirations and the lack of clarity of its structure, represents a blueprint for a new society. Charles and his advisors took upon themselves responsibility for the moral and spiritual well-being of the realm, which was primarily to be assured by correct preaching founded in Scripture and in canon law. The latter was here condensed to provide the bishops and the priests under their charge with a digest of what was regarded as its most significant elements. These were supplemented in the final section. At the same time, the correct working of secular justice was also recognised as being a pre-requisite for divine favour. This required not only the king's judges to deal justly and fairly, without favour, but also for other forms of violent dispute settlement, such as feud, to be eliminated.

It is obviously a matter of considerable interest to know who may have been influencing Charles, not only in the selection and formulation of the contents of this document, but also in persuading him to think of the nature of his role and his responsibilities as ruler in this way. As with virtually all legislative and diplomatic documents of this period, the only authority displayed is that of the king, and the role of his advisors or attendants is almost entirely concealed. Only by the analysis of literary style is it possible to get some idea of the names of those who may have been involved in the drafting of such texts. In this case, as in that of several other central instruments of both administrative and ideological significance, the hand of Alcuin has been detected.[34] This is by no means proof that he was the principal or sole influence behind these significant developments in royal self-awareness, but it is at least the best hypothesis that the evidence allows.

Alcuin was a deacon of Northumbrian birth who had been educated in the cathedral school at York. By his own account he succeeded his former teacher Aelbercht as Master of the school when the latter became bishop of York in 767.[35] In 781 he was sent to Rome to collect the *pallium* (a strip of lambs' wool worn liturgically and only by papal gift as a sign of approval) for Aelbercht's successor, archbishop Eanbald (780–96). On the journey home he encountered Charles and his entourage at Parma, in March 781.[36] In consequence, he was persuaded to return to the Continent to join the Frankish court for an extended period after he had completed his mission for archbishop Eanbald. It is often taken that this residence at the Frankish court began in 782, but the precision of the dating of the Parma meeting given in the *Vita Alcuini* may have led to its importance being over-emphasised, and it has been suggested that it was still several years before Alcuin became permanently attached to Charles's entourage.[37] He cannot be securely located there much before his probable involvement in the drafting of the *Admonitio Generalis*.

His stylistic traits have also been detected in some of the official letters written in Charles's name, and in particular in the undated circular letter known as *De Litteris Colendis*.[38]

Whatever the problems of dating Alcuin's first extended stay at Charles's court, it is known that he was back in Northumbria in 790 and that he stayed there until possibly as late as 793. It may have been the preparations for the great ecclesiastical council to be held at Frankfurt in 794 that led to his return to Francia. During his first residence at the court he had been invested with the offices of abbot of St Lupus at Troyes and of Ferrières.[39] Despite some speculation on this subject, it seems most unlikely that he was himself a monk, but in such cases holding the office of abbot involved special interest in and oversight of a monastery but not necessarily residence in it or responsibility for its day to day running. However, when in 796 Alcuin received in addition the abbacy of the very important monastery of St Martin in the suburbs of Tours, he retired from the court and spent his remaining years there. This did not stop him from visiting the court, though increasing bodily weakness served to limit and ultimately put an end to this. He continued to exchange frequent letters with Charles and with numerous friends he had known at the court. His correspondence for his final years, from 796 to his death in 804, greatly outweighs that which has survived from earlier in his life. Responsibility for the preservation of much of this collection lies with one of his correspondents, archbishop Arn of Salzburg, whose exchanges of letters with Alcuin are thus the most frequent of any in the extant corpus.

Although Arn's collection of Alcuin's letters was not unique, as other smaller such sets of his correspondence are known, by its sheer size it could seem to have helped distort the nature of the evidence for the court in the 790s.[40] The survival of 311 letters from or to Alcuin far outweighs the number of those that have survived and which are associated with any other member of the Carolingian court at this time, including Charles himself, and thus might seem to give Alcuin a prominence that he did not necessarily deserve. However, according to Einhard, writing about a quarter of a century after his death, Alcuin had indeed played a special role and was 'the most learned man anywhere'.[41] He was said to have instructed Charles in 'rhetoric, dialectic and astronomy'.[42]

Others had preceded him into royal favour, including Paulinus, who became Patriarch of Aquileia in the early 780s, Peter, who became bishop of Pisa in 781, and the Lombard historian and later monk of Monte Cassino, Paul the Deacon. Another Italian who benefited from Charles's patronage was Fardulf (d. 806), who in 793 was rewarded with the abbacy of Saint-Denis for betraying a major conspiracy against the king.[43] It is hardly surprising, in view of the

Lombard campaigns and Charles's visit to Rome in the Winter of 773/4, that it was to Italy that he first looked for foreign scholars. Nor that it should be Rome that was expected to be the source of authoritative texts of works of canon law, liturgy and theology.[44] Amongst the first and most important of these was the manuscript of the 'Dionysio-Hadriana' collection of conciliar canons and papal decretals, which was excerpted in the *Admonitio Generalis* of 789. It contained an expanded version, devised for pope Hadrian I, of the canon law collection formed by Dionysius Exiguus (Dionysius the Lesser), a monk from the Dobrudja in the first half of the sixth century. This had included Latin versions of the canons of the ecumenical and other councils regarded as authoritative by the western Church and a series of papal letters dating from the pontificate of pope Siricius (384–99) to that of Anastasius II (496–8). It became the sole authoritative text of canon law in Charles's dominions, and the manuscript itself may have been referred to thereafter as the *codex authenticus*.[45]

Another area in which Charles and his advisors felt that there should be standard practice and in which Rome might be expected to provide a clear direction, was that of liturgy.[46] Uniformity and correctness in the performance of the services of the Church and the administration of the Sacraments was considered essential to the maintenance of divine favour. The different regional Churches in both east and west had developed their own liturgies from at least the third century onwards, albeit with much mutual interaction and influence and with a large measure of agreement as to what the liturgical calendar and the sacraments consisted of. There were local and regional variations and consequent disputes, the most famous of which in the west was that over the dating of Easter, which had divided northern Britain and the north of Ireland from most of the rest of Christendom until the Synod of Whitby in 664 and the final acceptance of the common practices by Iona in 715. There was also considerable variation in the texts of the liturgy as used by different Churches.[47] While it was once held that in the early Church there had existed uniformity in liturgical practice and wording, following the lead of Rome, which had given way to a period of centrifugal regional development from the fifth century onwards, it is now understood that local diversity was the original condition, and that moves to establish greater uniformity come much later, not least in the Carolingian period.

At the beginning of Charles's reign, a number of different liturgical texts could be found being used in different parts of his kingdom. Some of these, such as the *Missale Gallicanum* and the *Missale Gothicum* (which, despite its name, was composed in north-east Francia around 750) were of indigenous Gallic origin, albeit much diluted by Roman borrowings.[48] Similarly, the

Spanish territories and the former Septimania used liturgies that had developed in the Visigothic period, and even in northern Italy marked differences could still have been found between the liturgical usages of such traditional centres as Milan and the text of the Roman sacramentaries. Even Roman practices were far from fixed, and considerable variety was still to be found in the Churches and monasteries of the city. Private versions of liturgical texts were also still being written as late as the seventh century.[49]

An attempt seems to have been made by Pippin III to abolish the use of the (already quite Romanised) Gallican rites, in favour of purely Roman ones, as represented by Sacramentary wrongly ascribed to pope Gelasius I (492–6).[50] This only added to the confusion, as variant and interpolated versions of this Mass book then began to proliferate in Francia alongside the Gallican ones.[51] Pippin had also, around the year 760, obtained copies from Rome of the Antiphonary and of the Book of Responses used by the papal court. Charles tried to revive his father's scheme for liturgical uniformity by obtaining another service book from Rome. Around 786 he sent the Lombard historian Paul the Deacon to Hadrian I, requesting that the latter send him a copy of the Sacramentary supposedly devised by pope Gregory the Great (590–694).[52] Various delays then ensued. When, around 790, this manuscript was eventually received in Francia, numerous copies of this authoritative text seem to have been made for distribution to the major ecclesiastical centres of the kingdom.[53] In itself this sacramentary was not fully comprehensive, being intended primarily for papal use, and therefore containing materials not suitable for other Churches. It was necessary for this to be supplemented in various ways. In some manuscripts material from the eighth-century Frankish versions of the Gelasian Sacramentary was added to the Gregorian. Likewise a substantial body of new liturgical texts together with a preface was subsequently appended to the latter, clearly with official backing, to provide prayers for feasts and ceremonies that were observed in Francia but which were not catered for in the Roman volume. It was long thought that this appendix was compiled by Alcuin and that he wrote the preface, but it now seems certain that it was the work of the influential abbot Benedict of Aniane (d. 821) early in the reign of Louis the Pious.[54] The Gallican service books were far from being immediately eliminated by Charles's measures, any more than they had by Pippin's, and the expanded Gregorian Sacramentary probably never gained unique authority as a Mass book in the Frankish Church.

It has been thought that a further area in which Charles sought to establish uniformity of practice around the basis of a single authoritative text was that of monastic life.[55] Here the key document would have been the *Rule of St. Benedict.* This was produced in central Italy around 540 by an abbot

Benedict, whose real fame was largely generated by the account given of him in the second book of Gregory the Great's *Dialogues*, written in 593. But for the latter, hardly anything would have been known of Benedict's life, and it seems reasonable to suppose that the great and rapid popularity of the *Dialogues* served, incidentally, to arouse interest in the monastic rule that the principal subject of Book Two was there said to have written. Without this, it is unlikely that Benedict's *Rule*, for all its intrinsic merits, would have come to acquire its status as the pre-eminent set of western monastic regulations. Other monastic founders, such as Benedict's anonymous near contemporary who is known as 'the Master', also wrote sets of rules. Those of the Irish abbot Columbanus (d. 615), who founded both Luxeuil in the kingdom of Burgundy and Bobbio in Lombard, northern Italy, were particularly influential, even beyond his own monasteries. In some monasteries in Francia a 'Mixed Rule', combining elements from the *rules* of both Benedict and Columbanus, were followed, in itself testimony to the growing influence of the former in the Merovingian period. On the other hand, the *Rule* of Benedict made no headway whatsoever in Spain before the tenth century, and was not in common use amongst the monasteries of the city of Rome until even later. At the other extreme, the special veneration accorded to Gregory seems to have led to Benedict's *Rule* becoming the norm for serious-minded monastic founders in England, where it was adopted not least by Benedict Biscop for his monasteries of Wearmouth and Jarrow. This in turn served to intensify the influence of Benedict's work in the Frankish kingdoms, when Anglo-Saxon missionaries such as Boniface began establishing monasteries on the Continent.

In 786 Charles made a point of stopping at the monastery of Monte Cassino, which Benedict had founded and where his relics were then preserved, on his way from Rome to Capua.[56] Here he encountered what may have been or more likely what was thought to have been Benedict's own manuscript of his *Rule*, and around 787 Charles obtained a copy of this from the abbot.[57] Several of the monastic canons promulgated by the Council of Frankfurt in 794 specifically name the *Rule* of Benedict as their source and as the authority for what was being commanded. [58] Similarly, one of the questions that Charles wished to put to the different groups of participants in an agenda for an assembly, probably that to be held in 811, was whether anybody other than someone following the *Rule* of Benedict deserved the name of a monk. Unfortunately, only the questions survive; not the answers. However, if there had been any intention at that time of establishing the *Rule* as the sole normative text for the monasteries of the Frankish empire, it was not pursued. Not until early in the reign of Louis the Pious, who had close monastic advisors such as Benedict of Aniane and Helisachar in his court, would such an attempt be made, at the synod held at Aachen in 816. Something approaching this had been tried in 802, when at the great assembly that produced the 'Programmatic Capitulary', the abbots and monks present held a separate meeting of their own, at which the *Rule* of Benedict was read out and a verbal commentary was delivered on it. The *Rule* was also here declared to be the yardstick against which contemporary monastic practices were to be measured.[59] The same procedure was followed at the episcopal synod of Rheims in May 813.[60] However, as again in 811, this does not seem to have led to an attempt to ensure that the *Rule* was known and observed fully and exclusively in the monasteries of the empire.

A final work for which a standard text may have been sought, if not obtained, was the Bible.[61] Although the 'Vulgate' text of the Latin Bible that had been produced by Jerome (d. 419) had become increasingly widely distributed in the west, there still existed a considerable variety of alternative, earlier translations, which collectively are known by the general name of the *Vetus Latina*, or 'Old Latin' version.[62] Criticisms existed of features of the style of the 'Vulgate', not all of which had been completed by Jerome. Also, unsurprisingly, different regional forms of the text of the 'Vulgate' developed. Thus, by the late eighth century it might almost be said that the text of no one Bible manuscript would be identical to any other. It was thus not surprising that the passion for authoritative texts already expressed by Charles and his entourage should also have directed itself towards the Bible. It is not certain, however, that the various attempts made in this period to reform the standard text of the Bible were actually officially promoted. The first of these, carried out by Maudramnus abbot of Corbie (772–81), was almost certainly a private initiative. In 800 Alcuin presented Charles with a revised text of the Bible as the most appropriate present that he could offer to mark the latter's imperial coronation. In a letter earlier in the year that he had sent to Charles's sister Gisela, abbess of Chelles, and to the king's daughter Rotrud he stated that he was keeping busy emending the text of the Old and New Testaments, on Charles's order.[63] The precise interpretation of his words remains debatable, and it is not necessarily accepted that his work was part of an official royal project to produce a single authoritative text.

It was an undertaking of his last years, carried out at St Martins Tours, where subsequent manuscripts of his Bible text would be produced throughout the ninth century. Alcuin knew hardly any Greek and no Hebrew, so his work was directed towards stylistic and orthographic improvements to Jerome's 'Vulgate', rather than constituting a new attempt to translate the Bible *ab initio*. The same is equally true of a version produced in the last part of Charles's reign by bishop Theodulf of Orléans. His text was based on previous Italian forms of the Latin Bible rather than on the Northumbrian ones primarily used by Alcuin, while Maudramnus's version shows Spanish textual influences.[64] Yet another revised text seems to have been produced at or close to Charles's court, as this was the one found being used in a series of lavish and finely executed illuminated Gospel books and pericopes (books with the Gospel texts divided up for liturgical reading), known collectively as the 'Ada' group.[65] However, even if a product of royal inspiration and used in the luxury manuscripts prepared at court, this version was far from satisfactory. It was Alcuin's revised Vulgate, circulated from Tours, that became by far the most significant of the various textual forms, but the extension of its influence was a gradual process over several decades.

It is possible that the revision associated with the 'Ada' manuscripts was the one referred to in a circular, known as the 'Letter to the Readers', which was sent out from the court at some point after 786.[66] In this letter to the *Lectores* Charles referred to his having had the text of the books of both the Old and the New Testaments corrected, rescuing them from corruptions introduced by careless copyists. The *Lectores* or 'Readers' referred to were the clergy, both secular and monastic, who had responsibility both for reading out Biblical passages in the performance of the liturgy and for delivering sermons. The latter would not be expected to be original compositions of their own, but rather be liturgically appropriate homilies drawn from the substantial bodies of such works produced by recognised and revered authorities from the past, such as Ambrose, Augustine and Caesarius of Arles. The question of the literacy and of the intellectual capabilities of the clergy in later eighth-century Francia was important not least because of the fear that an unlearned priesthood could unwittingly mislead the congregations entrusted to them in doctrinal matters, and that poorly educated scribes would corrupt the texts that they had to copy, leading to the loss and distortion of the original works. In the circular letter addressed to the *Lectores* or 'Readers' of the kingdom, Charles complained of such errors and textual corruptions that he had found in the texts of the readings used in the nocturnal offices. He also objected to the loss of the names in some manuscripts of the authors from whose works those readings had been taken. From this, it seems likely that at least this extant version of the circular was being sent primarily to the monasteries of Francia, as it is hard to imagine a regular pattern of nightly readings in any other context.

Charles explained that to remedy this problem he had commissioned a homiliary, or book of readings, capable of being used for all of the major feasts of the ecclesiastical calendar, and having now examined it, in this circular letter he authorised the use of this work in the churches throughout his kingdom.[67] This task had been entrusted to the Lombard Paul the Deacon, and it must have been completed before the latter returned to Italy and the monastery of Monte Cassino in 786. Paul, from Friuli, had once been part of the Lombard court at Pavia and was the author of a revision and extension to the sixth century of the abbreviated Roman History of Eutropius (Consul in 387).[68] He had come to Francia in 782, to try to secure the release of his brother, who had been implicated in Hrodgaud's rising in 776.[69] While attached to Charles's court he produced an abbreviated edition of the *De Significatione Verborum* ('On the Meaning of Words') of Sextus Pompeius Festus, which he dedicated to the king.[70] He also wrote a history of the bishops of Metz, at the request of the current incumbent of the see, archbishop Angilramn (768–91).[71]

Alcuin's work on the Bible text had derived not least from his own earlier work on the reform of current spellings and word forms then in use in Francia. His book *De Orthographia* ('On Orthography') was essentially a new edition and expansion of that of Bede (d. 735), which had been produced in the context of a Northumbria in which Latin was an alien language that had to be learnt.[72] There was thus considerable concern for the use of correct forms of spelling that came as close as possible to what were thought to be proper Roman usages. Spanish and Italian practices, while displaying some variations, also remained relatively close to forms inherited from Rome. In Francia, on the other hand, the indigenous tradition had become increasingly idiosyncratic, from the later sixth century onwards. Spellings were used, in which for example 'ae' or 'e' could be substituted for 'i' or 'o' interchanged with 'u'. These practices were sufficiently consistent in their application for the texts in which they appeared to have been perfectly comprehensible to an indigenous readership, whatever size that might have been, but to outsiders and those familiar with Roman forms and with the writings of the classical grammarians such spellings would have seemed bizarre and barbarous. Very much like the change in handwriting, a reform of spelling in manuscripts produced in Francia was effected around the turn of the century. It took longer to take hold in certain regions or particular monasteries. Individual scribes could find it hard to shake off the orthographic habits in which they had been brought up, and some manuscripts clearly required drastic correcting to bring them into line with what was coming to be accepted as best practice. But it can be said that in a relatively short period a wholesale reform of Frankish spelling was achieved. What is more, like the comparable reform of the script, no evidence survives that this was court directed or officially promoted.[73] It may be thought that Charles and his advisors were behind both, but it is far from being capable of being proved. Nor did the two necessarily develop in tandem. The revised spelling can be found in use in most parts of Francia by about 800 at the latest, while the unification of script required something like another generation to become general.

The search for authoritative texts and the attempts to make them normative could only succeed in so far as those required to use them were able to understand them. It was not long before Charles and his advisors realised that here was a problem indeed. The educational level of the clergy, both secular and monastic, had fallen considerably in comparison not only with the Late Roman period but even with that of the early Merovingians. The degree to which lay literacy survived is debatable, but is likely at best to have been confined to the uppermost levels of society and to have been limited in character.[74] Einhard, who is never entirely to be taken at face value, reports that Charles himself only tried to learn to write later in his life, even keeping writing tablets for his exercises in letter formation under his pillow, but made little progress. On the other hand, he is also said to have been capable of understanding and making astronomical calculations, and to have enjoyed being read to. *The City of God* of Augustine of Hippo (d. 430) was apparently his favourite book.[75] If these statements are true, it is clear that in this period intellectual ability and the capacity to read and write are not identical.

That the problem of poorly educated or inadequately trained scribes continued to worry the king and his advisors can be seen from an administrative mandate. This has been given the name *De Litteris Colendis* ('That letters – i.e. grammar – ought to be cultivated'). Only one copy, that sent to abbot Baugulf (779–802) and the monks of Fulda, has survived, but it is clear from the text that it was in principle being sent to all monasteries and cathedral chapters.[76] At the end of the text the recipients are ordered to make copies to be sent on to other bishops and monasteries. So it may be assumed to have worked in something like the fashion of a 'pyramid selling' operation, with a select group of initial recipients being required to pass it on to another, more numerous series of addressees, and so on down the line. In the document Charles complained that he had over the years received many letters and addresses from the monasteries of his kingdom, all containing 'worthy sentiments' but often written in 'ill-educated language'. The date of this circular letter is not certain, other than that it has to precede the imperial coronation in 800. Alcuin's influence on it would make a date after 793 likely.

The intention of the mandate was to make the study and teaching of grammar a regular part of normal monastic and clerical life. How far it, and other exhortations and commands like it, may have succeeded in its task probably depended upon the previous disposition towards learning of the individual monastery or cathedral chapter. It is clear that a number of them already had active scriptoria, in which an increasing number of texts were copied.

Others show little signs either before or after of taking seriously the provision of teaching for their members and the development of schools within the institutions. Amongst the most active were, not surprisingly, those monasteries most closely connected with the court, and whose abbots had been appointed by the king. These included St Riquier or Centula, whose abbot since 789 was Angilbert (d. 814), a central figure at court and *de facto* son-in-law of Charles, and Corbie, under the abbacy of the king's cousin Adalhard (d. 826). St Riquier in particular benefited from the patronage of Angilbert, who built up a substantial and sophisticated library for the monastery, of which perhaps only one manuscript now survives.[77] He also carried out a major programme of rebuilding, which included a complex design for the interior of the main Church, to accommodate liturgical processions of his own devising.[78] Corbie likewise assembled an impressive library in this period, developed its own distinctive forms of script, and began writing codices for other monasteries.[79]

St Amand was given to Alcuin's friend, the Bavarian Arn in 782, and under Alcuin himself Tours became an important centre of writing and study. On the other hand, while the library at St Gallen was clearly starting to expand around the end of the eighth century, it was not until the abbacy of Gozbert (816–37) that it became an important centre of learning. Reichenau, in Lake Constance, was slightly slower than St Gallen in starting to write manuscripts in its own scriptorium, but under its abbots Waldo (786–806) and Heito I (806–22), who also became bishop of Basle, an important library was built up by about 820.[80] Heito's abbacy also saw the beginning of an important period of construction, especially in the abbey Church of the 'Mittelzell' complex.[81]

Probably the most important centre of all, however, was the royal court itself. The king's entourage had long served as a source of teaching and experience for the sons of the aristocracy. The skills induced would be various, and more likely to be military than intellectual, but in certain instances the latter seems to have been given as much prominence as the former. Thus, the Visigothic royal court at Toledo in the seventh century and the Lombard one at Pavia in the eighth were both known for the educational attainments of some of those attached to them and of some of those who may have been formed by them.[82] The same may have been true at times of the Merovingian court under at least Chlotar II and Dagobert I.[83] It would be over a century before anything similar could be thought about another Frankish court, that of Pippin III. Even then, if Einhard be believed (which he all too often is), the king's elder son did not receive training in writing. This, though, was not quite the weakness that we would now hold it to be. A layman of high status did not need to write, other than perhaps to add some form of signature to documents. Texts would be written for him, even at his dictation, just as books could be read to him. The art of writing could remain a clerical preserve without its absence imputing a lack of learning to a layman.

Literary commissions might come from the court. One such was the *Commentary on the Octateuch* compiled by Wigbod at Charles's request from a variety of Patristic authors, notably Jerome (d. 419), Augustine (d. 430) and Isidore of Seville (d. 636).[84] On a smaller, but almost regular scale, a number of prominent lay and monastic writers received requests from Charles for some discussion, either of recent astronomical phenomena, such as comets, or of some theological topic that had been raised in his presence. Two such questions known to have been circulated and to which a variety of the replies received have been preserved related to baptism and to death. The surviving responses and other similar texts have helped to shape the current sense of how relatively sophisticated, and well endowed with texts from Antiquity and the patristic period, the court was in Charles's time.[85] Another favoured topic for such consultations, the discussion of unusual astronomical events, could relate to their quality as portents of forthcoming developments on earth. Einhard, in his account of the events preceding Charles's death, refers to eclipses and a black spot that was seen on the face of the sun for seven days as portents of his demise. It must be admitted that he is indulging in literary fancy abetted by hindsight, in that the episode of the black spot probably refers to an observation made in the year 807, seven years before the emperor's actual death. Einhard claims that it was no more than three years before.[86] This particular report in the annals, which comes in an unprecedentedly detailed astronomical section in the entry for that year, also gives clear evidence that a close watch was kept on the sky, probably at Aachen, as it also includes mention of a transit of the moon by Jupiter, an event that would have occurred between 2.40 and 4 o'clock in the morning. This was clearly the product of a wider programme of astronomical observation, of which some other hints can be found in the annals, whose purposes went beyond the looking out for signs and portents of terrestrial happenings.

The main difference between the courts of Pippin and of Charles may have lain not so much in the objectives pursued as in the means available to achieve them. The conquest of the Lombard kingdom opened up the way to more frequent and more direct contact with Rome, and the north Italian clerical élite that would have served the Lombard court needed to look to Francia for promotion and for influence. Thus, the itinerant entourage of the Frankish king came to take on for them some of the lure of Pavia. With the coming of the first Italian scholars in the late 770s, Charles's court became attractive to scholars from the conquered territories and in time even from beyond his own domains. These initially rather exotic visitors gave it its particular character and helped direct the king's interests in various projects, not least those concerning liturgical uniformity, textual emendation and the programme of moral and intellectual reform and revival, previously mentioned.

Although there remain some arguments over dating and over the precise influence of various individuals and their role in specific projects, the significance of Charles's acquisition of his foreign scholars and of their work at his court has long been understood.[87] Indeed, the very first account of it may be found in Einhard, who said that the king was particularly interested in the liberal arts and recruited an Italian deacon from Pisa called Peter to teach him the rules of (Latin) grammar. His teacher in other areas, notably 'rhetoric, dialectic and especially astronomy', was Alcuin.[88] This is much oversimplified, but may be something of a metaphor. The *trivium,* that included grammar as one of its three subjects, was regarded as the primary or elementary level in the Late Roman educational structure, while dialectic (or logic) and astronomy featured in the four subjects of the *quadrivium.* Not only were the topics assigned to Peter and to Alcuin in Einhard's account sequential, so too were the two men in chronological terms. Peter, who had once been a scholar attached to the Lombard court of king Desiderius, seems to have left Charles's service by 790, while the period from c. 789 to 802 saw the hey-day of Alcuin's influence. He may have lost favour in 802, over an episode in which his monks at Tours tried to resist the judicial authority of bishop Theodulf of Orléans, and his health was also by then in decline.[89] In the final phase of Charles's reign, from 802 to 814, it is much harder to say who the dominant figures at court actually were. Both the king's cousin Wala and Angilbert of St Riquier (d. 814) are likely to be amongst them, but not even Einhard gives any clear information about this.

The three phases in the history of Charles's court would thus seem to fall into the following chronological periods: firstly c. 774 to the later 780s, secondly, from then to the emperor's return from Italy in 801, and thirdly, the last 12 years of the reign. It is the second of these, in which Alcuin has been thought to have played the most important role, that has attracted the most attention, and in many ways has coloured the wider perception of the court. This was the time in which the attempts at establishing authoritative texts was mainly concentrated or initiated, and in which some very significant capitulary legislation was issued. The earlier period, which by 781 saw the first appearance of a court scriptorium capable of writing and illuminating de-luxe manuscripts, has come to be more fully appreciated recently.[90] The third period, which in some ways was marked by the most exciting extensions of some of the ideas developed in the 790s, remains relatively little explored, largely due to the limitations of the evidence. The ending of Alcuin's correspondence, in practice in 802, makes it hard to detect and delineate the personalities most influential at court in the crucial period following Charles's change of status from king to emperor in 800. This latter development, though, needs first to be seen from the perspective of the events that led up to it in the 790s.

8

FRANKFURT AND AACHEN, 792–4

The year 792 was in many respects a critical one for Charles; not least because it saw the second major conspiracy of the reign, and the first in which a member of his own family was implicated. This was his eldest son, Pippin, usually if unkindly known from Einhard's description of him as 'Pippin the Hunchback', who was born around 769. In the brief account of the conspiracy given in the *Lorsch Annals*, he is described as being Charles's son by a concubine called Himiltrude.[1] The author of these annals includes Charles's sons by his 'lawful' wife amongst the planned targets for the conspirators. Einhard also calls Pippin illegitimate, and it is he alone who rightly or wrongly describes him as being hunchbacked. The Reviser, on the other hand, omits any reference to Pippin as being illegitimate or his half-brothers as being intended victims along with their father. There are indeed grounds for suspecting, from a letter of pope Stephen III sent to Charles and Carloman in the Summer of 770, protesting against the rumoured plan that one or other of them was going to marry the daughter of the Lombard king Desiderius, that one or both of the Frankish kings had previously been married and had put aside his wife in the interests of this new union.[2] If that is true, it is quite possible that Charles had been married to Himiltrude prior to 770, and that Pippin was legitimate.[3] It is certainly notable that he had been given the name of Charles's own father, which from family tradition would imply at least provisional recognition of him as heir.

However, the possible divorce of his mother to enable Charles to marry firstly a Lombard princess (divorced 770/1) and then the Alamanic Hildegard (d. 781), may have left him politically sidelined. In 781 Charles had changed the name of his second son by Hildegard to Pippin, when the latter was baptised at Rome by Hadrian I, which must have been a clear signal that the elder Pippin's rights of inheritance were in question. In such circumstances it is perhaps not surprising that he should emerge as the figurehead, if not the leader, of a conspiracy. Why this took so long to develop is not clear, as the identity of his supporters is never revealed in the sources. The *Annales Regni Francorum* do not even mention the conspiracy. The more informative Reviser states that the main grievance of the plotters was the 'cruelty' of Charles's current wife, Fastrada (d. 794). What is meant by that is quite unknown, and the involvement of Pippin the Hunchback would seem to give more credence to the Lorsch Annalist's view that the primary aim was to put him on the throne from which his father and half-brothers seemed to have excluded him. In any event, the plot was revealed to Charles by a Lombard called Fardulf (d. 806), who was made abbot of Saint-Denis by way of reward, and the conspirators were seized. At an assembly held in Regensburg, probably early in 793, they were condemned. Pippin was confined to the monastery of Prüm, on which fate Einhard put a dubious gloss by suggesting that he had long shown signs of a monastic vocation. He died, still at Prüm, in 811. His co-conspirators were less fortunate: some being beheaded and the others hanged.[4]

One significant consequence of the discovery of the conspiracy was the determination to make effective a plan to impose an oath of loyalty on all of the leading men of the realm, both lay and clerical. This had first emerged as an idea in 789, probably as a consequence of the difficulties with Tassilo, against whom violation of a somewhat retrospectively interpreted oath of loyalty had been used as a justification for his removal. The minutes of an assembly held at Aachen, and dated to 23 March 789, include the text of an oath of fidelity to be sworn to the king and his sons.[5] No details are given as to whom would be required to take the oath or what procedures might be employed to impose it.[6] In consequence little if anything may have been done about it, and a more urgent and practical attempt was made to put it into practice four years later. This is the implication of part of a capitulary text prepared at the Regensburg assembly in the spring of 793, which took the form of notes for the *missi* who were being sent out both to explain and to impose the oath on their *missatica*.[7] They were instructed to tell their listeners that the justification for the oath was twofold. Firstly it was an ancient custom, and secondly it had been advanced in their defence by some of the recently detected and punished conspirators that they had not taken a personal oath of loyalty to Charles. This they thought would absolve them from the charge of *infidelitas* or disloyalty to the person of their ruler. That the making of such oaths of loyalty was indeed an ancient custom amongst the Franks seems proved by references in the seventh-century *Formulary of Marculf*, but the second reason given was probably the primary one.[8] A technical loop-hole had been exploited, albeit unsuccessfully, and Charles and his advisors were determined that no one else should feel it was available to them as a potential justification for supporting any other member of the royal house against the reigning monarch. The oath was now imposed on all bishops, abbots, counts and royal vassals, and also on various lower orders of clerics, such as archdeacons and the *vicedomini*, or bishops' deputies. The royal vassals were those lay landowners who had received estates, or 'benefices' from the king, for which they had commended themselves to him as 'his men', in a ceremony in which they placed their hands between his.[9] It is most probable that all or most of the lay conspirators of 792 would have fallen into these categories, but it is clear from their attempted defence that the oath that had been envisaged in the capitulary text of 789 had not been imposed upon them. In its absence they felt able to claim that they were not in any state of obligation to the ruler that transcended other sworn commitments, such as to their fellow conspirators or to another lord, such as another member of the royal family. This technical weakness was thus to be remedied by the effective imposition in 793 of the oath devised in 789. However, it only extended to the upper echelons of society, and, as will be seen, in 802 a new oath of a much more wide-ranging content would be imposed more generally.

Of rather longer-term significance if of lesser immediate note in 792 was the emergence in Francia of vocal but geographically limited support for a Spanish theology, already condemned by pope Hadrian I, that later became known as Adoptionism.[10] This was expressed in some form of treatise by a bishop Felix of the eastern Pyrenean see of Urgell. For this he was summoned to attend upon Charles at Regensburg, where he was convicted of error by an episcopal synod. While the theological arguments themselves and the subsequent stages of the controversy will be considered below, it is worth noting that it was probably this somewhat fortuitous emergence of support for a doctrine that the pope had judged heretical that gave Charles the occasion for summoning a large-scale ecclesiastical council, attendance at which was extended to include bishops from Italy and probably also from Britain. This council, once envisaged, was also able to extend its agenda to consider issues that might not otherwise have been appropriate to an ordinary Frankish episcopal synod. Plans for the great council of 794 must have begun to have been laid in the aftermath of Felix's appearance at Regensburg in 792, as the logistics of such a gathering were by no means simple. While these were being organised, Charles took himself off, in the Summer of 793, to supervise another of his long-cherished projects, albeit one that for technical reasons was to prove abortive. This was the construction of a canal between the Rhine and the Danube, of which some traces of the work undertaken in 793 can still be seen. The Winter of 793/4 may also have seen the most important reform of the coinage in the reign, with the introduction of a new style, heavier, silver *denarius*.[11]

It is not known why it was at Frankfurt that Charles decided to hold what became the most important ecclesiastical council of his reign. The Reviser, and the Lorsch annalist in their entries for 794, refer to Frankfurt as a *villa*, suggesting that it was a royal estate site rather than an urban settlement, however small. Although there had once been a Roman fort and settlement at Nida (abandoned c. 260) about 6 km north of the later town centre, the site of Frankfurt itself, located by a ford over the river Main, seems only to have become important in the late Merovingian period.[12] According to recent excavation in the area of the medieval cathedral, a small church was erected on the site around 678. This may have been built as a burial chapel, as the most significant feature of it was the inhumation within it of a young girl, who was buried with clearly high-status grave goods. It is possible that, as with the comparable child's burial under Cologne cathedral, this may have been a member of the Merovingian royal house, or at least someone of comparable local importance. The lack of any subsequent cult would seem to preclude this, or the Cologne burial, from being associated with a child saint. Whatever the reason for this initial interest in the location, it is clear that during Charles's reign the small Merovingian chapel had been replaced by a larger, but still architecturally simple, rectangular church. This it may be assumed was the place of meeting of the council in 794. It is noteworthy that Charles's wife Fastrada died in the course of the council, but she was sent for burial to the church of St. Alban at Mainz. Only under Charles's son and successor, Louis the Pious (814–40) did the church at Frankfurt receive transepts, and at the same time what was probably a royal residence was built immediately to the west of it.[13]

The *Annales Regni Francorum* record that Charles, for the only time in his reign, celebrated Easter here in 794, having spent Christmas at Würzburg. Here bishops from eastern and western Francia assembled together with two papal *missi*, the bishops Theophylact and Stephen, and Paulinus of Aquileia, Peter archbishop of Milan and other Italian prelates.[14] There were also some unnamed clergy, presumably bishops, from Britain.[15] From the perspective of the annalists, two major issues were discussed: the Adoptionist heresy and the reintroduction of the veneration of icons in Byzantium, that was authorised by the Second Council of Nicaea in 787. In practice the assembled bishops ranged more widely than just over these two questions, important as they were, and the *acta* of the council contain 56 clauses. These included some relating to issues of what might be thought to be primarily secular concern, such as the prices to be paid for corn, oats, rye and wheat and the value and acceptance of the new issue of royal silver coins (*denarii*).[16]

After the three opening matters, Adoptionism, icon veneration and the (renewed) confession of Tassilo of Bavaria, which may have been of particular interest to the monarch and his advisors, the order of business seems very haphazard, with episcopal and monastic regulations mixed up in no apparent order. Whether this reflects the actual organisation of the agenda or is just a peculiarity of the written record cannot be known for sure. Some of the clauses have been preserved only as headings, as for example with clauses 34 and 35, which read 'Concerning the crushing of avarice and greed' and 'Concerning the practice of hospitality', without giving any further indication of what was discussed, let alone what was decided. This would suggest that the text of the *acta* as we now have them has only been preserved in draft or outline form. It is possible that it may be little more than one individual's notes on the debates, reflecting a personal choice as to what was or was not thought particularly pertinent or significant. Even the major theological issues debated by the participants and the decisions on them that were taken are extremely briefly and rather crudely recorded.

The *acta* in their present form may not have been the expected documentary outcome of the proceedings. As will be seen, the Adoptionist issue was addressed in a separate synodal letter, and it may well have been intended that a similar independent text would represent the position taken by the bishops on the restoration of image veneration in Byzantium. A particular role in these discussions was clearly expected to be played by various clerics attached to the court. Some of these were not of episcopal or abbatial rank, and thus not normally qualified for inclusion amongst the participants of such a gathering. Special arrangements had to be made for such men. Thus, the last of the 56 clauses records the admission into the council as a member of Charles's principal ecclesiastical advisor, Alcuin, although he only held the rank of deacon.[17]

If the order of the *acta* be taken as an indicator, it seems that the first item of business was the dispute over Adoptionism, an issue in which Alcuin already seems to have taken a leading part. The issue was in many respects one of terminology. Around the year 781 archbishop Wilcharius of Sens, probably with the backing of pope Hadrian, had sent a cleric of Gothic origin called Egila into Spain, with some kind of roving episcopal commission. It seems likely that there were fears that the Spanish bishops under Arab rule were not taking a firm enough stand against Islam, which in western eyes was seen as a Christian heresy. However, perhaps in consequence, Egila appears to have become too closely involved with a rigorist and Romano-centric group amongst the Spanish Christians, who from what little is known of their beliefs had become heretical. The teachings of Migetius, the leader of this sect, were condemned by the Spanish episcopate in a council around 782/3, and pope Hadrian was obliged to repudiate Egila. However, in the denunciation of Migetius's doctrines, drawn up by bishop Elipandus of Toledo, whose church had enjoyed a primacy of honour over all the others in Spain since the Visigothic period, certain formulae referring to Christ as adopting his human nature aroused dissent.

This was led initially by the Asturian monk Beatus of Liébana and his disciple Etherius, who subsequently became bishop of Osma. When in October 785 Elipandus tried to use his primatial authority to have them silenced by the abbot of Liébana, this merely led to a widening of the dispute. Beatus and Etherius drew up a treatise denouncing Elipandus's use of the terminology of adoption in referring to Christ's human nature. A copy of this or a similar letter was probably sent to Rome, as Hadrian, while accepting the condemnation of Migetius, criticised Elipandus's Christology.[18] However, under the rule of the Umayyad Amirs of Córdoba, and with the continued backing of at least the majority of the Spanish episcopate, Elipandus remained immune to coercion. It may be, however, that attempts continued to be made by both sides to widen the basis of the support for their respective views. How soon Charles and his advisors came to be aware of the argument is not clear. It has been suggested that a clause in the *Admonitio Generalis* refers by implication to the dispute, thus indicating Alcuin's consciousness of it by 789, but the wording of the text is too general for this to be certain.[19] As previously mentioned, it was in or very soon before 792 that bishop Felix of Urgell, a small town in the eastern Pyrenees which had been under Frankish rule probably since at least 785, expressed his support for Elipandus's teaching.

This was the first and the only time that a bishop beyond the frontiers of *Al-Andalus*, or Arab Spain, declared himself to be a partisan of Elipandus's adoptionist theology.[20] However, his decision raised the danger that others might follow suit, and at the same time represented the first instance of heresy being propagated within the territories under Charles's rule. While it must be admitted that it was unlikely that Elipandus and Felix's adoptionist ideas would spread widely in Francia, not least because of the distinctively Spanish context of the argument and of the theological tradition that lay behind it, it was an almost axiomatic political concept that a Christian ruler had to prevent the spread of heresy to retain divine favour.[21] Thus, the stand taken by Felix in 792 provided the first opportunity for the arguments over Adoptionism to be given a formal condemnation in Francia and also required Charles to be seen to be acting vigorously against teachings that had already incurred papal censure for their unorthodoxy. While there are some grounds for feeling that the whole issue was in part blown out of all proportion and treated in a perhaps overly grandiose way to provide Charles and his court theologians with an opportunity of demonstrating on a wide stage both their theological orthodoxy and their learning, it has also to be accepted that the logic of the views that the king and his advisors held on his responsibilities made such reactions virtually inevitable.

It used to be thought that Elipandus's language and the ideas that lay behind it concerning the adoptive character of Christ's human as opposed to his divine nature reflected theological currents reaching Spain in consequence of its political absorption into the Arab world. In particular it has been held that his views were influenced by Nestorian teachings, which while long known had not previously been able to make themselves felt in Spain. Nestorian treatises in Latin translation have been detected as circulating amongst Christians in North Africa in the eighth century. Superficially this seems an attractive line of reasoning in that the teaching of Nestorius, patriarch of Constantinople (428–31), stressed the separateness of the human and divine natures in Christ, and this could be thought to be an implication of Elipandus's view of the former being adopted, and thus not intrinsic. However, recent rigorous examination of Elipandus's statements, contained not least in a series of letters arguing his case, and of the theological teaching behind them, has shown that he and his ideas belong firmly within a long-existing tradition within the Spanish Church, that was developed in the Visigothic period.[22]

One reason why this has not been recognised sooner is that Elipandus's opponents, not least Alcuin and pope Hadrian, thought in terms of Christological arguments that were essentially eastern Mediterranean in origin. While the Greek Church had been riven by such arguments over the nature, the person and the operation or 'energy' of Christ from the fifth to the seventh centuries, no such disputes had originated in the Latin west. The doctrinal literature, and such things as handbooks describing heresies, available in Latin and circulating amongst the western Churches, actually saw such arguments only in terms of the dichotomies over which their Greek counterparts had argued centuries before.[23] This was all the more true of the Anglo-Saxon Church, which had played no part in the original theological controversies of the Patristic period, and had received all of its doctrinal learning at second hand. On the other hand its tradition of learning would, through the person of Alcuin, take a leading role in interpreting and combating Elipandus. Thus, when in the eighth century western theologians encountered an argument over the divine and human natures of Christ, they could only see this as a reflection of the fifth-century conflicts over Nestorian and Monophysite teachings. They, as have their modern counterparts, could only interpret Elipandus's use of the word 'adoption' (by Christ of his human nature) as a sign of a Nestorian revival.

Felix had been rapidly brought to heel in 792/3. The Reviser, who was clearly interested in this issue and also saw it in the light of Nestorian theological ideas, provides an unusually detailed account of how Felix had responded to an enquiry from Elipandus by writing treatises in support of the latter's adoptionist view. For this he was brought before Charles and an episcopal synod at Regensburg, and was there condemned. This 'Council of Regensburg', as it is sometimes called, was probably just the ecclesiastical section of the general assembly that was held in Regensburg early in 793, which produced two extant capitulary texts.[24] Although normally dated to 792 on the basis of the text of the annals, it needs to be recognised that both the Annalist and the Reviser are here beginning their year after Easter, and thus events, such as the assembly, that took place in the Winter of 792/3 and prior to Easter 793 are located in the 792 annal, even if by a chronology that starts the year in January they really belong in 793. Felix was sent on to Rome under the tutelage of abbot Angilbert of Saint-Riquier; where – as at Regensburg – he repudiated his controversial views, and was then permitted to return to his diocese.

The calling of the Frankfurt ecclesiastical assembly provided the opportunity for a further, grander and even more formal condemnation of Felix (and also, in the secular sphere, of Tassilo of Bavaria). A synodal letter was composed, denouncing what was thought to be adoptionist theology, which was solemnly signed by all of the bishops present. This was almost certainly drawn up by Alcuin, who certainly conducted a long-range theological debate by letter with both Felix and Elipandus during the next few years. He also communicated with Beatus of Liébana, and the subject of Adoptionism features in several of his letters to friends at this time.[25] His later arguments were shaped by his discovery in Tours, where he went as abbot of Saint Martin in 796, of a manuscript containing a Latin translation of the acts of the Council of Ephesus of 431, which had condemned Nestorius. The influence of this can be seen in his 'Book against the Heresy of Felix', written in 797/8, and in the longer 'Seven Books against Felix of Urgell' of 798/9.[26]

An episcopal statement of similar tenor to that written by Alcuin for the bishops at Frankfurt was also produced by Paulinus of Aquileia. This *libellus sacrosyllabus* he had endorsed by the Italian episcopate, and he also presided over a synod of the northern Italian bishops at Cividale that condemned Adoptionism. Paulinus went on to write what has come to be regarded as the most sophisticated anti-adoptionist treatise, his 'Three Books against Bishop Felix of Urgell'.[27] He too continued to see the issue primarily in terms of the revival of Nestorian ideas. While some of the defence of their position put up by both Elipandus, who was now over 80 years old, and by Felix have survived in the form of a handful of letters, there is a sense in which the debate within the Frankish kingdom and its Lombard appendage had ceased to have much to do with them directly. It went its own way, dictated in part by the desire of prominent clerics such as Alcuin and Paulinus to use the opportunity for displays of their theological erudition. It may thus be suspected that when, after Felix's death in 818, Agobard of Lyons claimed to have found further writings amongst his papers defending Adoptionism, which he then felt necessary to rebut, the archbishop may merely have been inventing an excuse for some theological showmanship of his own. It must be admitted, though, that the idea that Felix was still recalcitrant in spite of the best efforts of Alcuin, Paulinus and others is most appealing.

The second issue discussed by the bishops at Frankfurt in June 794 was the question of the veneration of images, in the light of the decisions taken at the Second Council of Nicaea in 787. Like Adoptionism this had a considerable, and indeed much longer, pre-history. The growth of the cult of icons, which had formed a marked feature of the piety of the Greek and other eastern Churches in the sixth and seventh centuries, had generated a counter-movement, that had its intellectual roots in another long-standing Christian tradition, which took the Second Commandment literally. There had been doubts, for example enunciated in the *Panarion* of bishop Epiphanius of Salamis (d. 403), as to the permissibility of the depiction of the sacred in the medium of secular art. Others feared that the veneration of icons confused the distinction between the Divine Persons and their images. The emergence of prohibitions on figurative art in Islam, especially associated with the Caliph Yazid II (720–24), may have also seemed to be a reproach to Christian attitudes to the subject, and to have influenced imperial policy at a time when Byzantium and the Caliphate were engaged in a critical struggle, that had dramatically favoured the latter for nearly a century.[28]

It is difficult to quantify or locate precisely the Iconoclast constituency in eighth-century Byzantium, as the ultimate triumph of image-veneration led to the elimination of most iconoclast texts and the historiographical distortion of the character and aims of those, not least the emperors, who had supported it. It was under the emperor Leo III (717–41) that official support for iconoclasm first manifested itself, leading through rapid stages in the 720s to a prohibition on image-veneration, the destruction of many icons, and also an increasing estrangement from the Church of Rome, which by and large supported the iconodule, or image-venerating, position. Not until the reign of Charles's contemporary, the empress Irene (780–802) would the dominance of official iconoclasm be challenged. While it has been suggested that her Athenian background made her more naturally a supporter of image-veneration than of iconoclasm, it has been countered that she was unlikely to have been chosen as the wife of Leo IV (775–80) by his father Constantine V (741–75) if any doubts had existed as to her theological orthodoxy in imperial eyes.[29] By this latter view, her decision in the 780s to try to reverse the iconoclast legislation and to reintroduce the public veneration of icons could reflect the particular political circumstances that she then faced. A first attempt in 786 to hold a Church council in Constantinople that would effect this change had to be abandoned due to hostility on the part of the regiments of the imperial bodyguard stationed in the capital, who were largely loyal to the views of their former iconoclast masters Constantine V and Leo IV. However, this problem was overcome in 787 by the re-deployment and then disbanding of the rebel units and the siting of the council in the provincial city of Nicaea, the site of the first ecumenical council of the Church, held under the presidency of the first Christian emperor Constantine I (306–37) in 325.[30]

Preparation for the council clearly involved communication with Rome. From the papal perspective, as seen in the *Life* of Hadrian I in the *Liber Pontificalis*, the Byzantine synod was actually a response to an apostolic letter from the pope urging Irene and her son Constantine VI to 'set up the sacred images, as they are orthodoxly venerated in the holy catholic and apostolic Roman Church by the warrant of the Scriptures and the traditions of the approved Fathers from olden times to the present'.[31] The Byzantine bishops, on the other hand, saw themselves as forming an ecumenical council acting under imperial patronage, but whatever the differences in the views on the authority under which they were acting, the outcomes of the deliberations were equally satisfying to both sides. Iconoclast legislation was repealed, the then patriarch of Constantinople and other prominent iconoclasts were replaced, and image-veneration was reinstated. It remained triumphant, despite a briefer iconoclast revival under Leo V (813–20) and his two successors Michael II (820–9) and Theophilus (829–42).[32]

In the light of clear papal approval and positive enthusiasm for what had happened at Nicaea in 787, it is surprising to find that Charles and the Frankish Church reacted with marked hostility to the decisions taken at that council. A good three years after the holding of the Nicene council work began on a great denunciation of what was thought to be the heretical doctrine on image-veneration that it had propounded. This took the form of the treatise always known by its post-medieval name of *Libri Carolini* ('Charles's Books').[33] Composition of the work, which survives in only two manuscripts, one probably the original draft and the other a copy made directly from it, is attributed in the heading in the manuscripts to the king himself.[34] However, this seems to be no more than a formal fiction, and it is infinitely more likely that a variety of members of the court contributed to the final version. None of these are named. In the drafting of the original form of the text, though, the role of one dominant authorial personality has been detected. This has been claimed to be that of Alcuin, although it is known that he was absent in Northumbria throughout almost the whole period of the gestation of this work. A more convincing candidature is that of bishop Theodulf of Orléans, and despite prolonged and indeed bitter controversy over the matter, he is generally recognised now as the principal begetter, on Charles's orders, of the *Libri Carolini*.[35]

Like the treatises generated by Adoptionism, this great compilation, which is widely regarded as the finest product of early Carolingian controversial theology, served to test and display the erudition and also the argumentative skill of the luminaries of the court. It may well have been expected to serve as the definitive statement that would be accepted and endorsed by the bishops who would gather in Frankfurt in 794. To have been entrusted with its composition was clearly a mark of high royal esteem and trust. Theodulf (d. 821) is known from one of his own poems to have been a Goth, in other words to have originated either in Spain or in 'Gothia', the Frankish marcher territory north-east of the Pyrenees that had been conquered by Pippin III, and which corresponded with the former Septimania.[36] There is a danger of some circularity in the arguments concerning Theodulf's authorship of the *Libri Carolini,* in that the Hispanic palaeographic practices and clear reminiscences of Spanish biblical and liturgical texts clearly present throughout the work have been in fairly close order made to serve both as proof that Theodulf wrote the *Libri Carolini* and as illumination of his own cultural and intellectual background. He had become bishop of Orléans by 798, which suggests that he may have been born in the later 760s. It is possible that he was brought back into Francia in the aftermath of Charles's campaign along the Ebro in 778, but greater probability must favour an origin in Gothia. Certainly the view that he originated in or around Zaragoza has no foundation.[37]

The *Libri Carolini*, prepared on Charles's orders and clearly discussed and shaped at his court, had reached an almost finished state and had been subjected to stylistic and orthographic revision, probably following Alcuin's return from England, when the whole project was apparently suddenly shelved late in 793. The work was never circulated, although it was later known to archbishop Hincmar of Reims (d. 882), and its arguments may have had limited influence on the resolutions passed by the bishops assembled at

Frankfurt in 794. The sudden abandonment of this major undertaking on the eve of the occasion for which it was probably intended and its relegation to obscurity in the court library is surprising, to say the least. At Frankfurt in 794 the Frankish and Italian bishops apparently contented themselves with a denunciation of 'the recent synod of the Greeks which they held at Constantinople concerning the adoration of images and in which it was set down in writing that they judged anathema those who did not devote worship and adoration to the images of the saints as to the Holy Trinity'.[38]

Even from this brief statement it would seem that there was a certain measure of confusion in the minds of the Frankish bishops, not least concerning the location of the 'synod of the Greeks'. Here it is located in Constantinople rather than Nicaea. This is doubly surprising in that it is clear that the Frankish bishops were reacting to what they held to be a written statement of what the Byzantine council had decreed. It also emerges from the Frankfurt *acta* that the westerners thought that the Greek bishops were trying, at least liturgically, to elevate the status of icons to the same level as that of the Persons of the Trinity. In other words, they were declaring that images of the saints were as worthy of acts of worship as the Divinity itself. Such a view, if it had been held, would have been heretical in the extreme, but it is certain that this was not what the Greek bishops meant. The difficulty lay in cultural differences and in linguistic misunderstanding. The Nicene *acta* would in their original form have been in Greek, a language known to a handful at most of the bishops assembled at Frankfurt. It is clear, therefore, that the latter were relying on a Latin translation of the conciliar *acta*. One such is known to have been made in Rome soon after the holding of the Council of Nicaea, on the orders of pope Hadrian I. It has been suggested that this, not very adequate translation, was what by a round-about means had come into the hands of Charles and his court theologians, and that they did not recognise that this was not an official and original version of what the Greek bishops had actually said and decided. They were equally unaware that Rome had warmly welcomed the decrees made at Nicaea, as being in full accord with its own teachings. It has been argued that it was not until 793 that Charles was informed of the real Roman view on the Second Council of Nicaea, and that he then, in consequence of an unwillingness to oppose Rome doctrinally, stopped the work on the *Libri Carolini* and contented himself with the condemnation at Frankfurt of one extreme interpretation of what the Greek bishops had been thought to have said.[39]

The year 794 is significant not just for the holding of the Council of Frankfurt, but because it is also taken to mark the beginning of Charles's semi-permanent residence at Aachen, which is thereafter seen as the fixed point for his court and the political centre of his empire. The notion of such a 'capital' would have been alien to his Frankish predecessors, since at least the late sixth century, although it had been a long-standing tradition for their Visigothic and Lombard contemporaries, whose regimes were firmly associated with the towns of Toledo and Pavia respectively.[40] This did not mean that the Lombard and Visigothic monarchs were permanently resident in these cities, any more than Charles would be in Aachen after 794. But these were the centres of government, where the rulers would spend a significant if unquantifiable part of each year. The Merovingians had developed similar associations with certain towns in the sixth century, and Gregory of Tours in describing the division of territories that followed the death of Chlotar I in 561 names each of the new kings' principal urban centre. Whether these towns, which included Paris, Orléans, Metz and Soissons, really became or remained the administrative and court centres for their respective royal regimes is open to question, but there is little evidence either way. However, the same kind of links to a nameable capital cannot be made for their seventh-century successors, and the emergence of charter evidence in that period indicates that more often than not the later Merovingians were holding their courts in rural residences rather than in towns.

This statement is equally true of their early Carolingian successors. Certain royal villas appear to have been especially popular. Many late Merovingian kings are found residing at the villa palaces of Clichy near Paris and Compiègne near Soissons, while Attigny near Rheims emerges as a favourite site for Charles's father Pippin III. Obviously, such things could not have been determined on the basis of personal taste alone. The location chosen for an assembly or the place selected for the ruler's current residence would as often as not reflect military or political necessities or imminent plans for campaigns. This can be seen most clearly in Charles's own itinerary. For example, his protracted stay in Regensburg from the beginning of the winter of 791 to the spring of 793 was related to the Avar campaign of 791 and the plans for a second one in 792, as well as to internal reorganisation in Bavaria.

In Francia at least, the distinction between urban and rural residences should probably not be overdrawn. Although the evidence is distinctly patchy, the general impression that can be drawn from the archaeology of early Carolingian towns is that they were very small indeed. This applies not just to the few new foundations such as Paderborn and Münster, but also to much older towns of Roman origin, in which the inhabited core appears in most cases to have shrunk considerably. On the other hand, the rural royal villas that were particularly favoured by the monarch could develop numerous appendages to house courtiers, servants, guards, visitors and so forth, and could in consequence come to extend over relatively large areas. While the study of early medieval palace sites has been a major area of interest, especially for German archaeologists, only a few of the Carolingian ones have been even partly recovered.[41] To some extent this confirms the point just made. Medieval and modern towns grew up on the site of such former royal residences as Thionville and Aachen from the initial development of their palaces and related service areas. The later developments both destroyed evidence of the original constructions and limit archaeological access to them.

Even so, some sites have proved capable of moderately detailed investigation. One of these is Ingelheim, south-west of Mainz, where Charles spent Christmas in 787 and the Easter of 788, and which later became one of the favourite residences of his son Louis the Pious.[42] Excavations conducted between 1909 and 1914 seem to have revealed the ceremonial core of the palace complex, in the form of a series of interrelated buildings of very Late Roman appearance. Two of these on the south side are basilican in shape, placed at right angles to each other and separated by a square colonnaded courtyard. There was a smaller group of buildings on the north side, also including one of very ecclesiastical appearance. This, like the larger of the basilicas on the southern side, was oriented towards the east, but had a rectangular nave with a trefoil apse. This makes it more reminiscent of such contemporary Carolingian structures as Theodulf of Orléans's chapel at Germigny-des-Prés, built in 806, than the presumed Church on the south side of the palace, which in plan looks more like the kind of ecclesiastical basilica that had developed in the city of Rome from the fourth century onwards.[43] The two groups of buildings were apparently linked on the eastern side by a great semi-circular construction, fronted by a colonnade.[44] It has to be confessed that the early date of the excavations and a certain element of wishful thinking in the reconstructions based upon them leaves the evidence of this site as being at best provisional.

The presence of at least one substantial royal chapel and the likely existence of some form of throne hall, in which the major civil ceremonies of the court, as opposed to the ecclesiastical ones, would be performed seems to be confirmed by the more substantial evidence of Aachen itself. Here, fortunately, the original palace chapel was almost entirely preserved, to become incorporated into the later cathedral as its nave.[45] It survives not least as significant testimony to architectural borrowings from Italy as well as intellectual ones, as the plan of the Church of San Vitale in Ravenna, built with the financial assistance of the emperor Justinian around 548, has been seen as underlying that of the Aachen chapel. However, perhaps the best known feature of the latter, the placing of the ruler's throne in the first-floor gallery, over the entry and facing directly across the central space to the sanctuary on the east side, seems to be the product of an Ottonian reorganisation dated to 936, and not original to the Carolingian period. The throne itself, like the bronze railings around the upper story, is of almost certain Carolingian origin, and may thus have been moved to its present location from another site.[46]

It has been suggested that the primary influence on the plan of the palace at Aachen may have been that of the papal palatine and ecclesiastical complex in Rome, known as the Lateran.[47] In that these buildings would have been familiar to Charles from his visits to the city in 773/4 and in 781, this seems plausible. Some traces of stone work of that time survive in walls around the western entry to the cathedral, and excavations carried out between 1910 and 1914 also recovered something of the plan of other parts of the central section of the palace complex. In particular, a rectangular building with apsidal end, apparently linked to the chapel by a covered walkway, has been identified as the royal throne room.[48] This is similar in appearance to the ground plan of the building in the south-west corner of the palace at Ingelheim, and to the still-extant basilica at Trier, which was originally built as the throne hall of the emperor Constantine the Great (306–37).[49] Here the Roman emperor, enthroned in the apse behind curtains that would be opened or closed at various crucial stages, was the centre of a complex, rigidly controlled and very hierarchical series of diplomatic, administrative and power-displaying ceremonies. For the buildings of similar plan at Aachen and Ingelheim to be used in this same way would argue for a surprising continuity in ruler ceremonial between Late Antiquity and the Carolingian period, as well as for the survival of traditions concerning the previous use and associations of earlier buildings. Constantine's basilica at Trier, which had also long since ceased to be an imperial residence, had been taken over for use as a Church, possibly as early as the fifth century, and there was thus total discontinuity between its use for secular imperial rituals up to that point and its ecclesiastical liturgical employment in Merovingian and Carolingian times.[50]

There is no evidence at all that the kind of throne hall that was used in the court ceremonial of Late Antiquity could have filled a similar function under the Carolingians.[51] Einhard records that Charles wore only a bejewelled sword on the great liturgical feast days of the year and when receiving foreign envoys.[52] No mention is made of other regalia. Indeed, as the act of coronation was first used for Frankish rulers in 781 and then only in Rome, it would seem that Carolingian royal ritual was quite limited, and much less formal than it would become under the Ottonians. It was also much more concentrated on ecclesiastical occasions, with a primary location in Church rather than in a secular ruler's throne hall.[53] What might be called the civil ceremonial of the court was primarily directed at such communal acts as feasts and hunting. While both of these activities might provide hedonistic pleasures of various kinds, they also served as ways of bonding the members of the ruler's entourage together, and thus serving an important political function.[54] Thus, it may be that the basilican ground plans of Ingelheim and Aachen are those of churches rather than of throne rooms.

Another Constantinian association has been seen in Charles's plans for Paderborn, the site of another palace dating to his reign. This was revealed as a consequence of bomb damage to the town in the Second World War, and excavation has led to the uncovering not only of the ground plan of the Carolingian palace but also rather more substantial remains of its Ottonian successor.[55] The palace is located immediately to the north of the nave of the medieval cathedral begun by bishop Meinwerk (1009–36), within the roughly rectangular area of the Carolingian settlement. There is certainly a large rectangular building at the heart of the site, which has been identified as a throne hall, but it lacks the apsidal end of its Aachen and Ingelheim equivalents. Some traces have been found of the interior decoration of the palace, including small sections of painted plaster, some of which contain fragments of inscriptions as well as naturalistic designs.[56] There are grounds for suspecting that at one stage Charles thought of Paderborn, where construction of the palace and of a Church dedicated to the Saviour began in 776/7, as a possible future capital, as it is believed that this is the 'City of Charles' (*Urbs Caroli*) or 'Karlsburg' referred to in some of the minor annals.[57] This could be seen as a rather premature, even presumptuous, attempt to imitate Constantine the Great's foundation (in AD 327) of his new imperial capital of Constantinople.[58]

9

THE IMPERIAL CORONATION OF 800, AND ITS AFTERMATH

In December 795 pope Hadrian I died.[1] He had enjoyed a lengthy pontificate, which had coincided with much of Charles's reign over the Franks. According to Einhard, the king regarded the dead pontiff as a friend, even though their aspirations and policies had rarely coincided.[2] Following the overthrow of the Lombard kingdom, Charles had not restored papal rule over all the territories that the Church of Rome claimed, nor had Hadrian seen the reinstatement of icon veneration in Byzantium as the resurrection of heresy, in the way that the Frankish Council of Frankfurt had wished to regard it. Even so, relations between king and pope, as evidenced in the correspondence between them preserved in the collection known as the *Codex Carolinus*, were normally good, and Hadrian's standing in Rome had been generally secure and free from any hint of scandal.[3] The same could not be said of his successor, Leo III (795–816).

Leo was proclaimed on 27 December 795, the day after his predecessor's burial in St Peter's. Of Roman origin, he had risen in the bureaucracy of the papal administration and was in charge of the *vestiarium* of the Lateran at the time of his election on 26 December.[4] Formally this office of *vestiarius* implied responsibility for the papal vestments and liturgical vessels, but in practice it also extended to responsibility for the main Churches of the city and thus control of much of the wealth of the Roman Church.[5] Although the *Liber Pontificalis* makes out that Leo's election was both unanimous and popular, the truth of this would seem to be questioned by subsequent events. By November 798 Alcuin was hearing from one of his regular corespondents, archbishop Arn of Salzburg, that there were disturbances taking place in Rome directed against the pope.[6] Worse was to come. While leading one of the

141

regular processions around the churches of the city, known as the *Litania Maior*, Leo was attacked by a group of conspirators on 25 April 799. Those involved included two of the leading members of the papal administration, the *primicerius* Paschal and the *sacellarius* Campulus, both of whom were close relatives of the previous pope. The former was one of the three principal office holders in Rome and was in charge of the secretariat, while the latter was one of the two chiefs of the papal financial administration. Leo was attacked on a public occasion, suggesting that the attackers expected a measure of public support for their actions, which involved attempting both to blind him and cut out his tongue. Leo was then dragged into the monastery Church of Saints Stephen and Sylvester and there subjected to a further attack that left him 'half-dead and drenched in blood in front of the altar'.[7]

While these mutilations were intended to render Leo incapable of continuing in his office, there seems to have been a very half-hearted quality to the attacks, despite their apparent savagery. For when Leo was taken from Saints Stephen and Sylvester and imprisoned in the monastery of Saint Erasmus, it was discovered that he could still both see and speak. This the *Liber Pontificalis* would later attribute to a miracle, and it certainly proved vital to his continued political survival. For when he was rescued from St Erasmus by the papal chamberlain Albinus and other supporters, he was able to appear in St Peter's, outside the walls of the city.[8] There his manifest ability still to see and to speak led to his gaining the backing of duke Winigis of Spoleto, who had brought an armed force to the city on hearing of the coup. Rome itself seems to have been in the hands of the conspirators, and the duke, unable to take the city by force, took Leo back to Spoleto, whence he soon set out for Francia to try to gain Charles's backing for his restoration.[9]

Although the attempt to eliminate Leo had clearly been bungled and he had managed not only to escape but to gain some local support, there were clearly serious issues still to be resolved. The *Liber Pontificalis* ignores the fact that, to justify their actions, the conspirators had levelled charges of fornication and perjury against Leo. This presented problems that have affected the historical records of these events. That the laudatory 'Life of Leo III' compiled soon after his death and included in the *Liber Pontificalis* should have omitted reference to these accusations is not surprising. However, they also fail to be mentioned explicitly in the Frankish annals. In part this must reflect the fact that Leo was soon to be exonerated, and all of the annal accounts were written after the event. Beyond that, though, there was a real problem about jurisdiction. In the course of a disputed papal succession at the beginning of the sixth century, known as the Laurentian schism, there had been much consideration given to the question of who, if anyone, would be competent to sit in judge-

ment on a pope. The most influential view, enunciated not least by bishop
Ennodius of Pavia (d. 517) was that no-one had a higher authority and not
even a council of bishops could pass judgement on their ecclesiastical superior.[10] This line of argument had been thereafter promoted assiduously by
papal theorists. For Charles, therefore, the approach of a pope driven from his
own see and accused of malpractices presented some difficulties.

Alcuin, when he had heard from the king in June 799 about the attack on
Leo, had immediately urged Charles to give up his projected campaign in
Saxony and to intervene in Italy.[11] Charles did the opposite, and it may well be
that, by continuing his expedition into Saxony, he gained time to take advice
about what to do with Leo. He certainly seems to have thought of sending
Alcuin to Rome in July, a task from which the latter begged to be excused.[12] A
plan to send instead some former pupils of Alcuin was also discussed but
seems to have lapsed. By August if not earlier, Alcuin was aware of the nature
of the accusations being levelled against Leo. Even so, he clearly did not feel
that any other authority was competent to sit in judgement on the pope. In
a letter sent to Arn in the same month, he quoted the 'Canons of Sylvester',
and the acts of another unnamed council, actually the text known as the *Synodi
sinuessanae gesta*, to justify the view that a pope could not be judged. He
would not have known that both of these were spurious works, forged by partisans of pope Symmachus during the Laurentian schism (498–506).
Symmachus, like Leo III, had been accused of sexual improprieties, as well as
financial irregularities.[13] Paradoxically, it is only thanks to the survival of this
and of another of Alcuin's letters that we know the details of the charges made
against Leo.[14] It is likely that Alcuin used the accepted (if spurious) authority
of these 'Canons' to try to persuade Charles that he should give his support to
Leo irrespective of any accusations made against him.

Certainly, when the king and the pope did meet at Paderborn later in the
year, the latter was received with full honours, although the Frankish annals
and the *Liber Pontificalis* contradict each other in respect of describing who
showed the greater deference to whom.[15] The Frankish accounts of the papal
stay at Paderborn are exceedingly brief, and only the *Liber Pontificalis* mentions that envoys from the conspirators in Rome also appeared there to present
the charges against Leo. The same source alone adds that an assembly of lay
and ecclesiastical notables was then held at Paderborn, which advised Charles
to reinstate Leo. This he decided to do, sending the pope back to his city with
numerous gifts and accompanied by two *missi*, and no doubt an armed escort,
to restore him.[16] Arn of Salzburg was one of the two *missi* thus despatched,
and although the chronicle sources make no reference to this, it is clear from
an exchange of letters with Alcuin that their role also involved investigation of

the accusations made against Leo. Arn seems to have sent Alcuin a copy of the report that he made to Charles on his enquiries in Rome. This Alcuin destroyed, after reading it, to avoid the dissemination of scandal.[17]

While the issue of papal culpability may have consumed some of the discussions that preceded and accompanied Leo's visit to Paderborn, in the longer term a far more significant idea may also have been discussed at this time, that of an imperial title. The antecedents of Charles's coronation at the hands of Leo III in Rome on Christmas Day in the year 800 remain obscure and debatable. Little credence is now given to the statement in Einhard's *Vita Karoli* that Charles declared that he would never have entered the Church that day if he had known what was to happen.[18] The idea of the king being taken unawares when a Christmas Mass was suddenly transformed without prior arrangement into an imperial coronation is hard to credit, and Einhard is thought merely to be conforming to the tradition of 'the refusal of power' that was a standard feature of political rhetoric and probably even of ceremonial in Late Antiquity and the Early Middle Ages.

This convention made the acceptance of office, both secular and ecclesiastical, something that had to be forced on the recipient. A classic example is that of Ammianus Marcellinus's account of the elevation of the emperor Julian in 360, and the same tradition can be seen in Julian of Toledo's description of the choosing of Wamba as Visigothic king in 672.[19] In both cases the candidates are said to have tearfully refused the offices that were being offered to them, until forced to accept by threats of death as the only alternative. For both Julian and Wamba there are no grounds for suspecting that this particular piece of pantomime was sincere. Similarly, at least since the time of Augustine there had been a tradition that ecclesiastical office was not an honour to be sought but only a burden to be accepted reluctantly. The improbable story of Gregory the Great taking to flight and having to be brought back to Rome when elected pope in 590 belongs in this tradition.[20] What is not certain is whether such acts of refusal were just literary devices or whether they reflect the actual conduct that was deemed necessary on the part of those offered high secular or ecclesiastical office. While Einhard does not attempt to portray Charles engaging in such a ritual of refusal, the words that he puts into his mouth would have seemed appropriate.

If it be accepted that Charles indeed knew what was going to happen, and that the plan for an imperial coronation at the hands of the pope had previously been discussed and agreed, it may be asked when this occurred. Once more the annals fail us. There is no explanation given for the coronation so vividly described in the opening section of the entries for 801 in the *Annales Regni Francorum* and its Revised version. Only the contemporary *Lorsch*

Annals give any indication of a preceding stage of discussion, which is said to have taken place at an assembly in Rome in late November 800.[21] Once again the context is that of the attack on and the accusations made against pope Leo, with which the whole episode of the coronation is so intimately linked.

In 799, after Leo had been sent back to Rome with the *missi*, Charles had remained in Saxony before returning to Aachen. In the Spring of 800 he had toured the coastal region of northern Francia, where he had also initiated construction of a fleet against Danish raids. He was at the monastery of Saint-Bertin on 26 March and spent Easter (19 April) at the monastery of Saint-Riquier, of which Angilbert was the abbot.[22] The latter's experience and advice, as a former royal *missus* in Rome in both 792 and 796, may have been of particular value at this time.[23] After this Charles proceeded via Rouen to Tours, Alcuin's residence since 796, where his wife Liutgard died, and was buried on 4 June.[24] The king rounded off this journey, which was the only one he had paid so far to northern France, by returning to Aachen via Orléans and Paris. While the growing threat of piratical raids by the Danes might have been sufficient justification, the purely defensive nature of the work did not require Charles's presence in person and the rest of the itinerary might suggest that these first-ever visits to some of the major monasteries of Neustria was an end in its own right. Charles also spent time with a number of influential counsellors, including Alcuin, Angilbert and Theodulf of Orléans. It is a reasonable suspicion that these visits involved both the making of offerings at such influential shrines as the tombs of Saint Martin at Tours and Saint Denis outside Paris and the taking of advice.

In August Charles held an assembly at Mainz, where he announced his imminent departure for Italy; another reason for the renewal of the defences along the Channel earlier in the year. He proceeded across the Alps to Ravenna, which again was a rather circuitous way of approaching Rome and may reflect a need for further consultation, this time with his son Pippin, the king of the Lombards, who was then despatched southwards into the duchy of Benevento with the army that Charles had brought with him. He himself continued to Ancona, which is where he parted from Pippin, and thence to Mentana, where he was met by Leo III. The location of this meeting is significant in that it took place at the twelfth (Roman) milestone from Rome.[25] This was traditionally the place where the emperors were received when making a formal entry or *Adventus* into the city.[26] The pope's coming out of the city to greet the king at such a point could be another indicator that the imperial coronation was already planned. Discussions took place between them before the pope returned to Rome to prepare for Charles's formal reception into the city, which took place on 24 November.

A week after his arrival, which had culminated with an entry into the basilica of St Peter's, Charles held an assembly, at which he 'made clear to all why
he had come to Rome'.[27] This included a resolution of the problem of the
accusations made against Leo III. From the Annalist's account it is clear that
the Alcuinian view that no one was competent to judge the pope had been
accepted by Charles and his advisors, and a piece of theatre was devised to
shelve the issue permanently. Leo entered the pulpit in St Peter's carrying a
manuscript of the Gospels and there took an oath in the name of the Trinity
that he was innocent of all that was alleged against him.[28] While humiliating
for Leo, this allowed the immunity of his office to be preserved, and thus the
future consecrator of the emperor could emerge apparently justified. In consequence, whatever may have been thought privately about the accusations made
against Leo, his enemies who had tried to mutilate and depose him in 799 had
to be brought to trial. This took place in early in 801, when they were condemned to death for treason. On papal intervention this was changed to a
sentence of exile.[29]

The papal oath-taking was not the only piece of ceremonial planned for the
assembly initiated on 30 November. On the same day that Leo took his oath,
and this can hardly be a coincidence, envoys were received by Charles from
the Patriarch of Jerusalem, bringing him the keys to the Holy Sepulchre and to
the city itself. In theory Charles was thus made the defender of the Holy
Places. In practice this was a meaningless honour, in that Jerusalem had long
been under the authority of the Caliphs, now ruling from Baghdad. However,
the symbolic significance of these actions was high. The Patriarchate of
Jerusalem, although never as influential as those of Alexandria, Antioch and
Constantinople, had enjoyed great prestige from the Holy Places situated
within and around the city. Even after the fall of Jerusalem to the Arabs in
636, it was the emperors in Constantinople that its Church recognised as the
secular leaders of the Christian world. The sending of the keys of the city and
of the tomb of Christ to Charles was thus the equivalent of a transfer of formal
loyalty from the emperor in the east to the man who in a few days would be
crowned emperor in Rome.

If this be a reasonable supposition, then it has to be accepted that the patriarch was aware that a new emperor was about to be made. This fact he might
have discovered through the ambassador that had been sent by him to Charles
at Aachen the previous winter. This envoy was a monk who brought greetings
from the patriarch to the Frankish king, together with some unspecified relics.
For this to have been followed up a year later by the far more significant gift
of the keys and for their presentation to have been so carefully worked in with
the lead up to the imperial coronation on Christmas Day certainly argues both

careful planning and a greater symbolic significance to the patriarch's gesture than is sometimes allowed.[30] It would thus seem probable that the plans for the coronation were being laid at least a year before the event itself, and in all probability even earlier than that.

That the coronation was not just a rapid and unforeseen development that grew out of Charles's visit to Italy is also implied by the words of the Annalist. Having stated that the king had informed the assembly that gathered on 30 November of the reasons for his visit to Rome, the annal then mentions the resolving of the accusations made against Leo as being the first and most difficult of these objectives, but does not specify any others. Although the date then changes and thus a new annal begins, there is no reason why the narrative of the coronation, with which the entry for 801 begins, should not also be understood to relate to the previous claim that the king explained his purposes for being in Rome to the assembly that met on 30 November 800. This would confirm the specific statement in the *Lorsch Annals* that the decision to give Charles the imperial title was agreed upon at that council.[31] All in all, it looks as if there are good grounds for suspecting that the royal visit to Rome and its culmination in the imperial coronation on 25 December had been planned at least as early as 799, quite possibly during Leo III's visit to the court at Paderborn. Apart from Einhard's words there would be no grounds for doubting such a degree of preparation for so significant a step. But it still needs to be considered why Charles and his advisors were prepared to take it.

That the motivation behind the acceptance of the imperial title was a romantic and antiquarian interest in reviving the Roman empire is highly unlikely. No explicit evidence exists to support such a view in any of the texts of Charles's reign. Although an interest in and concern for the preservation of the literary and artistic heritage of Antiquity would grow in the Carolingian period, this tendency was still in its infancy. Far more influential were the Christian writings of the fourth and fifth centuries and the ideals of reform that had been generated from the works of Patristic authors such as Augustine and were transmitted through Gregory the Great, Bede, Boniface and others.[32] There may have even been an element of distrust of the pagan heritage of Antiquity making itself felt in Charles's court.[33] His own favourite book, Augustine's *De Civitate Dei,* would certainly have warned him of this, and it has been shown that the classical as opposed to Patristic learning of many of his scholars was quite limited. Alcuin, for example, may have known little more than Vergil of the Roman poets.[34] Theodulf of Orléans, who was unique in showing knowledge of the verses of Ovid, took a lead in warning against the seductive non-Christian legacy of Rome.

It has been suggested that Charles's interest in acquiring his imperial title derived from more practical and immediate needs than some of the older views on the question allowed for. In particular, he needed some new constitutional status to legitimate his rule over the recently conquered Saxons.[35] They, unlike the Lombards, did not have a monarchy that Charles could take as his own to validate his exercise of rule over a recognisably non-Frankish people. By exercising *imperium* over different ethnic groups by virtue of his new imperial status, it is argued, Charles could turn his *de facto* control of the Saxons and their lands into an authority that would be acceptable to at least the leaders of their society. However, it has to be said that this had not been a problem for earlier generations of Frankish kings, who had ruled over the Saxons and received tribute from them. The Frankish literary sources all concur in regarding Saxon opposition to Merovingian and Carolingian rule as rebellion. Thus, Charles and his predecessors thought they already had the right to rule Saxony as much as Bavaria or Aquitaine, and the various submissions made by the Saxons in the course of the wars would have seemed to validate this. The argument might be better applied to Italy. The limited geographical extent of Lombard royal power, the questionable ownership of the lands of the former Exarchate of Ravenna, the status of the Papacy and its territories, and the emergence of a Beneventan principality all meant that no unitary authority existed in Italy, in theory or practice. The imperial title at least gave Charles the right to try to impose his rule over the whole of it.

That there was an element of military and political risk in Charles's taking of the imperial title should not be doubted. Byzantium was bound to oppose such a move on the part of one who would inevitably be regarded as an upstart barbarian. Even while the Roman Empire in the west still existed, for an emperor in one or other half of the Empire to declare himself unilaterally led more often than not to civil war. In theory the Empire remained a unity even if authority was being exercised by more than one emperor, and thus mutual acceptance or *Concordia Imperatorum* was essential. Nor in theory had the Empire, although reduced in size by 800 to little more than Asia Minor and the southern sections of the Balkans, recognised any diminution of either the emperor's *de jure* sovereignty over all its former territories or his position as God's sole vicegerent on earth. That the Byzantine imperial administration would refuse to recognise a unilateral proclamation of an emperor in the west was probably long realised.

On the other hand, there was an argument to be made that the throne in Constantinople was then vacant, and there was thus no imperial partner whose consent was needed to validate the proclamation of Charles. After considerable political tension induced both by his remarriage and by his moves towards the re-imposition of Iconoclasm, the emperor Constantine VI had been overthrown in a coup in 796 led by partisans of his mother Irene. He had been blinded to render him incapable of resuming the imperial office. Unlike the attempt on Leo III in 799 this had been carried out with such brutal thoroughness that the deposed emperor had died. His mother, who had been the consort of Leo IV (775–80) and regent for her son for many years, now attempted to rule in person. This was the first time that an empress had tried to exercise imperial authority in her own right, and this may have contributed to her political difficulties.[36] The fate of Constantine VI also left her regime on an unsound footing, and such factors may explain the willingness of so traditional an adherent of Constantinople as the Patriarch of Jerusalem to look to a new Roman emperor in the west. There was thus both an argument from theory, that the eastern throne was vacant, and the practical reality of the weakness of Irene's political position that might have made the proclamation of Charles as emperor an attractive possibility from 796 onwards.

Indeed, it has been argued that what happened on 25 December 800 in St Peter's was not in itself a constitutive act but a purely liturgical recognition of a state that already existed.[37] That is to say that Charles had already fulfilled the necessary preconditions for holding imperial rule, and that in the light of the theoretical vacancy created by the killing of Constantine VI no other rival candidate existed. Thus, what Leo III did in the Christmas liturgy was to give ecclesiastical recognition to something that was already in being. This view, which was in part based on a document subsequently shown to be a forgery, has been vigorously challenged, and it is generally accepted that both Leo III and Charles regarded the coronation as the constitutive action that conferred the imperial title upon the new emperor.[38] Where they might subsequently have differed was the degree to which such a papal and liturgical context was necessary for future transfers of imperial authority. When in September 813 Charles felt his end approaching he summoned his only surviving son Louis to an assembly at Aachen and there crowned him as emperor with his own hand.[39] It was Louis who would later and definitively put the imperial coronation firmly back into papal hands, with dangerous future consequences.[40]

Another area of difficulty would have been the question of how acceptable this move might prove to the Franks. Charles's primary title had always been that of 'King of the Franks'.[41] For the new emperor to make drastic changes to the traditional styles and procedures of government, let alone to concentrate his attentions on Italy or on Mediterranean concerns more generally, risked alienating the Frankish nobles who attended the annual assemblies and provided most of the military manpower for the royal campaigns. In practice Charles seems to have been alive to this danger. He had already shown that the conquest of the Lombard kingdom would not deflect his attention from concerns that were primarily east Frankish: the campaigns against the Saxons, the Slavs and the Avars. Thus, while he remained in Italy for several more months in 801, dealing with military and administrative matters in Rome, Spoleto, Ravenna and Pavia, he then returned to Aachen in time for Christmas of that year.[42] He never came back to Italy for the rest of the reign.

Equally significantly, he very quickly changed the style of his imperial title. It seems that in Rome he had been crowned by Leo III under the title of *Imperator Romanorum* or 'Emperor of the Romans'. This was on the one hand doubly offensive to Constantinople, in that the Byzantines thought of themselves as the *Romaioi* or Romans, and on the other it was ill-suited to Frankish views on ethnicity. The Franks had if anything reinforced their own sense of a special Frankish identity in the course of the eighth century. The Gallo-Roman element that had formed an important part of the population in the Merovingian period had been absorbed into Frankish society in Neustria and Austrasia, while the ethnic distinctiveness of other elements of the population, such as the Burgundians and the various peoples east of the Rhine, had been reinforced by the proliferation of separate legal codes. For the Franks the Romans were essentially the inhabitants of the city of Rome or in a broader sense those peoples, such as the Aquitanians, who used Roman codes, such as the *Breviarium* of Alaric, as their 'national' law. Thus, for Charles to be *Imperator Romanorum* was almost meaningless in a Frankish political context.[43] A more acceptable formula, that of *Romanum gubernans Imperium* ('governing the Roman Empire'), seems to have emerged very quickly, and was in use by the date of the first surviving imperial diploma issued by Charles at Reno near Bologna on 29 May 801. Although previously thought to be a novelty, this title has been shown to be of Late Roman origin, and in regular use in Italy until the mid-eighth century.[44] Charles was also careful not to let his royal Frankish title be subsumed into his new imperial one, and thus frequently appears in his documents as *Rex Francorum* and as *Imperator*.[45] These developments helped in due course to make his imperial status diplomatically more acceptable to Byzantium too, but their primary purpose must have been to put the new dignity into an essentially Frankish context. After the conclusion of peace with the emperor Michael I in 812, Charles seems to have dropped the use of the 'Governing the Roman Empire' element in his title in diplomatic exchanges with Constantinople.[46]

At the simplest level, Frankish kings had always served as the military leaders of the people, and their role in law-making and as leaders of the army had to be expressed in the very public context of the annual assembly, the 'Marchfield'. Frankish ideas of rulership were very ethno-centric, and never extended to wider conceptions that might embrace non-Frankish subject peoples within a sense of a common political identity. There was no equivalent in the west in the eighth century to the Roman idea of citizenship as a common bond that transcended mere ethnic origin. Roman imperial traditions of rule were thus of little appeal to the Franks, and indeed probably little known to them or capable of being understood by them. There also existed a strong historiographical tradition, equivalent to one found amongst the Visigoths in Spain, that saw the Franks as both victors over the Romans and also, as orthodox Christians, their superiors as defenders of the faith.[47] Thus, the prologue to Pippin III's issue of an enlarged version of *Lex Salica*, that has been dated to 763/4, saw the Franks as having 'fought against and thrown from their shoulders the heavy yoke of the Romans'. They had also 'from the knowledge gained by baptism, clothed in gold and precious stones the bodies of the holy martyrs whom the Romans had killed by fire, by the sword and by wild animals'.[48] In such a tradition the title of 'Emperor of the Romans' could have little appeal, and might even seem derogatory to Frankish self-esteem.

These uncertainties over the title and the degree of rethinking that was required would suggest that such questions had not formed a significant part of the initial planning for the imperial coronation. One of the features that has given support to the view that it was rather a hurried or ill-conceived move has been the lack of evidence of such preparing of the ground. There are no traces of discussions in detail between Charles and his advisors prior to the Italian expedition of 800 of what the new title might mean and how it might best be expressed. The nearest that the evidence seems to come to such issues are references in some of the letters of Alcuin to the *Imperium Christianum* or 'Christian Empire'.[49] Was this an alternative view to that of a revival of a Roman Empire? Just as the inhabitants of the latter had been united by a common Roman citizenship (at least after AD 212), so, might a common faith in Christ provide a political bond for a new empire? It is hard to deduce a firm programme of this sort from Alcuin's words, and *imperium* is a much more malleable concept than is the title *imperator*. It had served a variety of purposes in Alcuin's native Northumbria, notably in the writings of Bede (d. 735).[50] A ruler could exercise *imperium*, in the sense of rule over more than one ethnic group, without holding the title of emperor, which was a claim to a universal authority.[51]

It has to be admitted that much of the source material that might have been expected to reveal such discussions and arguments over the plan for the imperial coronation and its significance is missing. Of written materials it is only Alcuin's letters that provide some hints as to discussions predating the coronation. It is also probable that much of the debate would have been conducted orally, without leaving any written record of itself. That the planning was longer term than often believed has already been argued. It could even be suggested that Charles's ambitions had been stirred even before 799. As early as 797 he had made diplomatic contact with the 'Abbasid Caliph Harun al-Rashid (786–809), sending three envoys to Baghdad. They may also have opened the contacts with the Patriarch of Jerusalem that led to his despatch of emissaries to Charles in 799 and 800.[52]

For the Franks, Harun was *Rex Persarum* ('King of the Persians'), though they also knew his Arabic title of *Amir al-Mu'minin* or 'Commander of the Faithful'.[53] The distance between the Frankish kingdom and the Caliphate made communication slow, but it may not have just been this problem that led to the arrival of ambassadors from Harun in Italy in 801. Also represented was the 'Abbasid's viceroy in Tunisia, Ibrahim ibn al-Aghlab (800–12). The envoys from Baghdad were able to report that Charles's own emissaries were on the way back to him, apart from two who had died *en route*, and that they were bringing appropriate gifts from the Caliph. These included an elephant called 'Abolabas' (Abu al-Abbas), which to the Franks may have been a curiosity, but was also an important and long-established symbol of authority in the near east, from Hellenistic times onwards.[54]

For Harun to sent such a gift and to have involved his newly appointed deputy in the west, the Aghlabid ruler, in the diplomatic exchanges would suggest that he too, like the Patriarch of Jerusalem, had been informed of Charles's imperial intentions at some earlier time. It has also been suggested that the Patriarch is likely to have sought the Caliph's permission before making the significant gesture of sending the keys of the city to Charles.[55] It is thus conceivable that some such plan had been in the air as early as 796/7, when the Byzantine throne became theoretically vacant and when Charles secured control of the Avar treasures, and became thereby a figure of increasing note in the east. For the 'Abbasids the Frankish ruler became a potentially useful counterweight both to Byzantium and to the rival Umayyad dynasty in Spain, which had previously held the Caliphal title in Syria until 750 and still might have hoped one day to recover it. It cannot be certain that Charles had made firm plans to secure an imperial title for himself as early as 796, but a number of developments both within the Frankish orbit and beyond in the final years of the eighth century made such an idea more worthy of consideration than it would previously have been. This is not, however, the same as saying that the implications of such a title and its practical and other significance had been carefully worked out. The problem over nomenclature and the rapid changes in the form of the title in the years 800 to 802 is proof enough of that.

Diplomatically, while Charles might have enjoyed receiving recognition from Baghdad, he could expect only hostility from Constantinople. Only the political and military difficulties of Byzantium limited the degree of opposition that could be expressed to the new developments in the west. The empress Irene, whose position had been weak since her killing of her son in 796, was prepared to negotiate an end to the conflicts in southern Italy, and did not react directly to Charles's imperial coronation. The Byzantine *Chronicle of Theophanes*, which is very favourable to Irene, claims that in 802 Charles sent envoys offering her a proposal of marriage, which she was planning to accept. But before she could respond, she was deposed in a coup and replaced by her former finance minister, who became the emperor Nicephorus I (802–11). No Frankish source mentions this scheme, but it may have been devised as a formal way of validating the anomalous status as 'Roman Emperors' of both Charles and Irene. Although negotiations continued into 803, the new emperor in Constantinople was unwilling to accept the title of his would-be western colleague. Fighting broke out in the Adriatic 806–7 and in 809, to be followed by further negotiations in 811. Not until 812, under the exceedingly weak regime of Michael I (811–13), did a ruler in Constantinople consent to use an imperial title in referring to Charles, probably under the style 'Emperor of the Franks'.[56] The Byzantines regarded this title as little better than meaningless, still considering the imperial office as one and indivisible and not to be linked to an ethnic rulership. 'Emperor of the Franks' was thus as exotic as 'Khagan of the Turks', and equally distanced from the real emperorship of the *Basileos* in Constantinople.[57]

For Charles on his return to Francia in the Autumn of 801, it is clear that his new status required some particular new governmental acts. Einhard records that his imperial office made Charles attempt to reconcile the differences between the two Frankish law codes and to reform their texts, and at the same time to have 'the laws of all nations under his rule ... written down'.[58] The former task apparently did not progress with any great speed, and Einhard refers, rather dismissively, to a few enactments in rough draft (*capitula ... inperfecta*) being added to the Frankish codes. This gives a rather misleading impression of the amount of such legal activity that has been assigned to the last decade of Charles's reign. This sense of limited purpose and achievement is made all the stronger in that the only other concerns of Charles that Einhard relates to his new-found imperial dignity consisted of a plan to have 'the ancient and barbaric songs concerning the deeds and wars of kings' consigned to writing, the commissioning of a grammar of his native tongue (i.e. the German dialect of eastern Francia), and the production of Germanic equivalents for the Latin names of the months. While Einhard gives no precise chronology, it has been assumed that the process of writing out versions of the laws of the subject peoples was initiated soon after Charles's return to Francia from Italy. Some of the capitularies of 802 reinforce the view that this process of revising existing laws and committing others to writing was one of the emperor's primary concerns at this time. Those legal codes not previously known to have existed in written form, such as the *Lex Frisonum*, are thus taken to have been compiled and written down around the year 803. This was far from being the only major administrative undertaking of these years, and Einhard's image of Charles otherwise being engaged only in various pieces of footling philology is entirely deceptive.[59] Indeed even these need to be seen in the context of the emperor and his advisors trying to develop a significance for the imperial role in a Germanic Frankish context. It is the capitulary evidence that is the best source of information for Charles's concerns in this period.

An assembly held at Aachen in March 802 produced one of the most lengthy and substantial sets of legal and administrative decrees of the reign, in a text which has come to be called 'the Programmatic Capitulary'.[60] It consists of 40 chapters, and was linked to the despatch of panels of *missi* across the empire. The *aide-memoires* or notes issued to the *missi* have also been preserved, and these can be compared with the text of the decisions of the imperial assembly in the Programmatic Capitulary. As many as six of these sets of notes have been found.[61] Their list of 19 chapters, which is little more than a series of headings, coincides with many of the main items in the Programmatic Capitulary itself, although the ordering is rarely the same. However, not all of the contents of the latter are included and there are one or two clauses in the *missi*'s list not to be found in the larger document. This seems to be a good example of how a central governmental programme might be modified or abridged in the course of its transmission to the regions.[62]

The concern for legal reform and the proper administration of justice, mentioned by Einhard, forms not only the opening subject of the Programmatic Capitulary but is a theme that runs throughout the whole work. The *missi* are required to assure the inhabitants of the regions to which they are sent that they are guaranteed the use of their traditional laws, but these are to be inspected and where elements in them are found to be other than just and equitable they are to be referred to the emperor for revision. The *missi* are also adjured by the fidelity they have sworn to Charles to enquire into all complaints that are put before them. Their second major task was to oversee the administration of a new oath and to explain its significance to those required to take it.

The oath is to be taken by all those who had previously promised fidelity to Charles as king of the Franks. They are now to take a comparable oath to him as 'Caesar', in other words as emperor. In addition all freemen over the age of 12 who had not yet taken an oath were now to do so. Two examples of the oath itself, taken on the relics of saints and very similar to an oath of vassalage, have been preserved in another document.[63] The implications of the fidelity that is promised are spelt out in considerable detail in the Programmatic Capitulary. It is expected that the oath takers will understand that what they have sworn encompasses protecting the emperor's life, not assisting his enemies, and not keeping silent when aware of treasonable plans or actions on the part of others. However, it is then explained in a sequence of seven successive chapters that fidelity now also includes avoiding cheating the emperor financially, neglecting a benefice received from him, not attempting to evade military service, not opposing or ignoring the emperor's commands and intentions, and not acting to thwart the proper working of justice. It also carried the obligation on the individual not to inflict any harm on Churches, widows and orphans, or pilgrims (*peregrini*), and the first requirement of all was that everyone must strive 'to maintain himself in God's holy service, according to God's command and his own promise; for the lord emperor cannot himself provide the necessary care and discipline for each man individually'.[64]

This is an extraordinary and novel extension of the use of the oath as an instrument of government. It effectively sought to tie all of the subject's duties towards the ruler into a relationship of obligation based upon supernatural sanction. Older, Roman, ideas of *maiestas* or treason could be found in the earlier oath, which confined itself to the protection of the ruler from conspiracy and from his subjects' aiding and abetting his external or internal enemies. The 802 oath, however, also sought to make any action that was economically detrimental to the emperor a treasonable one. It made mere passivity, as in failing to turn out for military service or in not looking after property provided by the monarch, an act of equal disloyalty. It equated the protection of the Church and of certain categories of persons under the emperor's special protection with fidelity to the ruler. Most strikingly of all, an individual's religious obligations were made political ones too. The thinking behind this latter extension of the meaning of fidelity would seem to have been that the emperor by virtue of his office was responsible for the spiritual well-being of those entrusted to him, but in practice was unable to exercise the kind of personal oversight of his subjects that this would require. This responsibility for leading the Christian life he therefore had to entrust to them to carry out individually, and where they failed to do so they were deemed to be betraying him.

This is a remarkable attempt to construct a basis for political and moral obligation. It was extended in other clauses of the Programmatic Capitulary to embrace different kinds of cleric and also monks and nuns. All of these were required to live according to the precepts of canon law, which was seen as their own particular *lex* or legal code. Reports of fornication and sodomy in monasteries particularly incensed the emperor, who demanded strict adherence to the monastic Rule. Judges and counts were also required to observe the law in their own dealings and to administer it justly in their courts. A number of offences were singled out for specific mention and prohibition. These included incest, patricide and stealing the emperor's game (clauses 33, 37 and 39). Homicide was also to be punished severely, but to prevent the proliferation of violence those who have killed were here ordered to make a financial composition with the relatives of the victim as soon as possible. They for their part were forbidden to reject a proper offer of monetary compensation. Feud was thereby to be avoided. Practice is all too likely to have fallen short of these injunctions, and the governmental machinery at Charles's disposal was insufficient to impose a real end to feuding occasioned by killing.[65] It was more the attempt, placed within the context of the ruler's responsibility for warding off divine anger from the people under his charge, that is notable. Similarly, although some subsequent capitularies emphasise the need for those who have not yet taken the oath now to be made to do so, the implications of the new interpretation of infidelity do not make themselves felt in the evidence relating to Carolingian government in Charles's final years.[66]

Another striking, if possibly impractical, feature of the Programmatic Capitulary is the way in which a number of particular offences were henceforth to be reserved for trial in the emperor's own court. These embraced such matters as cases of incest or sodomy amongst the clergy, but also could include what must seem like lesser misdemeanours, such as those of clerics accused of going hunting with dogs (a practice prohibited as early as Pippin's Soissons capitulary of 744).[67] While most of the crimes to be brought before the imperial court were of what might be called a moral character, and thus be thought to be central to Charles's view of his own responsibility to God for his subjects' conduct, in practice the need to send the parties from all over the Empire to Aachen and the resulting increase in the number of cases that could only be heard before the emperor must have greatly slowed down the central workings of justice in Francia.

Another problem that needed to be confronted in the aftermath of the imperial coronation was that of the succession and the nature of any territorial division that might have to be undertaken between Charles's sons. From a letter of Alcuin it is clear that Charles arranged a coronation at the hands of pope Leo for his eldest son before they left Rome in the Spring of 801.[68] The 'Life of Leo III' in the *Liber Pontificalis*, composed after his death in 816, states that

the younger Charles was anointed by the pope in the course of the same ceremony in which his father received his imperial crown on Christmas Day 800.[69]
Whether the details of the two sources are contradictory or complementary is
not clear, but that Charles was the focus of some king-making rituals in Rome
seems certain. In 789/90 he had been entrusted with responsibility for a part of
the old kingdom of Neustria, but while one set of annals calls this a *regnum* or
kingdom, the only other one to mention it merely refers to it as 'the dukedom
of Le Mans'.[70] While the two younger sons, Pippin and Louis, had been provided with nominal kingdoms of their own in Italy and Aquitaine as early as
781, the younger Charles had remained in Francia with their father, with the
expectation that he would in due course succeed to the Frankish monarchy.
With the imperial elevation of his father, it became possible to make the elder
son's status equivalent to that of his brothers. While Charles invested his sons
with royal titles and with responsibilities for designated regions, he retained a
superior authority over them. Even after the coronation in 800 he continued to
use the titles of 'King of the Franks' and 'King of the Lombards' in tandem
with his new imperial one. This can be seen not least in the detailed plan for
the division of the territories of the empire between his sons that was promulgated in 806.

This document, known as the *Divisio Imperii* ('Division of the Empire')
was issued at the royal palace at Thionville, and is dated 6 February.[71] In this
Charles, whose fears of being forgotten by posterity have been assuaged by
God's gift of three sons, formally recognises them as partners in his kingdom
while he continued to live and as his heirs after his death. To prevent future
disputes, he now divided up his lands between them. The eastern frontiers of
Louis's Aquitanian kingdom, which included Gascony, Septimania and the
newly conquered territories across the Pyrenees, required precise definition.
Most of Bavaria was added to Pippin's Italian kingdom, which thereby
became less of a Lombard realm. Some minor territories once held by Tassilo
III on the fringes of Bavaria in Alamannia were detached to form part of the
younger Charles's kingdom which, comprising Burgundy and all the rest of
Francia, formed the lion's share of the territories.[72] How the partnership in
power that is referred to in the *Divisio Imperii* worked thereafter is not clear.
Pippin and Louis had their own realms, although under close supervision from
their father, and all three brothers had taken increasingly prominent military
roles as their father grew less able to campaign in person, but whether the
younger Charles thereafter gained greater authority in Francia itself is by no
means clear. What has also aroused much comment is that no mention is made
in this document of the imperial office. Argument over this has included
the suggestion that Charles viewed this as a personal rather than a heritable

distinction. Alternatively, he may have seen it as essentially different in kind and not directly related to the territorial division being conducted in 806.

Certainly he did not in the end allow the imperial title to lapse with his death, as he summoned his son Louis to Aachen from Aquitaine in 813 and there crowned him emperor with his own hands. By this time, though, there were few hard choices to make. Pippin had died in 810 and the younger Charles in 811. The territorial division envisaged in 806 had ceased to be fully applicable. However, Charles seems to have decided that his grandsons should be able to inherit their fathers' portions. Pippin's son Bernard was sent to Italy in 812, and given a royal title in 813, in the course of the ceremonies in which his uncle Louis was crowned emperor.[73] The younger Charles appears to have left no heirs. Indeed, he is not known to have married, which is rather surprising in the light of his expected succession to the greater part of the Frankish empire. Thus, in 813 there was only one of the three sons left, and a grandson had acquired one of the portions. Whether or not Charles had planned it in this way all along, in the circumstances the entrusting of all the imperial territory other than the Italian kingdom to Louis, who already had three sons of his own, must have been inevitable. Whether the imperial title was then used by Charles in 813 to ensure that Louis had an authority that extended beyond those kingdoms to embrace that of his nephew Bernard or whether this was something with which he would have invested the senior surviving son in any case cannot be known. What is certain, though, is that it proved a dangerous and difficult inheritance.[74]

On the subject of Charles's intentional legacy, i.e. his plans for the disposition of his personal possessions and possibly even of the Frankish royal treasure, Einhard seems to offer guidance. Following the model of Suetonius's *Vita Augusti*, he concluded his *Vita Karoli* with an account of the emperor's will, drawn up early in 811.[75] He even tells his readers that he is giving them the very words of the document itself, and he certainly seems to provide an authentic list of its lay and ecclesiastical witnesses. However, the text that accompanies this list, and which purports to be the very will itself, is clearly nothing of the sort. It is absurdly brief and imprecise, and is cast in the third person. While third person wills recording the dispositions of a dying testator who was unable to have them committed in writing are known, they invariably make their character clear.[76] In comparison with any other extant dispositive wills from both this time and the preceding Merovingian period, this purported testament of Charles is entirely anachronistic in both form and content, and far too short.[77] It is also exceedingly vague and imprecise, and is contradicted by all of the other, briefer, accounts of Charles's will to be found in the historiography of the reigns of Louis the Pious and Charles the Bald. Einhard, misleading again, is giving his version or memory of the contents of the will, and not its precise text. The variant accounts of it, and other indicators, firmly suggest that Charles's testamentary intentions were never fully carried out by his less than satisfactory successor.[78]

10

FRONTIERS AND WARS, 793–813

Saxony and Beyond

In the light of the relative speed or indeed positive despatch with which the Lombard monarchy and the Bavarian duchy, and even the Avar khaganate, had been eliminated by Charles in the course of rapid and largely bloodless campaigns, the protracted and violent nature of the wars with the Saxons may seem surprising. However, this is not to compare like with like. The principal difference between the Saxons and Charles's other opponents in the closing decades of the eighth century lay in their social and political organisation. With a sophisticated and moderately well centralised governmental and administrative organisation such as that of the Lombard kingdom in northern Italy, the capture of the person of the king and of his capital put control of the governmental machine in the hands of the conqueror. While the individual regional Lombard dukes may have had an incentive to resist, none of them had the personal military power at their disposal, and attempts to form a confederacy could only expect limited success, as Hrodgaud's revolt proved. In the case of the Bavarians and the Avars internal divisions played into Frankish hands, and again there was limited potential for local resistance once the rulers had been killed or captured. With the Saxons, however, conditions were very different.

Something of the social and political organisation of Saxon society has been preserved in the earliest version of the *Life of Saint Lebuin*. This account of this Anglo-Saxon missionary, who worked in the area of western Saxony and who died about 780, was written at some point during the next 50 years. It may not entirely represent the realities of an earlier generation, but the picture it paints is both coherent and credible. It describes Saxon society as being essentially organised into regional communities, each of which had its own elected leader. These met together annually, each accompanied by 12 representatives of each of the three social classes amongst the population: nobles, the free and the 'half-free' or *lati*. At the assembly new laws were discussed and judgements were given in legal disputes. Plans, either military or peaceful, were also made for the whole community for the coming year.[1] The anonymous author of the *Vita* states that the assembly met at Marklo near the river Weser. Whether this was really for all sections of Saxony or merely represents the regional assembly of the Weissgau which might have been matched by similar meetings in the other Saxon lands cannot be known. If, however, the leader and 36 other representatives came from every region (*pagus*), it must have been a substantial gathering.

In such circumstances, while the almost continuous warfare of the period 772 to 785, and in particular Charles's final savage winter campaign, may have cowed the Saxons and imposed a ten-year period of peace, unless this was followed up by major changes in the government of the Saxons and in their culture, resistance to Frankish overlordship and the religious and other changes that were being demanded was almost bound to reassert itself. It does not seem that there was a major influx of Frankish population into Saxony, and Charles's administrative and religious reforms continued to be imposed from a small number of fortresses, that remained no more than alien enclaves in the Saxon rural landscape. Saxon levies were increasingly called upon to take part in Frankish wars, such as the campaign into Bavaria in 787, that against the Slavic Wiltzi in 789, and the Avar expeditions of the 790s. This obligation could be resented and evaded, but this only aroused Frankish wrath. Thus, the non-appearance of Saxon levies at the 795 assembly was taken as a sign of their 'infidelity' and the indication that they should be attacked yet again.[2] Thus, although the details of the fighting that resumed in the mid–790s suggest that it was the Saxons in the north, who were somewhat less affected by the earlier campaigns and were furthest removed from Frankish cultural influence, who took the lead in trying to break free of Carolingian rule, opposition to the latter may have been widespread in Saxon society.

It was in 793 that the first sounds of revived Saxon discontent were heard, in the form of a report from a *missus* delivered before an assembly at Regensburg. The Reviser calls this 'a general defection of the Saxons'.[3] Although it seems to have been too late in the season for any action to have been taken, after the conclusion of the great ecclesiastical council at Frankfurt in 794, Charles led a two-pronged expedition into Saxony, before which the

Saxons apparently capitulated without further resistance, surrendering hostages and taking yet more oaths.[4] This probably represented an unwillingness to take on the Franks in open battle, as the conflict was renewed the following year. The Annalist reports that the Saxons broke their agreement about the acceptance of Christianity, which they clearly continued to regard as a symbol of the Frankish yoke.[5]

The Reviser suggests that Charles, from bitter experience, was aware that the Saxons might resume the fighting in 795, and so ordered an assembly to be held at Kostheim am Main, so that an expedition could be launched into Saxony if needed. He also arranged for the Saxons' enemies to the east, the Slavic people known as the Abodrites, who lived across the Elbe, to join his campaign. They had already proved useful allies for the Franks in a campaign against another Slav confederacy, that of the Wiltzi, in 789.[6] However, this time the Abodrites fell into a trap crossing the river and their king Witzan was killed by the Saxons.[7] This, we are told 'acted like a goad to the king's resolve, spurring him to the swifter crushing of the Saxons, and provoked him to greater hatred of that perfidious people'.[8] A campaign of devastation followed, terminated as so often before by a Saxon submission and the surrender of hostages.[9] That a further devastation then proved necessary in 796 indicates that the cycle of resistance and terror continued unabated. The *Lorsch Annals* note that Charles took 'innumerable' Saxon captives.[10]

The 796 campaign appears to have been no more successful than its predecessors in actually breaking Saxon resistance, and another expedition was launched under Charles's own command the following year, which reached as far as the North Sea coast between the mouths of the Elbe and the Weser before returning to Aachen. He received hostages from both the Saxons and the Frisians, perhaps suggesting that the two had been co-operating against him.[11] No doubt following the successful precedent of the 784/5 campaign, Charles decided to launch a second attack on Saxony later in 797 and to spend the winter there with his army. He established his own winter headquarters on the Weser, near its confluence with the Diemel, at a place that he had named 'Herestelle' or 'Meeting Place of the Army', and he scattered his forces across Saxony, basically to hold down the countryside.[12] As the Reviser revealingly explains, early in the spring of 798 before fodder for the horses could be obtained and thus before the army could leave its various winter quarters, a group of Saxons to the east of the Elbe indicated their continued defiance by capturing and killing or holding for ransom a number of Frankish nobles. Amongst these was a royal *missus* called Godescalc, who was returning from an embassy to the Danish king Sigifrid. The Saxons involved then went on to attack the Franks' Abodrite allies, but were apparently defeated by them in a battle at a place called Suentana.[13] This has been possibly identified as Bornhöved, known in the later Slavic chronicle of Helmhold as 'Zuentineveld'.[14] The Reviser indicates that a Frankish *missus* called Eburis commanded the Abodrite right wing, perhaps indicating the presence of Frankish forces in the battle. He is said to have reported back to Charles that 4000 Saxons were killed in the first encounter. The contemporary *Lorsch Annals* offer the slightly smaller and more precise figure of 2901 dead Saxons.[15] The king in the meanwhile, apparently enraged by the Saxon killing of his *missi*, had been ravaging the whole area between the Weser and the Elbe.

This series of events, together with the Frankish alliance with the Abodrites, led to the imposition of another harsh peace on Saxony. Charles was in Paderborn in 799, re-establishing his administrative order in Saxony when the news of the attempt to overthrow pope Leo III in Rome reached him. This was the beginning of the process that led to his imperial coronation in Rome on 25 December 800. It is worth noting that the pacification of the Saxons through the campaigns of 795 to 798 was probably a precondition for his being able to march into Italy in August of 800.[16] No further trouble with the Saxons is recorded until 802.[17] In this year, Charles, who had just returned from Italy, had an army gathered from amongst the Saxons and sent it against their fellow Saxons across the Elbe, where it 'brought devastation upon them'.[18] A final solution remained for these still-resisting Saxons. As early as 799 Charles had begun expelling Saxon families from their lands and redistributing these amongst his own men. The dispossessed Saxons were sent as serfs, unfree labourers, to other parts of the Frankish empire.[19] This process was taken a step further in 804, when the emperor led an army in person into Saxon territory beyond the Elbe, and apparently rounded up the entire population and removed it into Francia. The Saxon lands east of the Elbe were then handed over to the Abodrites. As the *Chronicle of Moissac* put it: 'the emperor sent his *scarae* ... into Wihmodia, both into Ostogau and into Rosogau, to take the people there away, out of their homeland; and he also removed the Saxons beyond the Elbe from their homes, and he dispersed them within his kingdom where he saw fit'.[20]

No more is heard of Saxon resistance to Frankish rule. The western Saxons had been largely crushed by 785, and it is not known how far any of them were stirred to further resistance nearly a decade later. At that time it was the various Saxon groups in the area of the Elbe and the Weser who both conducted the resistance to Frankish rule and imposed Christianisation, and who felt the consequences of it. A final hard core of resistance across the Elbe was eliminated in 804. Thereafter, when Saxons are mentioned in the annals they appear as contingents fighting in the Frankish armies on the eastern frontiers.[21] In that sense it could be said that in 804, after over 30 years of nearly continuous fighting, the Franks's Saxon problem had at last been solved. But this was at a cost, probably hardly recognised at the time.

The earlier phase of the Saxon wars had already seen Charles and his armies campaigning both eastwards and northwards as far as the valley of the Elbe. Leaders of Saxon resistance, such as Widukind, on a number of occasions took refuge beyond the frontiers of Saxon territory. In the second period of the war various groups of Slavs to the east of the Saxons, particularly the Abodrites, were brought into play by the Franks. In 804 Charles, in his camp in Saxony, chose a certain Thrasco to serve as king of the Abodrites.[22] At the same time he made them a gift of the lands once occupied by the Saxons across the Elbe. This would imply that he had no intention at this point of extending direct Frankish rule across the Elbe, preferring to work through a compliant Slav ruler of his own choosing. Whether there was any expectation that this special relationship with the Abodrites might lead to missionary activity and the attempt to convert them is uncertain and has been positively denied.[23] Apart from some suggestions in a letter of Alcuin written in 789, referring to the Wiltzi and the Wends, no attempts to evangelise the Slavs seem to have been made in Charles's reign.[24]

Thrasco is mentioned as a *dux* of the Abodrites in 798, but the account in the *Annales Mettenses Priores* implies that in 804 Charles was trying to create a single ruler for the people, previously divided under several leaders.[25] This represented an attempt to make a significant change in Abodrite social and political organisation. It may not have worked, as in 808 Thrasco is called no more than *dux* again, but the attempt was significant. In other words, these campaigns did not just affect the Saxons. Other neighbouring peoples were involved for better or worse and the effects of the events in Saxony will have had consequences well beyond the region itself. The Bohemians, for example, may have accepted a single leader in this period, in response to Frankish expansion. This in turn led to campaigns being directed against them in 805 and 806.[26]

Above all the activities of Frankish armies and the arrival of refugees seem to have had significant repercussions in Denmark. The Danish peninsula had largely been beyond the ken of the Frankish and other chroniclers writing before the late eighth century, and as Danish society was then, and would remain for some time pre-literate, little historical information exists concerning this region. Later traditions, recorded in such works as the *Gesta Danorum* or 'Deeds of the Danes' of Saxo Grammaticus inspire little confidence.

Archaeology provides some ways into the understanding of Danish society in the period before the reign of Charles. In particular, the existence of a major earthwork across the narrowest part of the Jutland peninsula, known as the *Danevirke*, indicates the existence of a fairly sophisticated social and political order by at least the middle of the eighth century.[27] This structure was thought to have been erected in the time of Charles's Saxon wars, to delineate and defend the Danish frontier against the growing power of the Franks. However, dendrochronological analysis of wood used in its construction indicates a date at least half a century earlier. For such a thing to have been built, it may be assumed that the area it crossed was in the hands of a single political authority; one, moreover, that was able to assemble the resources of materials and manpower required to undertake this major task of construction.[28] Simply put, this has been taken as indicating the existence of a Danish kingdom, extending at least over Jutland, in this period.

While their western neighbours may not have known much about what was happening in the Danish homelands, or at least not recorded it, this does not mean that contact had not been made.[29] Trade with the Baltic had existed since Roman times at the very least, both by land and sea. Early trading stations are known both in Denmark and elsewhere in Scandinavia, which had their counterparts in the Channel in the Roman and later Frankish ports of Boulogne and Quentovic. Cultural contact of various kinds with these regions across the North Sea has been diagnosed in eastern Britain, particularly in East Anglia, and there may well have been some movement of population as well.[30] Earlier Danish sensitivity to Frankish expansion in areas north-east of the Rhine may lie behind the account of a Danish attack on the coast at the time of the Merovingian king Theuderic I (c. 511–33) who, with his son Theudebert, was building up the first Frankish hegemony in this area. A Danish leader called Chrocilaic, who has been identified with the 'Hygelac' of the Anglo-Saxon poem *Beowulf*, was defeated and killed by Theudebert in the course of a naval raid on the Channel coast.[31] That the same phenomenon, not recorded in the intervening period, resumed at the time of Charles's Saxon wars may suggest similarity of cause and of response.

Danish concern with what was happening in Saxony is first mentioned by the Reviser in his annal for 782. The same source recorded Widukind's flight to the Danish king Sigefred in 777.[32] What was discussed between Charles and the Danish envoys at the sources of the Lippe in 782 is not revealed, any more than is the purpose of the embassy on which Charles sent his *missus* Godescalc to Sigefred in 798. By this time there may have been additional causes of friction, in that a Christian missionary centre had been created close to the frontiers of the Danish kingdom, in the form of the bishopric of Bremen.

This was established in 787. Its first incumbent was an Anglo-Saxon called Willehad, who had been sent around 770 with the backing of a Northumbrian synod to help evangelise the Frisians. In 780 Charles had transferred him to take part in the attempted conversion of the Saxons in the region between the rivers Weser and Elbe. He had to take refuge in 783 in the monastery of Echternach during the revolt led by Widukind, but returned to Saxony in 785 and became the first bishop of Bremen two years later. He died in 789, soon after the consecration of his cathedral.[33] An account of miraculous cures performed at his tomb was written by Anskar, who undertook missionary expeditions to the Danes and the Swedes in the time of Louis the Pious, and an anonymous *Vita Willehadi* was composed around 860.[34]

It is clear, not least from a letter of Alcuin to an unnamed abbot that was probably written in 789, that the hope then existed that the process of converting the Saxons might be extended both to the Danes and to the Slavic Wiltzi and Wends.[35] In practice the evangelising of Saxony proved to be an uphill struggle, as further letters from Alcuin that have been dated to 796 seem to confirm.[36] At that time he was advocating that the Saxons should not be subject to paying tithes, the tax of one tenth of annual income that was payable to the local church, as this obligation might have contributed to stiffening their resistance. The church of Bremen in this period may have lost much of its initial impetus. According to the much later *Deeds of the Bishops of the Church of Hamburg* written by Adam of Bremen (died c. 1085), Willehad was succeeded by one of his pupils by the name of Willeric, who held the see for nearly 50 years, dying in 839.[37] However, contradictions in his scanty sources of information relating to the episcopate of this Willeric led Adam to suggest that he did not become bishop until 804. This in turn caused him to suspect that the bishopric of Bremen was inactive or possibly not functioning for all or much of the period between 789 and 804. It is clear that Adam had very little hard information to fill in the gap between the brief episcopate of Willehad (d. 789) and the first missionary journey to the Swedes of Anskar, probably dateable to 829/30.[38] He does at least report on the basis of later records of the church that Charles established a bishopric in the Saxon settlement of Hamburg in 804, under a certain Heridag.[39]

While in practice these missionary bishoprics on the northern fringes of Saxony may have enjoyed only limited success in Charles's reign, their presence represented a cultural threat to the Danes and others who were within the radius of their influence. From an early stage in the Saxon wars the association between Frankish political power and conversion to Christianity had been made apparent. That these were inextricably linked in the minds of those living close to the Franks is made clear from the simultaneous offer of submission and conversion by the Avar Tudun in 795, which recognised that political allegiance and religious adherence were as one. Thus, Frankish territorial expansion and the establishment of the bishoprics in Bremen and then Hamburg represented a joint cultural and political threat both to the Slavs beyond the Elbe and to the Danes. Some of the Slav tribes may have been prepared to accept both Frankish hegemony and religion, for the advantages that this seemed to offer both against their old Saxon enemies and vis à vis other rival Slavic peoples, but the Danes seemed to regard gradual Frankish encroachment on their territories as nothing but a threat.

By 800, reports start to appear in the Frankish annals of piratical raids by *Nordmanni*, a term normally thought to apply to the Danes. In consequence, before heading south on the journey that would ultimately take him to Rome, Charles toured the Channel coast and had a fleet built to defend it.[40] Although few details are given, Charles's 804 campaign, which enhanced the power of the Abodrites and eliminated the Saxons east of the Elbe, seems to have considerably disturbed the Danes. A king called Godefred is recorded in the annals as assembling a fleet and a cavalry army in Schleswig, along the frontier between the Danish kingdom and the Saxons. Charles was at Hollenstedt on the Elbe and negotiations between the two, which were to have been face to face, were in the end conducted through envoys. Of the discussions the annals only reveal that Charles was trying to obtain the return of 'fugitives'.[41] These may well have been Saxons, but no further information is given as to the discussions or their outcome.

Whether it was the approach of Frankish power across the Elbe or that of their allies the Abodrites to the east of the river that seemed the most threatening is not clear. But it was the Slavs who were first to feel the Danes' reaction. In 808 Godefred, together with his allies the Wiltzi, attacked the Abodrites, drove out Thrasco, and captured and hanged another of their leaders called Godelaib, perhaps as a sacrifice to Oðin. A number of Slav forts were captured and the Annalist reports that at least two thirds of the Abodrites were made tributary to the Danes.[42] He also suggests that the 'mad' Danish king lost many of his forces, including his nephew Reginold in the war, but this may be little more than an attempt to make the best of a humiliating subjection of the Franks' main ally in this region.[43] The Frankish military response was muted, in that the younger Charles directed his forces, via a bridge that he built over the Elbe, not at the Danes themselves but at some lesser Slavic peoples called the Smeldingi and the Linones who had submitted to king Godefred. He devastated their lands and then withdrew to Saxony.

The growth of Frankish military involvement and the polarisation of the Slavic peoples in the area to the south and south-east of Denmark, seems to

have had significant economic and social consequences for the Danes. In his
entry for the year 808 the Annalist records that on his return from the campaign against the Abodrites, Godefred destroyed their trading post on the
Baltic, known to the Danes as 'Reric' and took the merchants there back with
him to the Danish port of Sliesthorp. He then built an earthwork all the way
along the southern frontier of his kingdom from the Baltic to the north bank of
the river Eider, with only a single gateway being constructed to allow passage
through it.[44] These two processes of the removal of trading stations and the
establishment of a fixed frontier with very limited points of communication
through it are linked, and are also extraordinarily reminiscent of the reactions
of other peoples in similar circumstances. In particular, attempting to control
economic and other contacts when faced by a perceived threat from an alien
society that is regarded as both culturally menacing and yet also alluring, was
a marked feature of the responses of steppe peoples to their sedentary neighbours.[45] Faced by the threat of Frankish military and cultural expansion the
Danish king was trying both to define the physical frontier of his territory and
to restrict contact between his people and the Franks and their subjects, a
process in which controlling the exchange of goods and the movement of
merchants played a key role.

In 809 Godefred sent a message to Charles through merchants, whose
importance as diplomatic as well as cultural intermediaries is here underlined.
He wished to forestall any Frankish reaction to his attack on the Abodrites
the previous year, and claimed that it was they who had broken the treaty
made in 804. A meeting was arranged between his representatives and those
of Charles between the Elbe and the Danish frontier, probably at Beidenfelth
on the river Stör.[46] Although Franco-Danish questions seem to have been
left unresolved, some form of agreement was reached between the Danes and
the Abodrites, with Thrasco surrendering a son to Godefred as a hostage.
However, this left the Abodrite leader with a free hand to seek his revenge
on the Wiltzi, whom he proceeded to attack, ravaging their territory. He then
obtained assistance from the Saxons in a raid on the Smeldingi, leading to the
capture of the settlement known to a Frankish chronicler, though probably not
to its Slavic inhabitants, as *Smeldingconnoburg*.[47] Probably in response to
these clear provocations, Godefred arranged for his men to murder Thrasco at
Reric, which had recently been re-established.

The real causes of friction, within the wider context of growing Frankish
military, cultural and commercial involvement in the southern Baltic region,
lay in the conduct of the allies of the two greater powers. Rivalries and feuds
between the various Slav peoples were exacerbated and given the opportunity
for wider expression in the wake of the Frankish conquest of Saxony and the

escalating Danish reactions to it. The events of 808 and 809 in this frontier zone between the Frankish empire and Denmark and reports of threats made by the Danish king led Charles to respond in the same year by establishing a military frontier of his own. A fortified settlement was created with Saxon assistance on the river Stör at 'Esefelth' (probably Itzoe) under a count Egbert.[48] This was occupied by Frankish forces brought as a show of strength through the frontier district of Frisia. Once again Frankish boundaries, recently established on the Elbe, were having to be expanded further, primarily in response to the reactions to their previous advance.[49] This was a process that was being dictated more by events on the frontiers than by any long-term strategy being devised in Aachen. It had little to do with what from hindsight might be perceived to have been the real needs or interests of the Frankish empire.

The year 810 proved to be one of crisis for the Danish kingdom, facing an ever closer advance of Frankish power. The Abodrite attacks on the Wiltzi and the Smeldingi and then Godefred's murder of Thrasco in 809 may have weakened the Slav participants on both sides, and the creation of the fortress at Itzoe brought a Frankish military settlement to within 30 km of the Danish frontier line. There was no longer a buffer zone between the two realms. A raid on Frisia by 200 Danish ships saw the devastation of the islands off the coast, and the landing of an army, which defeated the Frisians and forced them to pay a tribute of 100 pounds weight of silver. This was provocation on a large scale, and Charles gathered an army and advanced through Saxony to the confluence of the rivers Weser and Aller. This was one of the very few campaigns of his later years that he led in person. He seems to have been told that Godefred wanted to take him on in pitched battle, again a very rare occurrence by this time, and may have felt that such a challenge required his personal participation.[50]

In practice this was to be a turning point, but not in the way that might have been anticipated. Godefred was murdered by one of his own men and his fleet withdrew from Frisia. Godefred's immediate successor, Hemming, began negotiations for a peace. An interim agreement seems to have been made in 810, and was sworn to by the Danes on their weapons. In 811 a group of Frankish counts, led by Charles's cousin Wala, negotiated a more formal and final accord with some Danish emissaries led by Hemming's brothers.[51] There followed, from what little the Frankish sources were able to record of it, a period of considerable turmoil and upheaval in Denmark, with various rivals vying for power and the kingdom splitting into various parts. For the rest of Charles's reign and the opening years of that of his successor the Danes would present no threat, and on occasion Frankish help or recognition would be sought by claimants to the Danish kingdom. It seems likely that these dramatic changes were connected to Godefred's murder and the policies he had been pursuing. That Hemming sought an immediate peace rather than pursue his predecessor's threat of resolving the issues by battle would seem to indicate at least a division of opinion on the issue amongst the leading Danes. The state of siege that Godefred had generated by the attempt to eliminate the trading settlement of 'Reric' and the closing of the frontier may have contributed to a collapse of confidence in his ability to resist. It is possible, too, that the disruption to normal commercial activity caused by the events of these years contributed directly to the growth of piracy and the ensuing movement overseas of elements of the Danish and other Scandinavian populations. The lack of internal evidence and the limited nature of Frankish knowledge of what was happening within Denmark, let alone the other Scandinavian kingdoms, makes it impossible to draw hard and fast conclusions, but it is hard to believe that Viking activity in western Europe in the ensuing decades was not related to this period of conflict in Frisia, Saxony and the Slav lands to the south of Denmark in the first decade of the ninth century.

For Charles the unexpected elimination of Godefred would in practice put an end to the problems with the Danes as far as his own reign was concerned. However, even as he was still waiting encamped on the Weser, news was brought him of three disasters of different scale and significance. Firstly, the Wiltzi, allies of Godefred, had captured the fortress of Höhbeck on the Elbe, which had been held by a garrison of Saxons commanded by the imperial legate Odo.[52] This would be re-occupied by the Franks in 811. Secondly, his son Pippin king of Italy was reported to have died on 8 July. Indeed this was the second family tragedy of the year, as Charles's daughter Rotrud had died on 6 of June. A third loss was that of the elephant the emperor had received from Harun al-Raschid in 801.[53] At the same time, a cattle pest had killed off all the herds that had been brought to feed the expedition. This bovine disease spread throughout Francia in the course of the year.

The sea-borne threat which the Danes had posed in recent years still seems to have remained a potential threat in the emperor's mind, in that amongst the tasks he is reported to have carried out in person in 811 was an inspection of a fleet that he had ordered to be built at Boulogne the previous year.[54] Here he also restored the Roman lighthouse, which had been an important navigational aid for shipping in the Channel in the Late Empire. Charles then travelled to Ghent on the river Scheldt, where more ships for his fleet were under construction. These would not be needed for immediate purposes, as another embassy from the new Danish king met the emperor on his journey back to Aachen to bring gifts and renew assurances of peaceful intentions. The threat of Danish raids in fact was to be lifted for over 20 years, resuming when the Frankish empire was torn by civil war between Louis the Pious and his sons in 834.[55] By that time Charles's war fleet of 810/11 may have rotted away, as no attempt was later made to fight the Danish raiders on the sea.

Decline and Failure? A Historiographical Debate

Verdicts on Charles have been mixed amongst modern admirers as well as amongst his contemporaries. In particular, the final phase of his reign, following the imperial coronation, has come in for criticism. François Louis Ganshof, one of the most prolific and distinguished of twentieth-century students of the Carolingian period, characterised this as an 'Une décomposition'.[56] Around the same time he also wrote a brief article summing up what he called 'L'échec de Charlemagne', which in the English version was translated bluntly as 'Charlemagne's failure'.[57] This period, immediately after the ending of the Second World War, was in many ways the nadir of Charles's reputation. It also saw published the influential *Das Karolingische Imperium* of the Austrian historian Heinrich Fichtenau, which received an abridged English translation in 1957.[58] The history of an empire-building process in central Europe recalled too many recent horrors, even if Charles's standing amongst the Nazis had at best been ambiguous.[59] For Ganshof, Charles's failure lay in the inability to create an adequate administrative apparatus to ensure the transmission and enforcement of the ruler's will. He allowed that such measures as the enhanced and extended use of oaths and of *missi* represented steps intended to compensate for the inadequacies of the existing bureaucratic machinery, but recognised them as being at best partial and incapable of being transformed into a properly institutionalised basis for government. In consequence the administrative structures of the Carolingian empire remained incapable of being self-motivated and self-supporting. They were not capable of sustaining the government of weak or incapable rulers, or even ones just lacking the confident assurance and dynamism of Charles himself. In the longer term the failure to generate a suitable administrative machinery on the part of the Carolingian state was seen by Ganshof as a fatal legacy for those monarchies that saw themselves as its heirs or borrowed their ideas on government and its institutions from it.

Within this broader context, which applied to the whole reign, he saw the final period as marking a 'decomposition' because so much depended upon the emperor's personal decision making and inspirational powers. As his physical faculties inevitably started to fail, so did the inadequacies of the governmental machinery become more and more apparent. At the same time, the new imperial dignity clearly meant for Charles greatly enhanced responsibilities, which he felt incapable of delegating. He thus demanded increased reference to himself, especially in judicial matters, at a time when he was personally less able to bear it, and the limited functioning of the central administrative machinery became more and more congested. This same period was also one of mixed fortunes militarily and diplomatically for the Carolingian state. In particular, an unnecessary war in Italy and the Adriatic was largely generated by the taking of the imperial title, and the conflict with the Danes had dangerous consequences in both the longer and shorter terms. Finally, the imperial title in itself was a legacy of dubious worth, which in 806 Charles might have regarded as strictly personal to himself and not something to be passed on to one or more of his heirs. This view or decision was clearly reversed in 813, when Charles sent for his only surviving son Louis and crowned him with his own hands at Aachen.[60] For Ganshof this could only be attributed to a powerful influence working on Charles to change his earlier idea on the matter, and this strong but misguided influence he believed was that of the emperor's cousin Wala (d. 836).

Some of this analysis has been questioned.[61] In particular it has been pointed out that the lack of continuing territorial expansion does not in itself imply decline, and in the Spanish March at least some further if limited extension of Frankish territory was achieved. After the conquest of Barcelona in 801, an advance down the Mediterranean coast to Tarragona, which had been abandoned in 797 by its Berber garrison after it had massacred the indigenous population, and on to Tortosa was attempted. However, the former could not be held and an attempt in 810 to take the latter failed. More significant was the gradual infilling by resettlement of displaced fugitive *Hispani*, Spaniards from the south or from Arab-held lands in the Ebro valley, of the region between Barcelona and the Pyrenees. This process, linked to the building of numerous small fortresses, eventually created a dense and secure enough Christian population for further advances to be undertaken by the indigenous comital dynasty founded by Wifred the Hairy (d. 897).

Such slower but steadier developments on the frontiers form part of a transition away from the 'smash and grab' style of Frankish expansion that had been a feature of both sixth- and eighth-century conquests.[62] These had greatly rewarded the leading men and their followers who had provided the military manpower for the Frankish army and upon whom the kings also relied for internal support. However, the enriching of such men with lands in newly conquered territories and in some cases with administrative offices in them gave

them new interests and responsibilities, and led to a tendency towards con-
solidation at the expense of expansion. The limited nature of the apparatus of
central government and of communications also tended towards eventual
inertia, as it became harder and harder for the ruler and his court to remain
well informed about developments on the frontiers. In some cases other local
features made the establishing of fixed boundaries increasingly necessary.
Linguistic, cultural and ecological differences made the absorption of Slav
populations into the Frankish Empire or an advance out onto the steppe north
of the Danube impractical. It seems clear that the Elbe was intended to mark
the limit of Frankish expansion north-eastwards after the conquest of the
Saxons, but, as has been discussed, the complex relations with the Danes and
various Slav peoples that ensued led to unsought further involvement beyond
that river. In due course similar causes would draw the eastern Franks further
and further into the Slav lands beyond Bavaria, though not in Charles's day.

Thus, while lack of expansion might not be indicative of decay, it was
accompanied by significant social and political consequences as far as the
ruling classes of the Frankish empire and its central administration were concerned.[63] An increasing defensiveness of outlook and attitude replaced the
earlier aggression, leaving the newly created empire increasingly vulnerable to
the attacks of more virile predators, notably the Arabs and the Vikings. At the
same time, where expansion of a sort did occur, it was often unplanned and
unwanted, as in the case of the lands beyond the Elbe, or could not be sustained, as with the attempts to take Tarragona and Tortosa in 810. The military
achievements and territorial aggrandisement of Francia under Charles are
undeniable, but it is legitimate to question whether he left his heir a legacy that
could not be sustained, because once territorial expansion decreased, as it
inevitably had to, it was doubtful whether or not the Carolingian state had the
administrative or the ideological capacity to maintain what had been conquered and to forge a viable political entity out of it. From the perspective of
hindsight, it clearly did not.

The contrast between short-term achievement and the lack of a longer-term
potential to sustain it may be seen in numerous ways. For example, in military
terms it has been suggested that Charles's naval activities in his final period
are particularly notable.[64] Not only did he undertake a major fleet-building
programme at Boulogne and on the Scheldt in 810/11 to meet the threat
from Denmark, but he also engaged in maritime ventures in the western
Mediterranean, occupying the Balearic islands at their inhabitants' request in
798, and resisting Arab naval raids on those islands in 799 and on Corsica and
Sardinia in 806 and 807. Admittedly, Arab raids from Spain on Corsica in 809
and 810 encountered no resistance, and Sardinia was ravaged. However,

further Carolingian naval victories over Arab fleets were recorded in Sardinia and Majorca in 812 and 813.[65] The final phase of Charles's reign saw the Carolingian empire turned into a major maritime power in both the Channel and the western Mediterranean. But this proved short-lived. No fleet resisted Danish attacks on the Channel ports and rivers in the 830s. A Carolingian fleet was still defending Corsica in 828, and it even raided the North African coast west of Carthage in the same year, but it is not heard of thereafter.[66] Arab raids that seemed to threaten Rome itself came to play a crucial role in the papacy's use of the imperial title as a lure to draw rival Carolingian rulers into the defence of Italy in the second half of the ninth century.[67]

Thus, in the longer term, Ganshof's general argument may continue to command assent. Had the administrative organisation of the Empire been comparable to that of Byzantium in the same period, there are good reasons to suspect that such fleets could have been maintained on a permanent basis rather than be allowed to disappear.[68] The argument applies more broadly to most aspects of the military capacity and the political organisation of the Carolingian lands in the ninth century. The Byzantine empire was able to face and survive raids from the 'Abbasid caliphate of a much larger and more potentially destructive kind in its very heartlands than those posed by Viking and Arab activities in the West. Its government was able to tolerate periods of political upheaval and the rule of individual emperors of a wide range of capacities and competencies.[69] Centralised administration remained firm, and even protracted civil wars in disputed successions did not lead to the territorial division of the Empire. This could not be said of the heirs of Charlemagne.

NOTES

1 The Frankish Inheritance

1. Einhard, *Vita Karoli*, 22, ed. L. Halphen, p. 66.
2. On Einhard see A. Kleinklausz, *Einhard* (Paris, 1942); a new book on him is being written by David Ganz. For the arguments about the date of the work see Heinz Löwe, 'Die Entstehungzeit der *Vita Karoli* Einhards', *DA*, 39 (1963), pp. 85–103.
3. Suetonius, *De Vita Caesarum II: Divus Augustus*, ed. J. C. Rolfe (rev. edn, London, 1951), chs 79–81, pp. 244–6; W. S. M. Nicoll, 'Some Passages in Einhard's *Vita Karoli* in Relation to Suetonius', *Medium Ævum*, 44 (1975), pp. 117–20. See also Andrew Wallace-Hadrill, *Suetonius* (London, 1983), pp. 50–72.
4. Roger Collins, 'Reviser Revisited', in A. C. Murray (ed.), *After Rome's Fall: Narrators and Sources of Early Medieval History* (forthcoming). Why Einhard was so unusually detailed in his account of Roncesvalles is not clear. He may have had family ties with one of the Frankish commanders killed in the battle, the seneschal Eggihard.
5. *Vita Karoli*, prologue, ed. Halphen, pp. 2–6. An edition of the work made by Gerward, the palace librarian of Louis the Pious first mentions Einhard as its author in a short verse finale (ed. Halphen, p. xvi).
6. 'Lest I offend the spirits of the fastidious with novelty' (Einhard, *Vita Karoli*, ed. Halphen, p. 2).
7. For a recent attempt to redate the *Vita Karoli* to c. 817/18 see Rosamond McKitterick and Matthew Innes, 'The Writing of History', in R. McKitterick (ed.), *Carolingian Culture* (Cambridge, 1994), pp. 193–220.
8. *Gregorii Turonensis Episcopi Historiarum Libri Decem*, ed. Bruno Krusch and Wilhelm Levison, *MGH SRM*, 1 (rev. edn, Hanover, 1951).
9. J. M. Wallace-Hadrill (ed.), *The Fourth Book of the Chronicle of Fredegar* (London, 1960); also Roger Collins, *Fredegar* (Aldershot, 1996) for a survey of the work and the arguments over authorship, dating and purpose.
10. For the Continuations of Fredegar and their particular problems see Roger Collins, 'Deception and Misrepresentation in Eighth-Century Frankish Historiography: Two Case Studies', in Jörg Jarnut, Ulrich Nonn and Michael Richter (eds), *Karl Martell in seiner Zeit* (Sigmaringen, 1994), pp. 227–47. The text is in Wallace-Hadrill, *Fourth Book* (note 9 above), pp. 80–121.
11. Ed. Bruno Krusch, *MGH SRM*, II, pp. 214–328; see Richard A. Gerberding, *The Rise of the Carolingians and the 'Liber Historiae Francorum'* (Oxford, 1987).
12. For the history of this period see I. Wood, *The Merovingian Kingdoms* (London, 1994), pp. 255–92.
13. Irene Haselbach, 'Aufstieg und Herrschaft der Karolinger in der Darstellung der sogenannten Annales Mettenses Priores', *Historische Studien*, 406 (1970),

175

pp. 1–208; Adolf Gauert, 'Noch einmal Einhard und die letzen Merowinger', in Lutz Fenske *et al.* (eds), *Institutionen, Kultur und Gesellschaft im Mittelalter* (Sigmaringen, 1984), pp. 59–72.

14. François-Louis Ganshof, 'L'historiographie dans la monarchie franque sous les Mérovingiens et les Carolingiens', *Settimane*, 17 (1970), pp. 631–85, at pp. 667–74; also Louis Halphen, *Etudes critiques sur l'histoire de Charlemagne* (Paris, 1921), pp. 16–59.

15. *Annales Laureshamenses*, ed. Georg Pertz, *MGH SS*, I, p. 22, which (after a later interpolation concerning St Benedict) begins with a list of the deaths of four Irish clerics: Canan, Domnan (i.e. Adamnán of Iona), Cellan (Cellán mac Sechnusach the Wise) and Tigermal.

16. Wattenbach-Levison, *Deutschlands Geschichtsquellen im Mittelalter*, 2 (Weimar, 1953), pp. 180–92.

17. The first Irish annals may date to the mid- to late-seventh century: Kathleen Hughes, *Early Christian Ireland: Introduction to the Sources* (London, 1972), pp. 97–159, and A. P. Smyth, 'The Earliest Irish Annals', *Proceedings of the Royal Irish Academy*, 72C (1972), pp. 1–48.

18. Edited by F. Kurze, *MGH SRG*. See Wattenbach-Levison, *Deutschlands Geschichtsquellen* (note 16 above), 2, pp. 245–54.

19. Leopold von Ranke, 'Zur Kritik fränkisch-deutsch Reichsannalisten', *Abhandlungen der köninglike Akademie der Wissenschaften zu Berlin* (1854), pp. 415–35.

20. On this see Wattenbach-Levison, *Deutschlands Geschichtsquellen* (note 16 above), 2, pp. 254–7, and *ARF*, ed. Kurze, pp. xii–xiv.

21. Ibid.; P. D. King, *Charlemagne: Translated Sources* (Lancaster, 1987), p. 18, would like to see the debate re-opened.

22. Collins, 'Reviser Revisited' (note 4 above).

23. Max Manitius, 'Einharts Werke und ihr Stil', *NA*, 7 (1881/2), pp. 517–68, and footnotes to Kurze's edition.

24. See the *apparatus criticus* to *ARF*, ed. Kurze, pp. 117–78.

25. Collins, 'Reviser Revisited' (note 4 above).

26. Matthias Becher, *Eid und Herrschaft* (Sigmaringen, 1993), pp. 74–7.

27. *CLA*, X, no. 1482; there is a photographic facsimile in F. Unterkircher, *Das Wiener Fragment der Lorscher Annalen* (Graz, 1967).

28. Bernhard Bischoff, *Lorsch im Spiegel seiner Handschriften* (Munich, 1974), pp. 53 and 79, note 106.

29. MS Paris, Bibliothèque Nationale lat. 4886. Jean Dufour, *La bibliothèque et le scriptorium de Moissac* (Geneva, 1972), pp. 17, 40, 88–9. The text is edited by Georg Pertz in *MGH SS*, 1, pp. 282–313 and 2, pp. 257–9.

30. *MGH SRM*, vols I–VII, ed. Bruno Krusch. See also Paul Fouracre and Richard A. Gerberding, *Late Merovingian France: History and Hagiography, 640–720* (Manchester, 1996), which includes some translations.

31. For the most recent assessment of what forms the corpus of genuinely Merovingian *Lives* see Ian Wood, 'Forgery in Merovingian Hagiography', in *Fälschungen im Mittelalter*, V (*MGH Schriften*, 33: Hanover, 1988), pp. 369–84.

32. On Carolingian relics see Patrick J. Geary, *Furta Sacra* (2nd edn, Princeton, NJ, 1990), pp. 28–43.

33. Gerberding and Fouracre, *Late Merovingian France* (note 30 above), pp. 166–253. Strangely, more can be gleaned of Merovingian politics from the Northumbrian *Life of Wilfred* by Stephanus (c. 715) than from most of the lives of these significant Frankish bishops.

34. *Vita Alcuini*, ed. W. Arndt, *MGH SS*, 15, pp. 182–97; see Donald Bullough, 'Alcuino e la tradizione culturale insulare', *Settimane*, 20 (1973), pp. 571–600, at pp. 577–80.

35. Texts are in *PL*, 120, columns 1507–650. See B. Kasten, *Adalhard von Corbie. Die Biographie eines karolingischen Politikers und Klostervorstehers* (Düsseldorf, 1985), and L. Weinrich, *Wala, Graf, Mönch und Rebell* (Berlin, 1963); also David Ganz, 'The *Epitaphium Arsenii* and Opposition to Louis the Pious', in Godman and Collins (eds), pp. 537–50.

36. *Gesta Sanctorum Patrum Fontanellensis Coenobii*, ed. F. Lohier and J. Laporte (Rouen and Paris, 1936); Walter Goffart, 'Paul the Deacon's *Gesta episcoporum Mettensium* and the Early Design of Charlemagne's Succession', *Traditio*, 42 (1986), pp. 59–93.

37. Amongst the rare exceptions are the writing tablets from Vindolanda and from Carlisle; see Alan K. Bowman, *Life and letters on the Roman Frontier* (London, 1994).

38. Isabel Velázquez Soriano, *Las pizarras visigodas: edición crítica y estudio* (Murcia, 1989).

39. J.-O. Tjåder, *Die nichtliterarischen lateinischen Papyri Italiens aus der Zeit 445–700*, 3 vols (Lund, 1954–5; Stockholm, 1982).

40. Ian Wood, 'Disputes in Late Fifth- and Sixth-century Gaul: Some Problems', in Wendy Davies and Paul Fouracre (eds), *The Settlement of Disputes in Early Medieval Europe* (Cambridge, 1986), pp. 7–22.

41. *Chartae Latini Antiquiores*, vols XIII–XVI, ed. Hartmut Atsma *et al.* (Zurich, 1981–6); David Ganz and Walter Goffart, 'Charters Earlier than 800 from French Collections', *Speculum*, 65 (1990), pp. 906–32.

42. For the Merovingian period J. M. Pardessus (ed.), *Diplomata, Chartae, Epistolae, Leges ad Res Gallo-Francicas Spectantia* (2 vols, Paris, 1843); for Pippin III and Charles see Engelbert Muhlbacher (ed.), *MGH Diplomata Karolinorum*, 1.

43. On which see Paul Fouracre, '*Placita* and the settlement of disputes in later Merovingian Francia', in Wendy Davies and Paul Fouracre (eds), *The Settlement of Disputes in Early Medieval Europe* (Cambridge, 1986), pp. 23–44.

44. Margarete Weidemann, *Das Testament des Bischofs Berthramn von Le Mans* (Mainz, 1986); Patrick J. Geary, *Aristocracy in Provence* (Stuttgart and Philadelphia, 1985).

45. There are suggestions that one or two noble families in Spain have documentary collections relating to their holdings that extend back to the ninth century, but this is very exceptional.

46. Edmund E. Stengel (ed.), *Urkundenbuch des Klosters Fulda*, vol. I: *Die Zeit der Äbte Sturmi und Baugolf* (Marburg, 1958) for Fulda charters of 750 to 802, and H. Waartmann, *Urkundenbuch der Abtei St Gallen*, vols I–II: *700–920* (Zurich, 1863); also Rosamond McKitterick, *The Carolingians and the Written Word* (Cambridge, 1989), pp. 77–134.

47. David Ganz, 'Bureaucratic Shorthand and Merovingian Learning', in Patrick Wormald, Donald Bullough and Roger Collins (eds), *Ideal and Reality in*

Frankish and Anglo-Saxon Society (Oxford, 1983), pp. 58–75, especially pp. 61–7.

48. François-Louis Ganshof, *Recherches sur les capitulaires* (Paris, 1958); H. Mordek, 'Karolingische Kapitularien' in idem. (ed.), *Überlieferung und Geltung normativer Texte des frühen und hohen Mittelalters* (Sigmaringen, 1986), pp. 25–50.

49. For a comprehensive catalogue of the capitulary manuscripts see Hubert Mordek, *Biblioteca capitularium regum Francorum manuscripta. Überlieferung und Traditionszusammenhang der fränkischen Herrschererlasse* (Munich, 1995); for Ghaerbald's collection see Karl August Eckhardt, *Die Kapitulariensammlung Bischofs Ghaerbalds von Lüttich* (Göttingen, 1955), pp. 81–130.

50. For a recently discovered capitulary see Hubert Mordek, 'Recently Discovered Capitulary Texts Belonging to the Legislation of Louis the Pious', in Godman and Collins (eds), pp. 437–54.

51. Karl August Eckhardt, 'Die *Capitularia missorum specialia* von 802', *DA*, 12 (1956), pp. 498–516.

52. Ed. K. A. Eckhardt, *MGH Legum*, section I, 4, pp. 238–73.

53. Ed. A. Boretius, *MGH Legum*, section II, 1, items 39 and 41, pp. 111–14, 117–18. Item 68, pp. 157–8 contains *capitula* to be added to the Bavarian code, *Lex Baiuariorum*.

54. Ibid., item 40, clause 19, p. 116.

55. *MGH Legum*, series II, 1, ed. Alfred Boretius, items 10–18, pp. 24–43.

56. A. H. M. Jones, *The Later Roman Empire*, 3 vols (Oxford, 1964), 1, pp. 470–522.

57. J. F. Matthews, 'The Letters of Symmachus', in J. W. Binns (ed.), *Latin Literature of the Fourth Century* (London, 1974), pp. 58–99.

58. Peter Godman, *Poets and Emperors* (Oxford, 1987), and his *Poetry of the Carolingian Renaissance* (London, 1985).

59. E. Salin, *La civilisation mérovingienne*, 4 vols (Paris, 1950–9); see Laure-Charlotte Feffer and Patrick Périn, *Les Francs*, 2 (Paris, 1987).

60. P. Demolon, *Le village mérovingien de Brebières (VIe–VIIe siècles)* (Arras, 1972).

61. Claude Lorren 'Le village de Saint-Martin de Mondeville', in Patrick Périn and Laure-Charlotte Feffer (eds), *La Neustrie* (Rouen, 1985), pp. 351–62. On rural society in the eighth and ninth centuries see Chris Wickham, 'Rural Society in Carolingian Europe', in *NCMH*, pp. 510–37.

62. For example, Frans Theuws, 'Haus, Hof und Siedlung im nördlichen Frankreich (6–8. Jahrhundert)', in *Die Franken, Wegbereiter Europas*, 2 vols (Mainz, 1985), pp. 754–68.

63. Paris: M. Fleury, *Point d'archéologie sans histoire* (Oxford, 1988: Zaharoff Lecture for 1986–7).

64. Ludwig Berger, *Archäologischer Rundgand durch Basel* (Basel, 1981).

65. For example, Jean-François Reynaud, *Lyon aux premiers temps chrétiens: basiliques et necropoles* (Paris, 1986); *Premiers temps chrétiens en Gaule méridionale* (Lyon, 1986), pp. 35–100.

66. Jean-Maurice Rouquette and Claude Sintès, *Arles antique* (Paris, 1989), p. 64; cf. Continuations of Fredegar 20, ed. Wallace-Hadrill, p. 95, for destruction of southern towns by Charles Martel in 737/9. An exception to the tendency towards urban shrinkage, at least in area, may have been Cologne, which seems to have preserved its original and lengthy circuit of Roman walls: see Sven Schütte,

'Continuity Problems and Authority Structures in Cologne', in G. Ausenda (ed.), *After Empire: Towards an Ethnology of Europe's Barbarians* (Woodbridge, 1995), pp. 163–75.

67. F. Prinz, *Frühes Mönchtum im Frankenreich* (2nd edn, Darmstadt, 1988) provides distribution maps on pp. 666–83.

68. S. McK. Crosby, *The Royal Abbey of Saint-Denis* (New Haven, 1987), pp. 29–50.

69. For example, Wolfgang Erdmann and Alfons Zettler, 'Zur karolingischen und ottonischen Baugeschichte des Marienmünsters zu Reichenau-Mittelzell', in Helmut Maurer (ed.), *Die Abtei Reichenau* (Sigmaringen, 1974), pp. 481–522; for Saint-Denis see Crosby, *Saint-Denis* (note 68 above), pp. 51–84; Richard Hodges, *Light in the Dark Ages: The Rise and Fall of San Vincenzo al Volturno* (London, 1997); in general see Mayke de Jong, 'Carolingian monasticism: the power of prayer', in *NCMH*, pp. 622–53.

70. Wood, *Merovingian Kingdoms* (note 12 above), pp. 259–66; Gerberding, *The Rise of the Carolingians and the 'Liber Historiae Francorum'* (note 11 above), pp. 109–13, 158–9.

71. J. M. Wallace-Hadrill, *The Long-haired Kings* (London, 1962), pp. 231–48; Eugen Ewig, *Die Merowinger und das Frankenreich* (2nd edn, Stuttgart, 1988), pp. 142–72.

72. Eugen Ewig, 'Résidence et capitale pendant le haut Môyen Age', *Revue historique*, 230 (1963), pp. 25–72.

73. Juan Empar and Ignacio Pastor, 'Los visigodos en Valencia. Pla de Nadal: ¿una villa aulica?', *Boletín de Arqueología Medieval*, 3 (1989), pp. 137–79.

74. Kenneth John Conant, *Carolingian and Romanesque Architecture 800–1200* (2nd edn, Harmondsworth, 1966), pp. 59–60.

75. Paul Fouracre, 'Observations on the Outgrowth of Pippinid Influence in the *Regnum Francorum* after the Battle of Tertry (687–715)', *Medieval Prosopography*, 5 (1984), pp. 1–31; Gerberding, *The Rise of the Carolingians* (note 11 above), pp. 92–115; see also Paul Fouracre, 'Frankish Gaul to 814', in *NCMH*, pp. 85–109.

76. *De Ordine Palatii*, ed. Thomas Gross and Rudolf Schieffer, *MGH Fontes Iuris Germanici Antiqui*, 3 (1980). On Merovingian courts and administration see, in general, P. S. Barnwell, *Kings, Courtiers and Imperium: The Barbarian West, 565–725* (London, 1997), pp. 23–51.

77. J. M. Wallace-Hadrill, 'Archbishop Hincmar and the Authorship of Lex Salica', in his *The Long-haired Kings* (London, 1962), pp. 95–120.

78. For example, Gregory of Tours, *Historiarum Libri Decem*, III.xi, ed. Krusch and Levison, *MGH SRM*, 1, pp. 107–8.

79. Averil Cameron, 'How did the Merovingian Kings Wear their Heir?', *Revue belge de philologie et d'histoire*, 43 (1965), pp. 1203–16.

80. Timothy Reuter, 'Plunder and Tribute in the Carolingian Empire', *Transactions of the Royal Historical Society*, 5th series, 35 (1985), pp. 75–94.

81. L. Levillain, 'Campus Martius', *BEC*, 107 (1947/8), 62–8; B. S. Bachrach, 'Was the Marchfield Part of the Frankish Constitution?', *Medieval Studies*, 36 (1974), pp. 178–85. See, in general, Hans-Werner Goetz, 'Social and Military Institutions', in *NCMH*, pp. 451–80.

82. See Jean François Verbruggen, 'L'armée et la strategie de Charlemagne', in W. Braunfels (ed.), *KdG*, 1, pp. 420–36, and F. L. Ganshof, 'L'armée sous les Carolingiens', *Settimane*, 15 (1968), pp. 109–30.

83. F. L. Ganshof, 'Observations sur la date de deux documents administratifs émanant de Charlemagne', *MIöG*, 62 (1954), pp. 83–91.

84. Ed. Boretius, item 49, clause 2 (March 806), p. 136.

85. Jones, *Later Roman Empire* (note 49 above), I, pp. 411–69, and 2, pp. 607–86.

86. For arguments that a state system of taxation survived even as late as the ninth century see Jean Durliat, *Les finances publiques de Diocletian aux Carolingiens (284–889)* (Sigmaringen, 1990); also Walter Goffart, 'Old and New in Merovingian Taxation', *Past and Present*, 96 (1982), pp. 3–21, reprinted in his *Rome's Fall and After* (London, 1989), pp. 213–31.

87. Walter Goffart, *Barbarians and Romans AD 418–584: The Techniques of Accommodation* (Princeton, NJ, 1980).

88. On the royal estates and their administration see Wolfgang Metz, *Das karolingische Reichsgut* (Berlin, 1960), pp. 11–195, and more generally Janet L. Nelson, 'Kingship and Royal Government', in *NCMH*, pp. 383–430.

89. Alan M. Stahl, *Mérovingiens et royaumes barbares (VIᵉ–VIIIᵉ siècles* (Paris, 1994), pp. 45–80.

90. Josef Fleckenstein, *Die Hofkapelle der deutschen Könige*, 2 vols (Stuttgart, 1959), 1, pp. 11–43.

91. Pauline Stafford, *Queens, Concubines and Dowagers: The King's Wife in the Early Middle Ages* (London, 1983), pp. 93–114.

92. Karl Ferdinand Werner, '*Missus-Marchio-Comes* Entre l'administration centrale et l'administration locale de l'Empire carolingien', in Werner Paravicini and K. F. Werner (eds), *Histoire comparée de l'administration (IVᵉ–XVIIIᵉ siècles)* (Sigmaringen, 1980), pp. 191–239.

93. Janet L. Nelson, 'Dispute Settlement in Carolingian West Francia', in Wendy Davies and Paul Fouracre (eds), *The Settlement of Disputes in Early Medieval Europe* (Cambridge, 1986), pp. 45–64.

94. Paul Fouracre, 'Merovingians, Mayors of the Palace and the Notion of a "Low-born" Ebroin', *Bulletin of the Institute of Historical Research*, 57 (1984), pp. 1–14.

95. K. F. Werner, 'Bedeutende Adelsfamilien im Reich Karls des Grossen. Ein personengeschichtlicher Beitrag zum Verhältnis von Königtum und Adel im frühen Mittelalter', *KdG*, 1, pp. 83–142.

96. K. F. Werner, 'Les principautés periphériques dans le monde franque du VIIIᵉ siècle', *Settimane*, 20 (1973), pp. 482–514.

97. Roger Collins, 'Theodebert I, *Rex Magnus Francorum*', in Wormald *et al.* (eds), *Ideal and Reality* (note 47 above), pp. 7–33.

98. Michel Rouche, *L'Aquitaine des Wisigoths aux Arabes, 418–781* (Paris, 1979), pp. 87–132; Roger Collins, *The Basques* (Oxford, 1986), pp. 99–112.

99. *Chronicle of Fredegar*, IV, 87, ed. Wallace-Hadrill, pp. 73–4.

2 The Making of the Carolingian Dynasty, 687–771

1. For a recent restatement of the older views see Pierre Riché (tr. Michael I. Allen), *The Carolingians: A Family who Forged Europe* (Philadelphia, 1993), pp. 13–69; for the alternative see most recently Paul Fouracre, 'Frankish Gaul to 814', in *NCMH*, pp. 85–109.

2. Roger Collins, 'Deception and Misrepresentation in Early Eighth-Century Frankish Historiography: Two Case Studies', in Jörg Jarnut, Ulrich Nonn and Michael Richter (eds), *Karl Martell in seiner Zeit* (Sigmaringen, 1994), pp. 227–48.

3. For a highly tendentious, Carolingian re-telling of these events see the *Annales Mettenses Priores*, ed. B. de Simson, *MGH SRG*, pp. 1–13.

4. Jörg Jarnut, *Agilolfingerstudien* (Stuttgart, 1986), pp. 121–4.

5. *Chronicle of Fredegar*, IV.42, ed. J. M. Wallace-Hadrill, *The Fourth Book of the Chronicle of Fredegar* (London, 1960), pp. 34–6; Paul Fouracre and Richard A. Gerberding, *Late Merovingian France: History and Hagiography, 640–720* (Manchester, 1996), pp. 138–9 and n. 36.

6. Matthias Werner, *Der Lütticher Raum in frühkarolingischer Zeit* (Göttingen, 1980), pp. 396–7 and n. 2; Eduard Hlawitschka, 'Die Vorfahren Karls des Grossen', in W. Braunfels (ed.), *KdG*, I, pp. 51–82 does not consider this possibility.

7. Ed. Georg Pertz, *MGH SS*, II, p. 264.

8. *Annales Mettenses Priores* s.a. 688, ed. B. de Simson, *MGH SRG*, p. 3; see Janet Nelson, 'Gender and Genre in Women Historians of the Early Middle Ages', in *L'Historiographie médiévale en Europe* (Paris, 1991), pp. 149–63; reprinted in idem., *The Frankish World, 750–900* (London, 1996), pp. 183–98. It is, however, possible that these annals were not compiled until after 829: see Roger Collins, 'Reviser Revisited', in A. C. Murray (ed.), *After Rome's Fall: Narrators and Sources of Early Medieval History* (forthcoming). Gisela (died c. 810) is one of the many daughters of the royal house for whom no marriage was arranged; see p. 191 n. 53, and p. 194 n. 26. Was this a dynastic tradition?

9. Fouracre and Gerberding, *Late Merovingian France* (note 5 above), pp. 301–19.

10. *Vita Sanctae Geretrudis*, ed. Bruno Krusch, *MGH SRM*, II, pp. 447–74, with revisions in *MGH SRM*, VII, pp. 791–7; trans. Fouracre and Gerberding (note 5 above), pp. 319–26.

11. *Fredegar*, IV.86 and 88, ed. Wallace-Hadrill (note 5 above), pp. 72 and 75.

12. Bertram Colgrave (ed.), *Eddius Stephanus's Life of Wilfrid* (Cambridge, 1927), ch. 28, p. 55; Jean-Michel Picard, 'Church and Politics in the Seventh Century: the Irish Exile of King Dagobert II', in idem. (ed.), *Ireland and Northern France AD 600–850* (Dublin, 1991), pp. 27–52.

13. Matthias Becher, 'Der sogennante Staatsreich Grimoalds', in Jörg Jarnut, Ulrich Nonn and Michael Richter (eds), *Karl Martell in seiner Zeit* (Sigmaringen, 1994), pp. 119–47.

14. *Annales Mettenses Priores* s.a. 688, ed. de Simson, p. 2; Horst Ebling, *Prosopographie der Amtsträger des Merowingerreiches* (Munich, 1974), p. 168 for Gundewinus/Gundoin.

15. Matthias Werner, *Adelsfamilien im Umkreis der frühen Karolinger* (Sigmaringen, 1982), pp. 27–31.

16. Continuations of Fredegar 2–3, ed. Wallace-Hadrill (note 5 above), pp. 80–3; Richard A. Gerberding, *The Rise of the Carolingians and the 'Liber Historiae Francorum'* (Oxford), pp. 67–91.

17. Ian Wood, *The Merovingian Kingdoms, 481–75* (London, 1994), pp. 221–38.

18. Pardessus, no. 431, II, pp. 229–30; *Liber Historiae Francorum*, 48, ed. Bruno Krusch, *MGH SRM*, II, pp. 322–3; trans. Gerberding, *Rise of the Carolingians* (note 16 above), p. 178.

19. Gerberding, *Rise of the Carolingians* (note 16 above), pp. 93–4.

20. Pardessus, docs 436 and 456, II, pp. 237 and 261, for the last mention of Norbert and first reference to Grimoald as Mayor.

21. *Annales Laureshamenses* s.a. 708, *Annales Sancti Nazariani* s.a. 708, ed. Georg Pertz, *MGH SS*, 1, pp. 22–3; Continuations of Fredegar 7, ed. Wallace-Hadrill (note 5 above), p. 87; this may have been an act of vengeance for bishop Lambert of Liège, murdered in 705 by Pippinid supporters.

22. Continuations of Fredegar 6, ed. Wallace-Hadrill (note 5 above), p. 86; Waltraud Joch, 'Karl Martell – ein minderberechtiger Erbe Pippins?', in Jarnut *et al.* (eds), *Karl Martell* (note 13 above), pp. 149–69.

23. Wilhelm Levison, 'A propos du Calendrier de S. Willibrord', *Revue Bénédictine*, 50 (1938), pp. 37–41.

24. Continuations of Fredegar 10, ed. Wallace-Hadrill (note 5 above), p. 89; *Liber Historiae Francorum* 53, ed. Krusch (note 18 above), p. 327, does not mention Orléans.

25. *Chronicle of 754*, ch. 69, ed. José Eduardo López Perreira, *Crónica Mozárabe de 754* (Zaragoza, 1980), p. 84.

26. Continuations of Fredegar 10, ed. Wallace-Hadrill (note 5 above), p. 89.

27. *Annales Petaviani* s.a. 724, ed. G. Pertz, *MGH SS*, I, p. 9.

28. *Annales Sancti Amandi, Annales Tiliani, Annales Petaviani, Annales Laureshamenses* s.a. 721–30, ed. Pertz, *MGH SS*, I, pp. 6–9, 24.

29. Gerberding, *Rise of the Carolingians* (note 16 above), pp. 94–5, 137–9.

30. Wood, *Merovingian Kingdoms* (note 17 above), pp. 259–61.

31. Roger Collins, *The Arab Conquest of Spain, 710–797* (Oxford, 1989), pp. 86–91.

32. Edward Gibbon, *Decline and Fall of the Roman Empire*, ed. J. B. Bury (7 vols, London, 1898), VI, p. 15.

33. Continuations of Fredegar 20, ed. Wallace-Hadrill (note 5 above), pp. 93–5; *Annales Laureshamenses* s.a. 737 and 739, ed. G. Pertz, *MGH SS*, I, p. 24.

34. Patrick J. Geary, *Aristocracy in Provence* (Philadelphia and Stuttgart, 1985), pp. 120–30, 144–52.

35. Continuations of Fredegar 23, ed. Wallace-Hadrill (note 5 above), p. 97.

36. Rev s.a. 741, ed. Kurze, p. 3.

37. Boniface ep. 48, ed. M. Tangl, *MGH epistolae selectae*, 1 (Berlin, 1955), pp. 76–8.

38. *Annales Laureshamenses*, s.a. 741, ed. G. Pertz, *MGH SS*, 1, p. 24; for the identification see Collins, 'Deception and Misrepresentation' (note 2 above), pp. 229–35.

39. K. F. Werner, 'Les pricipautés péripheriques dans le monde franc du viiie siècle', *Settimane di studio sull'alto medioevo*, 20 (1972), pp. 482–514.

40. On Alamannia see Michael Borgolte, *Geschichte der Grafschaften Alemanniens in fränkischer Zeit* (Sigmaringen, 1984), pp. 21–8, and Jörg Jarnut, 'Untersuchungen zu den fränkisch-alemannischen Beziehungen in der ersten Hälfte des 8. Jahrhunderts', *Schweizerische Zeitschrift für Geschichte*, 30 (1980), pp. 7–28.

41. ARF and Rev. s.a. 742–4, 747–8, 753. These campaigns will be considered in more detail in subsequent chapters.

42. Reinhard Schneider, *Königswahl und Königserhebung im Frühmittelalter* (Stuttgart, 1972), pp. 183–6.

43. Eugen Ewig, 'Die Namengebung bei den ältesten Frankenkönigen und im merowingischen Königshaus', *Francia*, 18 (1991), pp. 21–69, at p. 68. *Gesta*

Abbatum Fontanellensium, IV.2, ed. F. Lohier and J. Laporte (Rouen, 1936), pp. 41–2 presents him as a son of Theuderic IV (721/2–37).

44. Claire Stancliffe, 'Kings who Opted Out', in Patrick Wormald, Donald Bullough and Roger Collins (eds), *Ideal and Reality in Frankish and Anglo-Saxon Society* (Oxford, 1983), pp. 154–76.

45. M. Becher, 'Drogo und die Königserhebung Pippins', *FS*, 23 (1989), pp. 131–53.

46. ARF and Rev. s.a. 746, ed. Kurze, pp. 6–7.

47. Ep. 79, ed. Tangl (note 37 above), p. 172 ' … ad filium Carlomanni.'; trans. Ephraim Emerton, *The Letters of Saint Boniface* (New York, 1973), pp. 141–2.

48. Becher, 'Drogo' (note 45 above).

49. ARF s.a. 748, ed. Kurze, pp. 6–9.

50. Continuations of Fredegar 35, ed. Wallace-Hadrill (note 5 above), p. 103 (my translation).

51. For example, Robert Folz, *The Coronation of Charlemagne* (London, 1974), p. 28.

52. Michael J. Enright, *Iona, Tara and Soissons* (Berlin and New York, 1988), pp. 108–19.

53. Continuations of Fredegar 33, ed. and trans. Wallace-Hadrill (note 5 above), p. 102.

54. ARF s.a. 749, ed. Kurze, p. 8; trans. Bernhard W. Scholz, *Carolingian Chronicles* (Ann Arbor, 1970), p. 39.

55. Ibid.

56. Einhard, *Vita Karoli*, 1–2, ed. Halphen, pp. 8–12.

57. Adolf Gauert, 'Noch einmal Einhard und die letzen Merowinger', in Lutz Fenske, Werner Rösener and Thomas Zotz (eds), *Institutionen, Kultur und Gesellschaft im Mittelalter* (Sigmaringen, 1984), pp. 59–72.

58. Ed. W. Gundlach, *MGH Epp.*, III, pp. 469–653. It was made because of the deteriorating state of the originals, which were in many cases probably written on papyrus, and the collection now survives in a single ninth-century copy, MS Vienna Osterreichische Nationalbibliothek 449, made for Archbishop Willibert of Cologne (870–89).

59. Jörg Jarnut, 'Wer hat Pipin 751 zum König gesalbt', *FS*, 16 (1982), pp. 45–57.

60. Enright, *Iona, Tara, and Soissons* (note 52 above), pp. 80–94.See also David Harry Miller, 'Sacral Kingship, Biblical Kingship, and the Elevation of Pepin the Short', in Thomas F. X. Noble and John J. Contreni (eds), *Religion, Culture and Society in the Early Middle Ages* (Kalamazoo, 1987), pp. 131–54.

61. Arnold Angenendt, 'Rex et Sacerdos. Zur Genese der Königssalbung', in Norbert Kamp and Joachim Wollasch (eds), *Tradition als historische Kraft* (Berlin/New York, 1984), pp. 100–18.

62. Continuations of Fredegar 36–37, ed. Wallace-Hadrill (note 5 above), pp. 104–7, relate the diplomatic and military causes and consequences of the papal visit, but make no mention of the anointing.

63. Roger Collins, 'Theodebert I, *Rex Magnus Francorum*', in Wormald *et al.*, *Ideal and Reality* (note 44 above), pp. 7–33.

64. Paul Goubert, *Byzance avant l'Islam*, 2, pt 1: *Byzance et les Francs* (Paris, 1956), pp. 16–22, 95–159.

65. David H. Miller, 'The Roman Revolution of the Eighth Century: a Study of the Ideological Background of the Papal Separation from Byzantium and Alliance with the Franks', *Medieval Studies*, 36 (1974), pp. 79–133; Jan T. Hallenbeck,

Pavia and Rome: the Lombard Monarchy and the Papacy in the Eighth Century (Philadelphia, 1982), pp. 15–61.

66. ARF s.a. 755 and 756, ed. Kurze, pp. 12 and 14; these campaigns will be considered in slightly more detail in ch. 4 below.

67. Roger Collins, 'The *Vaccaei*, the *Vaceti* and the rise of *Vasconia*', *Studia Historica*, 6 (1988), pp. 211–23; corrected reprint in idem., *Law, Culture and Regionalism in Early Medieval Spain* (Aldershot, 1992), item XI.

68. Michel Rouche, *L'Aquitaine des Wisigoths aux Arabes 418–781* (Paris, 1979), pp. 120–32.

69. Continuations of Fredegar 52, ed. Wallace-Hadrill (note 5 above), p. 120; ARF and Rev. s.a. 768, ed. Kurze, pp. 26–7; the precise date appears only in the *Annales Sancti Amandi*, s.a. 768, ed. Georg Pertz, *MGH SS*, 1, p. 12.

70. ARF s.a. 768, ed. Kurze, p. 28 for the date; Continuations of Fredegar 53, ed. Wallace-Hadrill (note 5 above), pp. 120–1.

71. Continuations of Fredegar, ibid.; Sumner McK. Crosby, *The Royal Abbey of Saint-Denis* (New Haven, 1987), pp. 52–6.

72. Continuations of Fredegar 53, ed. Wallace-Hadrill (note 5 above), p. 121.

73. On the conflicts between Charles and Carloman see Jörg Jarnut, 'Ein Bruderkampf und seine Folgen: Die Krise des Frankenreiches (768–771)', in Georg Jenal (ed.), *Herrschaft, Kirche, Kultur, Beiträge zur Geschichte des Mittelalters* (Stuttgart, 1993), 165–76.

74. Continuations of Fredegar 54, ed. Wallace-Hadrill, p. 121 gives the date as Sunday 18 September and gives no date for Pippin's death; ARF s.a. 768 gives 9 October. The latter was also the feast day of Saint Dionysius the Areopagite, patron of the monastery of Saint-Denis, where Pippin had been buried.

75. ARF and Rev. s.a. 768, ed. Kurze, pp. 28–9.

76. *Codex Carolinus*, no. 44, ed. W. Gundlach, *MGH Epp.*, III, pp. 558–60.

77. *Codex Carolinus*, no. 48, ed. Gundlach, pp. 566–7, where she is addressed by Stephen III as *Deo consecrata*.

78. Rev. s.a. 770, ed. Kurze, p. 31, which is fuller than ARF on this journey.

79. *Codex Carolinus*, no. 45, ed. Gundlach, pp. 560–3.

80. *Liber Pontificalis*: Stephen III, chs 29–32, ed. Louis Duchesne, *Liber Pontificalis* (2nd edn, 3 vols, Paris, 1955), 1, pp. 478–80; their deaths were reported to Bertrada and Charles by Stephen III in *Codex Carolinus*, no. 48, ed. Gundlach, *MGH Epp.*, III, pp. 56–67.

81. This is explicitly stated (by Desiderius) to have been part of the plan: *Liber Pontificalis*, Hadrian I, ch. 5, ed. Duchesne (note 80 above), 1, p. 487.

82. Ibid., Hadrian I, chs 6–16, ed. Duchesne (note 80 above), pp. 487–91. Hadrian I claimed that he had only wanted to save Paul's soul.

83. Just as very little is known of Carloman's reign in Francia. No capitularies of his have survived; for his charters see note 88 below.

84. ARF s.a. 771, ed. Kurze, p. 32; only the *Annales Mettenses Priores* refer to the destination being Desiderius's court.

85. Rev. s.a. 768, ed. Kurze, p. 33, refers to Wilcharius as archbishop of Sitten. Donald Bullough, 'The Dating of Codex Carolinus Nos. 95, 96, 97, Wilchar and the Beginnings of the Archbishopric of Sens', *DA*, 18 (1962), pp. 223–30, especially n. 29.

86. On these see Michael Borgolte, *Geschicte der Grafschaften Alemanniens in fränkischer Zeit* (Sigmaringen, 1984), pp. 64–6, 107–11, 154–6, and 249–50.

87. Alain Stoclet, *Autour de Fulrad de Saint-Denis (v. 710–784)* (Geneva, 1993), pp. 205–40.

88. Engelbert Muhlbacher (ed.), *MGH Diplomata Karolinorum*, 1, docs 43–54, pp. 61–76, including some forged or interpolated texts.

89. *Codex Carolinus*, nos 69, 71–2, 77, 82–3 and appendix nos 1–2, ed. Gundlach, pp. 598–9, 601–3, 609, 615–19, 654–7.

90. *Vita Karoli*, 18, ed. Halphen, p. 58.

91. David Ganz, *Corbie in the Carolingian Renaissance* (Sigmaringen, 1990), pp. 22–4.

3   The Saxon Wars, 772–85

1. W. Levison, *England and the Continent in the Eighth Century* (Oxford, 1946), p. 108, where he also hails Pippin III's almost equally violent Aquitanian wars as 'one of the bases of future France'.

2. For a variety of essays on early Saxon history, written over several decades of this century, see W. Lammers (ed.), *Entstehung und Verfassung des Sachsenstammes* (Darmstadt, 1967). It is notable that in Germany much scholarly attention was devoted to the Saxons in the 1930s.

3. Ammianus Marcellinus, XVII. viii.1–4, ed. J. C. Rolfe (rev. edn, London and Cambridge, Mass., 1950), pp. 232–4, which makes this a Roman success; in practice it was a recognition of the *status quo*.

4. J. Haywood, *Dark Age Naval Power* (London and New York, 1991), pp. 23–50 on Frankish and Saxon maritime raids.

5. Gregory of Tours, *Historiarum Libri Decem*, II.xviii, ed. Bruno Krusch and Wilhelm Levison, *MGH SRM*, 1, p. 65.

6. Gregory, V.xxvi, ibid., p. 232, describing the slaughter by the Bretons of a contingent of such Saxons fighting for the Frankish king Chilperic (561–84); they also appear fighting for his son Chlotar II in 590 in X.iv.

7. See R. Collins, 'Theodebert I, "Rex Magnus Francorum"', in P. Wormald, D. Bullough and R. Collins (eds), *Ideal and Reality in Frankish and Anglo-Saxon Society* (Oxford, 1983), pp. 7–33.

8. Gregory of Tours, IV.xiv, ed. Krusch (note 5 above), pp. 145–7.

9. Ibid., IV.xlii, pp. 174–7. This group was later settled as federates of the Austrasian king Sigibert I (561–75), and there may have been a re-establishment of the Frankish hegemony at this time; see below.

10. Fredegar IV.38, ed. J. M. Wallace-Hadrill, *Fourth Book of the Chronicle of Fredegar* (London, 1960), p. 31.

11. Ibid., IV.75, pp. 63–4.

12. Ibid., IV.54–5 and 78, pp. 44–5, 65–7.

13. A. Genrich, *Die Altsachsen* (Hildesheim, 1981), pp. 74–86.

14. The 'Chatuarii' are probably the same people as the 'Chatti', reported as living across the Rhine in the vicinity of Cologne: Gregory of Tours II.ix, ed. Krusch (note 5 above), p. 55.

15. *Annales Sancti Amandi, Annales Tiliani, Annales Laubacenses*, and *Annales Petaviani* s.a. 715, 718, 720, 729 (not all of the episodes are recorded in every one

of these annals): ed. G. Pertz, *MGH SS*, 1, pp. 6–7; also *Annales Laureshamenses* s.a. 718, 720, and 738: ibid., p. 24. There is a chronologically vague reference, probably to the 718/20 campaigns in the Continuations of Fredegar 12, ed. Wallace-Hadrill (note 10 above), p. 90.

16. *Annales Petaviani* s.a. 738, p. 9. The *Annales Sancti Amandi* are alone in reporting Saxon campaigns in both 733 and 734, while the others only record a single campaign in 733: *MGH SS* 1, pp. 8–9. The AD dates in these annals are not contemporary with the events themselves, and some chronological confusion may be expected.

17. Continuations of Fredegar 19, ed. Wallace-Hadrill (note 10 above), p. 93.

18. Ibid., 27, 31 and 35, pp. 99, 101 and 103; ARF and Rev. s.a. 743, 744, 747, 748, 753. These annal accounts are far less dependent on the Continuations of Fredegar than is usually believed.

19. Continuations of Fredegar 31, ed. Wallace-Hadrill (note 10 above), p. 101.

20. ARF s.a. 741 and 747, ed. Kurze, pp. 2 and 6.

21. S. von Schnurbein, *Untersuchungen zur Geschichte der römischen Militärlager an der Lippe* (Frankfurt am Main, 1981).

22. For the taking of oaths by the Saxons on their weapons, which were then clashed together, see Continuations of Fredegar, 74, ed. Wallace-Hadrill (note 10 above), p. 63. For the limited evidence on Germanic paganism see Ian Wood, 'Pagan Religions and Superstitions East of the Rhine from the Fifth to the Ninth Century', in G. Ausenda (ed.), *After Empire: Towards an Ethnology of Europe's Barbarians* (Woodbridge, 1995), pp. 253–79.

23. Ibid., 27 and 31, pp. 99 and 101.

24. *S. Bonifatii et Lullii epistolae*, ed. M. Tangl, *MGH Epistolae Selectae* 1, nos 21, 46 and 47, pp. 35–6 and 74–6; see T. Schieffer, *Winfrid-Bonifatius und die christliche Grundlegung Europas* (Freiburg, 1954), pp. 170–81. Despite the sentimental appeal to the Anglo-Saxon missionaries of a project to convert their continental Saxon relatives, Boniface made no real headway in this direction. See also K. Honselmann, 'Der Brief Gregors III an Bonifatius über die Sachsenmission', *Historisches Jahrbuch*, 76 (1957), pp. 83–106.

25. A similar phenomenon, slightly more fully explored in the historiography, applied to the conflicts with the Vikings in England and Francia in the ninth and tenth centuries. See Alfred P. Smyth, *King Alfred the Great* (Oxford, 1996), pp. 66–98.

26. ARF and Rev. s.a. 753, ed. Kurze, pp. 10–11, placing his death at the fortress or hill of 'Iuburg', which has been identified as Iburg near Osnabrück.

27. ARF s.a. 758, ed. Kurze, p. 16; the Continuations of Fredegar do not refer to this campaign at all. ARF refers to Pippin's capture of 'Sitnia', which Kurze identified as Sithen, between Wesel and Münster.

28. ARF s.a. 772, ed. Kurze, p. 34.

29. ARF and Rev. s.a. 775, ed. Kurze, pp. 40–1; trans. B. W. Scholz, *Carolingian Chronicles* (Ann Arbor, 1970), p. 51.

30. An early ninth-century manuscript in the monastery of St Paul in Carinthia in Austria records a list of 10 Westphalian, 15 Eastphalian and nine Angrarian hostages (*MGH Capitularia*, I, ed. Boretius, pp. 233–4). It also records the names of those individual Frankish bishops and nobles to whom they were entrusted.

31. I owe this suggestion to Dr M. Balzer; it was made to the Ethnogenesis conference held at Zwettel in 1985 in an unpublished lecture. The importance of Paderborn

will emerge from the discussion of subsequent events, and see note 29. For the events see ARF and Rev s.a. 776, ed. Kurze, pp. 42–9.

32. K. Hauck, 'Paderborn, das Zentrum von Karls Sachsen-Mission 777', in J. Fleckenstein and K. Schmid (eds), *Adel und Kirche: Gerd Tellenbach zum 65. Geburtstag dargebracht von Freunden und Schülern* (Freiburg, Basel, Vienna, 1980), pp. 92–140.

33. *Annales Mosellani* s.a. 777, ed. I. M. Lappenburg, *MGH SS*, 16, p. 496. This set of annals runs from 703 to 797, with its entries becoming relatively more detailed for the 780s and 790s.

34. ARF and Rev. s.a. 777, ed. Kurze, pp. 48–51; only Rev. refers to Widukind as a leader of the Westphalians and to his followers taking refuge with the king of the Danes.

35. Sigebert, *Vita Deoderici*, ed. G. H. Pertz, *MGH SS*, 4, p. 465. See Regine Le Jan, *Famille et pouvoir dans le monde franc (viie–xe siècle)* (Paris, 1995), p. 42.

36. ARF s.a. 743 and 744, ed. Kurze, p. 4.

37. For the identification see J. F. Böhmer, *Regesta Imperii: Die Regesten des Kaiserreichs unter den ersten Karolingern* (2nd edn, Innsbruck, 1908), p. 23.

38. ARF s.a. 778, ed. Kurze, p. 52, indicates that the news reached Charles when he was at Auxerre, but whether this was on the way or returning from Spain is not clear.

39. *Annales Mosellani* s.a. 780, ed. Lappenburg (note 33 above), p. 497; neither *ARF* nor Rev. mentions this.

40. ARF and Rev. s.a. 782, ed. Kurze, pp. 58–65; one of these is named as Halfdan.

41. *Capitularia*, ed. Boretius (note 30 above), item 26, pp. 68–70.

42. J. T. McNeill and H. M. Gamer, *Medieval Handbooks of Penance* (New York, 1938), pp. 194 and 291.

43. H. Dörries, 'Germanische Religion und Sachsenbekehung', *Zeitschrift für niedersächsische Kirchengeschichte*, 39 (1934), pp. 53–83.

44. A. Genrich, 'Archäologische Aspekte zur Christianisierung im nördlichen Niedersachsen' in H.-W. Krumwiede (ed.), *Vorchristlich-christliche Frühgeschichte in Niedersachsen* (= Beihefte 64 of the *Jahrbuch der Gesellschaft für niedersächsische Kirchengeschichte*, 1966), pp. 21–32.

45. The thirteenth-century cathedral of Münster and its Domplatz are fringed by houses, that in turn are surrounded by a ring of streets. The latter and the river on the west mark almost exactly the line of the Carolingian defences. See O.-E. Selle, *Mimigernaford-Monasterium: Sachsenort. Domburg. Bischofsstadt* (Münster, 1984).

46. W. Winkelmann, 'Ausgrabungen auf dem Domhof in Münster', in idem., *Beiträge zur Frühgeschichte Westfalens* (Münster, 1984), pp. 70–88 and plates 44 to 51.

47. They may now be seen in the Westfälisches Landesmuseum für Kunst und Kulturgeschichte in Münster.

48. For Frankish horse sacrifices in the late fifth century see R. Brulet, G. Coulon, M.-J. Ghenne-Dubois and F. Vilvorder, 'Nouvelles recherches à Tournai autour de la sépulture de Childéric', *Revue archéologigue de Picardie* 3/4 (1988), pp. 39–43. See also Rudolf Moosbrugger-Lau, *Die frühmittelalterliche Gräberfelder von Basel* (Basel, 1982), pp. 35–6. A similar horse burial, but of seventh-century date, may be seen in the archaeological museum in Frankfurt-am-Main.

49. Rev. s.a. 782, ed. Kurze, p. 63; ARF, characteristically, claims this to have been a Frankish victory, while admitting the deaths of the two *missi*.

50. ARF and Rev. s.a. 782, ed. Kurze, pp. 62–3. On this notorious episode see F. von Klocke, 'Um das Blutbad von Verden und die Schlacht am Süntel 782', *Westfälische Zeitschrift*, 93 (1937), pp. 151–92; for (ideologically inspired) arguments over the significance of the episode and the numbers of the dead see E. Rundnagel, 'Der Tag von Verden', *Historische Zeitschrift*, 157 (1938), pp. 457–90 and W. Schmitt, 'Das Gericht zu Verden 782', *Thüringisch-Sächsische Zeitschrift für Geschichte und Kunst*, 27 (1940), pp. 14–26. Hitler's SS commander, Heinrich Himmler, set up a monument to the Saxon dead.

51. *Annales Mosellani* s.a. 783, ed. Lappenburg (note 33 above), p. 497, trans. King, p. 134; for more detailed accounts see ARF and Rev. s.a. 783, ed. Kurze, pp. 64–7; the Old Testament reminiscences and phraseology of the annals were more than literary artifices.

52. Rev. s.a. 785, ed. Kurze, p. 69; trans. King, pp. 118–19.

53. Rev. s.a. 785, ed. Kurze, p. 71; on the importance of the godfather/godson relationship in this period see A. Angenendt, 'Taufe und Politik im frühen Mittelalter', *FS*, 7 (1973), pp. 43–68, and idem., *Kaiserherrschaft und Königstaufe* (Berlin and New York, 1984).

54. Rev. s.a. 785, ed. Kurze, p. 71; ARF ignores this conspiracy entirely.

55. Though it is probably unwise to see Widukind as a religious or prophetic leader of the Saxons: Wood, 'Pagan Religions' (note 22 above), pp. 263–4 and 268.

56. The battle and its location are described in *Annales Mettenses Priores*, s.a. 746, ed. B. de Simson, *MGH SRG*, vol. 10, p. 37; the massacre may be deduced from Continuations of Fredegar 29, ed. Wallace-Hadrill, p. 100.

57. Matthew Innes, 'Franks and Slavs c. 700–1000: the Problem of European Expansion before the Millennium', *Early Medieval Europe*, 6 (1997), pp. 201–16, at p. 210.

4 Italy and Spain, 773–801

1. Jörg Jarnut, *Geschichte der Langobarden* (Stuttgart, 1982), pp. 21–6; István Bóna, *The Dawn of the Dark Ages: The Gepids and the Lombards in the Carpathian Basin* (Budapest, 1976), pp. 83–92.

2. *Epistolae Austrasicae* 8: letter of bishop Nicetius of Trier to Chlodosuinth: ed. Wilhem Gundlach, *MGH Epp.*, III, pp. 119–22; on the collection see idem., 'Die Sammlung der Epistulae Austrasicae', *NA*, 13 (1888), pp. 365–87.

3. Walter Goffart, 'Byzantine Policy in the West under Tiberius II and Maurice', *Traditio*, 13 (1957), pp. 73–118.

4. Paul Goubert, *Byzance avant l'Islam*, 2, pt 1 (Paris, 1956), pp. 16–26.

5. Jarnut, *Geschichte der Langobarden* (note 1 above), pp. 55–66, and idem., *Agilolfingerstudien* (Stuttgart, 1986); Paul the Deacon, *Historia Langobardorum*, VI.54, ed. Georg Waitz, *MGH SRG*, p. 237.

6. T. F. X. Noble, *The Republic of St. Peter: The Birth of the Papal State 680–825* (Philadelphia, 1984), pp. 61–94.

7. Continuations of Fredegar 35, ed. J. M. Wallace-Hadrill, *The Fourth Book of the Chronicle of Fredegar* (London, 1960), p. 103.

8. ARF and Rev. s.a. 753, ed. Kurze, pp. 10–11.

9. Noble, *Republic of St. Peter* (note 6 above), p. 82 and notes 92–3. Rev., unlike ARF, exculpates Carloman from any blame, on the grounds that he was obeying his abbot, who in turn was acting on the orders of the Lombard king.

10. ARF s.a. 754, ed. Kurze, p. 12. Rev. adds that his body was then sent back to Monte Cassino for burial. Einhard, *Vita Karoli*, 2, ed. Halphen, p. 12, is misleading to the point of mendacity on Carloman's career after 747.

11. Continuations of Fredegar 36–8, ed. Wallace-Hadrill (note 7 above), pp. 103–8; Jan T. Hallenbeck, *Pavia and Rome: The Lombard Monarchy and the Papacy in the Eighth Century* (Philadelphia, 1982), pp. 63–85.

12. Noble, *Republic of St. Peter* (note 6 above), pp. 94–9.

13. *Liber Pontificalis: Hadrian I*, 28 and 30, ed. Duchesne, I, pp. 494–5.

14. The precise month is recorded in *Annales Mosellani* s.a. 774, ed. I. M. Lappenburg, *MGH SS*, 16, p. 496; also in the *Chronicle of Moissac* s.a. 774, ed. Georg Pertz, *MGH SS*, 1, p. 295.

15. ARF and Rev. s.a. 773 and 774, ed. Kurze, pp. 34–41, for the fullest account of the campaign. *LP*, Hadrian I, 44, ed. Louis Duchesne, *Liber Pontificalis* (2nd edn, 3 vols. Paris, 1955), 1, p. 496, refers to disease in Pavia.

16. H. Wolfram, *Intitulatio I. Lateinische Königs- und Fürstentitel bis zum Ende des 8. Jahrhunderts* (Graz-Vienna-Cologne, 1967), pp. 217–36. Desiderius and his wife Ansa were taken to Francia and detained in the monastery of Corbie: *Annales Sangallenses Maiores* s.a. 774, ed. G. H. Pertz, *MGH SS*, vol. 1, p. 75.

17. *MGH Diplomata Karolinorum*, I, doc. 80, pp. 114–15. Not least dubious is the name of the referendary, the official who supervised the drawing up and signing of royal documents. He is here named as 'Enrich'. All other documents from this period name (H)itherius, and in his absence deputies sign '*ad vicem Itherii*'; e.g. docs 81 and 82.

18. C. Cipolla (ed.), *Codice Diplomatico del Monasterio di S. Colombano di Bobbio fino all'anno MCCVIII*, 1 (Rome, 1918), doc. xxvii, pp. 128–31.

19. Boretius, doc. 82, p. 118. He is last recorded as being in Pavia in the document of 16 July 774: ibid., doc. 81, pp. 115–17.

20. See for example the way that Desiderius, then Duke of Tuscany, had deposed his predecessor Ratchis in 757: Hermann Frölich, *Studien zur langobardischen Thronfolge von den Anfängen bis zur Eroberung des italienischen Reiches durch Karl den Großen* (2 vols, Tübingen, 1980), 1, pp. 224–35.

21. Chris Wickham, *Early Medieval Italy: Central Power and Local Society, 400–1000* (London, 1981), pp. 47–55. Giovanni Tabacco, *The Struggle for Power in Medieval Italy* (Cambridge, 1989), pp. 109–24; and Giovanni Tabacco, 'L'avvento dei Carolingi nel regno dei Longobardi', in S. Gasparri and P. Cammarosano (eds), *Longobardia* (Udine, 1993), pp. 375–423.

22. For relations between Rome and Spoleto see Hallenbeck, *Pavia and Rome* (note 11 above), especially pp. 106–74.

23. On Franco-Beneventan dealings see above all Ottorino Bertolini, 'Carlomagno e Benevento', in *KdG*, I, pp. 609–71, and in general T. S. Brown, 'Byzantine Italy, c. 680–c. 876', in *NCMH*, pp. 320–48.

24. *Chronographia*, a.m. 6267, ed. C. de Boor, Theophanes: *Cronografia* (Leipzig, 1883), 1, p. 449. Adelchis is here known by the Greek name of Theodotos, which he adopted in Constantinople.

25. See for example the duchy of Trento: Jörg Jarnut, 'Das Herzogtum Trent in lango-bardischer Zeit', *Atti dell'Accademia roveretana degli Agiati*, 6 (1985), pp. 167–78.

26. On the Lombard duchy and the region of Friuli see H. Krahwinkler, *Friaul im Frühmittelalter: Geschichte einer Region vom Ende des fünften bis zum Ende des zehnten Jahrhunderts* (Vienna, 1992). On Hrodgaud see Stefano Gasparri, *I Duchi Longobardi* (Rome, 1978), pp. 71–2.

27. *Annales Petaviani*, s.a. 776, ed. Georg Pertz, *MGH SS*, 1, p. 16. On these dukes see Gasparri, *I Duchi*, pp. 61–2, 84–5, 98–100, 60 respectively.

28. *Codex Carolinus*, ep. 57, ed. Gundlach, pp. 582–3: in a letter probably sent in January 776 pope Hadrian warned Charles that these dukes were plotting with Hrodgaud to seize and despoil Rome. He may, however, have been hoping to enlist Charles's help by implying involvement in a wider plot. He certainly had other reasons for hostility to the duke of Chiusi: ibid., ep. 58 of February 776, ed. Gundlach, pp. 583–4.

29. ARF and Rev. s.a. 776, ed. Kurze, pp. 42–5.

30. *MGH Diplomata Karolinorum* 1, docs 111 and 112.

31. ARF s.a. 777, ed. Kurze, p. 48; Roger Collins, *The Arab Conquest of Spain, 710–797* (Oxford, 1989), pp. 175–80. Einhard, *Vita Karoli*, 9, ed. Halphen, p. 28, gives no explanation whatsoever for Charles's Spanish campaign.

32. For these episodes and other problems that 'Abd al-Rahman I had faced see Collins, *Arab Conquest of Spain*, pp. 113–40.

33. Roger Collins, *The Basques* (2nd edn, Oxford, 1990), pp. 90–5.

34. *Chronicle of Moissac* s.a. 759, ed. Pertz (note 14 above), p. 294; Eduardo Manzano Moreno, *La frontera de Al-Andalus en época de los Omeyas* (Madrid, 1991), pp. 74–7.

35. The Reviser (s.a. 778, ed. Kurze, p. 51) states that the 778 campaign was motiv-ated by the 'far from idle hope of gaining certain cities in Spain' (trans. King, p. 113).

36. *ARF* s.a. 778, ed. Kurze, p. 50; trans. Scholtz, p. 56.

37. Pedro Chalmeta, 'Invasión e islamización (Madrid, 1994); see also Roger Collins, 'Spain: the northern kingdoms and the Basques, 711–910', in *NCMH*, pp. 272–89.

38. José María Lacarra, 'La expedición de Carlomagno a Zaragoza y su derrota en Roncesvalles', in idem., *Investigaciones de historia navarra* (Pamplona, 1983), pp. 17–93 for a detailed account of the expedition; see also Manzano Moreno, *La Frontera de al-Andalus* (note 34 above), pp. 110–16.

39. Fernando de la Granja, 'La Marca Superior en la obra de al-'Udri', *Estudios de Edad Media de la Corona de Aragón*, VIII (Zaragoza, 1967), pp. 447–545, at pp. 461–3. There are disagreements between the Arab sources and between them and the Frankish annals over numerous points of detail. See Collins, *Arab Conquest* (note 31 above), pp. 175–80.

40. Einhard, *Vita Karoli*, 9, ed. Halphen, p. 30. For no obvious reason the name of Hruodland is omitted in the 'B' class of manuscripts of the *Vita*, which contain the edition of the work made for Louis the Pious by Gerward, his court librarian.

41. *MGH Poetae aevi Karolin*, 1, ed. Ernst Dümmler, p. 109. Einhard calls him the *regiae mensae praepositus* or 'prefect of the royal table'. He performed ceremonial functions at royal banquets and had easy access to the monarch.

42. *Liber Pontificalis*: Hadrian I, 33, ed. Duchesne (note 15 above), 1, p. 499.

43. C.-R. Bruhl, 'Chronologie und Urkunden der Herzöge von Spoleto', *Quellen und Forschungen aus italienischen Archiven und Biblioteken*, 51 (1971), pp. 1–92; see also D. Bullough 'The Writing-office of the Dukes of Spoleto in the Eighth Century' in D. Bullough and R. L. Storey (eds), *The Study of Medieval Records* (Oxford, 1971), pp. 1–21.

44. *Annales Mosellani* s.a. 781, ed. Lappenburg (note 14 above), p. 497, for the name change. Not only was Pippin the name of Charles's father but the latter had been the first of the Frankish rulers to receive the title of *Patricius Romanorum* from the Papacy.

45. ARF and Rev. s.a. 780 and 781, ed. Kurze, pp. 54–9. For Aquitaine see Leonce Auzias, *L'Aquitaine carolingienne* (Toulouse and Paris, 1937), especially pp. 1–75.

46. *Annales Sancti Amandi* s.a. 780, ed. Pertz, *MGH SS*, 1, p. 12.

47. F. Manacorda, *Richerche sugli inizi della dominazione dei Carolingi in Italia* (Rome, 1968).

48. R. Colins, 'The *Vaccaei*, the *Vaceti* and the rise of *Vasconia*', in idem., *Law, Culture and Regionalism in Early Medieval Spain* (Aldershot, 1992), item XI.

49. R. Collins, 'Pippin I and the Kingdom of Aquitaine', in Godman and Collins, pp. 363–90.

50. G. Roura, *Girona Carolíngia, del any 785 a l'any 1000* (Girona, 1988), pp. 18–26. Ramón d'Abadall I de Vinyals, 'El domini carolingi a la Marca Hispanica', in idem., *Dels Visigots als Catalans*, 2 vols (Barcelona, 1969), 1, pp. 139–52.

51. See pp. 126–7 below, and Mathias Becher, *Eid und Herrschaft. Untersuchungen zum Herrscherethos Karls des Großen* (Sigmaringen, 1993), pp. 88–194.

52. *MGH Diplomata Karolinorum*, 1, docs 156, 157 and 158, ed. M. Tangl *et al.*, pp. 211–16.

53. This, and a comparable refusal around 790 to send his daughter Bertha to marry the son of king Offa of Mercia, have sometimes been taken, alongside the account of Charles's devotion to them in *Vita Karoli*, 19, to indicate incestuous feelings or even acts between Charles and his daughters. If that had been the case, Einhard would never have mentioned it, and the central word in his account, *contuburnium*, has a totally unsalacious meaning in his model, Suetonius's *Divus Augustus* 89.

54. On these events see W. Treadgold, *The Byzantine Revival 780–842* (Stanford, 1988), pp. 75–89.

55. *Codex Carolinus*, 83, ed. W. Gundlach, *MGH Epp.*, III, pp. 616–19.

56. *Codex Carolinus*, 80 and 84, ed. Gundlach, pp. 611–14, 619–20.

57. Ibid., 82, ed. Gundlach, pp. 615–16; Bertolini, 'Carlomagno e Benevento', pp. 655–62.

58. Ibid., appendix 2, pp. 655–7. This is a letter to Charles from abbot Maginarius, January 788, papyrus original preserved at Saint-Denis, and now in the Bibliothèque Nationale.

59. Papal warnings: *Codex Carolinus*, 80 and 84, ed. Gundlach, pp. 611–14, 619–20; Erchempert, *Historia Langobardorum Beneventanorum* ch. 4, ed. Georg Waitz, *MGH SRL*, p. 236.

60. Rev. s.a. 788, where the decision is wrongly ascribed to Constantine VI alone. Theophanes s.a. 6281. See Treadgold, *Byzantine Revival* (note 54 above), pp. 89–92.

61. Treadgold, op. cit., pp. 92–5.
62. P. Grierson, 'Money and Coinage under Charlemagne', *KdG* 1, p. 516; reprinted in his *Dark Age Numismatics* (London, 1979), item XVIII.
63. ARF s.a. 800–802, ed. Kurze, pp. 110–17.
64. For the later history of this region see Barbara M. Kreutz, *Before the Normans. Southern Italy in the Ninth and Tenth Centuries* (Philadelphia, 1991), chs 1–4.
65. Collins, *The Arab Conquest of Spain* (note 31 above), pp. 200–7.
66. Rev. s.a. 793, ed. Kurze, p. 95; *Lorsch Annals* s.a. 793, ed. Georg Pertz, *MGH SS*, 1, p. 35.
67. Ibn 'Idhari, ed. E. Lévi-Provençal, *Al-Bayan al-Mugrib*, III (Paris, 1930) s.a. 177 (A.H.); *Chronicle of Moissac* s.a. 793, ed. Pertz (note 14 above), p. 300. See María J. Viguera, *Aragón musulmana* (2nd edn, Zaragoza, 1988), pp. 65–9.
68. Collins, *Arab Conquest of Spain* (note 31 above), pp. 141–67; Paulino García Toraño, *Historia de el Reino de Asturias (718–910)* (Oviedo, 1986), pp. 193–208.
69. *Vita Karoli*, 16, ed. Halphen, p. 46. There are no references to any such contacts in the late ninth-century chronicles of the Asturian kingdom.
70. ARF and Rev. s.a. 797, ed. Kurze, pp. 100–1.
71. ARF and Rev. s.a. 798, ed. Kurze, pp. 104–5; surprisingly, no reference is made to this in the late ninth-century Asturian *Chronica Albeldensia* and *Adefonsi Tertii Chronica* ('Chronicle of Alfonso III'), suggesting that it was not remembered as so great a triumph in the kingdom itself: Juan Gil Fernández, José L. Moralejo and Juan I. Ruíz de la Peña (eds), *Crónicas asturianas* (Oviedo, 1985).
72. Collins, *Arab Conquest of Spain* (note 30 above), pp. 210–12.
73. Josep M. Salrach, *El procés de formació nacional de Catalunya (segles VIII–IX)* (2 vols, Barcelona, 1978), 1, pp. 14–26.
74. Ermoldus, *In Honorem Hludowici ... Augusti* in Edmond Faral (ed.), *Ermold le Noir: poème sur Louis le Pieux et épitres au roi Pépin* (Paris, 1932), bk 1, lines 102–647, pp. 12–50; see Peter Godman, 'Louis "the Pious" and his poets', *FS*, 19 (1985), pp. 239–89, at pp. 253–71.
75. Collins, *The Basques* (note 33 above), pp. 123–32.

5 Tassilo III and Bavaria, 781–8

1. H. Wolfram and A. Schwarcz (eds), *Die Bayern und ihre Nachbarn*, 2 vols (Vienna, 1985); for a useful overview of Bavarian archaeology see H. Dannheimer, *Auf den Spuren der Baiuwaren: Archäologie des frühen Mittelalters in Altbayern* (Pfaffenhofen, 1987).
2. Herwig Wolfram, *Die Geburt Mitteleuropas* (Vienna, 1987), pp. 311–40; Ludwig Pauli, *The Alps: Archaeology and Early History* (Engl. tr., London, 1984), pp. 57–8.
3. H. Tatzreiter, 'Slawisch-deutsche Mischnamen im Donauraum von Ober- und Niederösterreich', in H. Wolfram and W. Pohl (eds), *Typen der Ethnogenese unter besonderer Berucksichtung der Bayern*, 2 vols (Vienna, 1990), 1, pp. 243–60.
4. F. Koller, 'Salzproduktion und Salzhandel', in Hermann Danheimer and Heinz Dopsch (eds), *Die Bajuwaren von Severin bis Tassilo 488–788* (Munich, 1988), pp. 220–2.

5. See the papers in vol. 2 of Wolfram and Schwarcz, *Die Bayern* (note 1 above); A. Sandberger, *Altbayerische Studien zur Geschichte von Siedlung, Recht und Landwirtschaft* (Munich, 1985).

6. G. Diepolder, 'Grundzüge der Siedlungsstruktur', in *Die Bajuwaren* (note 4 above), pp. 168–78.

7. On the Carantanians see Wolfram, *Die Geburt Mitteleuropas* (note 2 above), pp. 341–6; also the introduction and commentary to idem. (ed.), *Conversio Bagoariorum et Carantanorum* (Graz, 1979).

8. Paul, *Historia Langobardorum* III.10 and 30, ed. G. Waitz, *MGH SRG* (Hanover, 1890), pp. 118 and 133–5.

9. Ibid., IV.7 and 39, pp. 146 and 167. Jörg Jarnut, *Agilolfinger Studien* (Stuttgart, 1986), pp. 57–68.

10. Jarnut, *Agilolfinger Studien*, pp. 9–40.

11. *Fredegar*, IV.52 and 87, ed. Wallace-Hadrill, pp. 43 and 73; their names were Chrodoald and Fara.

12. Paul the Deacon III.30, ed. Waitz (note 8 above), pp. 133–5; Jörg Jarnut, *Geschichte der Langobarden* (Stuttgart, 1982), pp. 41–6.

13. J. Jarnut, 'Genealogie und politische Bedeutung der agilolfingischen Herzöge', *Mitteilungen des Instituts für Österreichische Geschichtsforschung*, 99 (1991), pp. 1–22.

14. J. Fleckenstein, 'Fulrad von Saint-Denis und der fränkische Ausgriff in den süddeutschen Raum', in Gerd Tellenbach (ed.), *Studien un Vorarbeiten zur Geschichte des großfränkischen und frühdeutschen Adels* (Freiburg, 1957), pp. 1–39; Wilhelm Störmer, *Adelsgruppen im früh- und hochmittelalterlichen Bayern* (Munich, 1972).

15. F. Prinz, 'Herzog und Adel im agilulfingischen Bayern. Herzogsgut und Konsensschenkungen vor 788', *Zeitschrift für Bayerische Landesgeschichte*, 25 (1962), pp. 283–311; modified by the arguments of A. Kraus, 'Zweiteilung des Herzogtums der Agilolfinger?', *Blätter für deutsche Landesgeschichte*, 112 (1976), pp. 15–29. See also W. Störmer and G. Mayer, 'Herzog und Adel', in *Die Bajuwaren*, pp. 153–59.

16. Alain Stoclet, *Autour de Fulrad de Saint-Denis (v. 710–784)* (Geneva, 1993), pp. 244–51 on the historiographical debate.

17. H. Wolfram (ed.), *Conversio Bagoariorum et Carantanorum* (Graz, 1979), and idem., *Die Geburt Mitteleuropas* (Berlin, 1987), pp. 109–63; also F. Prinz, 'Arbeo von Freising und die Agilulfinger', *Zeitschrift für Bayerische Landesgeschichte*, 29 (1966), pp. 580–90.

18. F. Prinz, *Frühes Mönchtum im Frankenreich* (2nd edn, Darmstadt, 1988), pp. 317–445; W. Störmer and H. Dannheimer, 'Die agilolfingerzeitlichen Klöster', in *Die Bajuwaren* (note 4 above), pp. 305–17, and W. Hartmann and Heinz Dopsch, 'Bistümer, Synoden und Metropolitanverfassung', ibid., pp. 318–26.

19. L. Holzfurtner, *Gründung und Gründungsüberlieferung. Quellenkritische Studien zur Gründungsgeschichte der Bayerischen Klöster der Agilolfingerzeit und ihrer hochmittelalterlichen Überlieferung* (Munich, 1984), pp. 169–71. On S. Candido see Stoclet, *Autour de Fulrad*, pp. 343–52, and for Kremsmünster the articles in Siegfried Haider (ed.), *Die Anfänge des Klosters Kremsmünster* (Linz, 1978).

20. Friederich Prinz, 'Arbeo von Freising und die Agilulfinger', *Zeitschrift für bayerische Landesgeschichte*, 29 (1966), pp. 580–90.

21. C. Bowlus, *Franks, Moravians and Magyars: the Struggle for the Middle Danube 788–907* (Philadelphia, 1995), pp. 33–45.

22. Stoclet, *Autour de Fulrad* (note 16 above), pp. 252–358.

23. *Annales Sancti Amandi, Annales Tiliani, Annales Laubacenses, Annales Petaviani* all s.a. 725, *MGH SS*, 1, pp. 8–9. They all report that this was his first campaign in Bavaria.

24. *Annales Sancti Amandi* and *Annales Tiliani* s.a. 728, ibid., p. 8; the *Annales Laubacenses* do not have an entry for this year, and the *Annales Petaviani*, ibid., p. 9, report that Charles fought in Saxony.

25. Fredegar Continuations, 12, ed. Wallace-Hadrill, p. 90.

26. Fredegar Continuations, 25, ed. Wallace-Hadrill, *Fourth Book*, p. 98. This is said to have been carried out on the advice of Swanachild and against the wishes of Pippin and Carloman. It is also worth noting that, as would later be the case with Charles's sister and with his daughters, no arrangement had been made for Chiltrude to wed during her father's lifetime.

27. ARF and Rev. s.a. 743, ed. Kurze, pp. 4–5; this was also the year in which they found it necessary to consecrate – or invent? – a new Merovingian king.

28. Fredegar Continuations, 26, ed. Wallace-Hadrill, p. 99.

29. ARF s.a. 748, ed. Kurze, p. 8. Lantfred duke of the Alamans is also recorded as one of Grifo's allies in 748.

30. Fredegar Continuations, 32, ed. Wallace-Hadrill, pp. 101–2.

31. Ibid., 39, ed. Wallace-Hadrill, p. 107.

32. ARF s.a. 757, ed. Kurze, pp. 14 and 16.

33. Matthias Becher, *Eid und Herrschaft. Untersuchungen zum Herrscherethos Karls des Großen* (Sigmaringen, 1993), pp. 35–45.

34. *ARF* s.a. 763, ed. Kurze, pp. 20 and 22; trans. Scholz, p. 44.

35. *ARF* s.a. 778, ed. Kurze, p. 50; this is not in Rev.

36. For Tassilo as son-in-law of Desiderius see Einhard, *Vita Karoli*, 11, ed. Halphen, p. 34.

37. Eigil, *Vita Sturmi*, 22, ed. G. H. Pertz, *MGH SS*, II, p. 375.

38. *Annales Iuvavenses maiores* s.a. 772, ed. G. H. Pertz, *MGH SS*, I, p. 87.

39. J. M. Wallace-Hadrill, *The Frankish Church* (Oxford, 1983), pp. 416–17; Wolfram, *Die Geburt Mitteleuropas* (note 2 above), pp. 143–5.

40. T. Bitterauf (ed.), *Die Traditionen des Hochstifts Freising* (2 vols, Munich, 1905–9), doc. 34.

41. *Annales Petaviani* s.a. 781, ed. G. H. Pertz, *MGH SS*, I, p. 16; *Annales Mosellani* s.a. 781, ed. J. M. Lappenburg, *MGH SS*, XVI, p. 497.

42. *ARF* s.a. 781, ed. Kurze, p. 58; cf. Rev. s.a. 781, ibid., p. 59.

43. ARF s.a. 781, ed. Kurze, p. 58.

44. On such relationships see Susan Reynolds, *Fiefs and Vassals: the Medieval Evidence Reinterpreted* (Oxford, 1994), pp. 17–74 and 84–105.

45. ARF s.a. 787, ed. Kurze, pp. 76–8.

46. *ARF* s.a. 787, ed. Kurze, p. 76. No mention is made of any of this in the *Liber Pontificalis*.

47. S. Krämer, 'Arn', *Lexicon des Mittelalters*, 1, pp. 993–4.

48. Quotations from *ARF* s.a. 787, ed. Kurze, p. 78.

49. Ibid. The young Pippin was ordered to accompany the Italian army only as far as Trento.

50. *ARF* s.a. 788, ed. Kurze, p. 80; trans. King, p. 86.
51. Rev. s.a. 788, ed. Kurze, p. 81.
52. *Annales Nazariani* s.a. 788, ed. G. Pertz, *MGH SS*, 1, p. 44; trans. King, p. 157.
53. *Annales Laureshamenses* s.a. 788, ed. Pertz, *MGH SS*, 1, pp. 33–4; these annals, like *ARF* and Rev., state that this was at Tassilo's own request. The *Annales Nazariani* claim that this was done 'against his will'.
54. Wolfram, *Die Geburt Mitteleuropas* (note 2 above), pp. 189–90; Michael Borgolte, *Geschichte der Grafschaften Alemanniens in fränkischer Zeit* (Sigmaringen, 1984), pp. 246–7.
55. *Annales Laureshamenses* s.a. 794, ed. Pertz, p. 36; trans. King, p. 141. See also clause 3 of the acts of the Council of Frankfurt: ed. Boretius, *MGH Legam*, item 28, p. 74.

6 Conflict on the Steppes: the Avars, 788–99

1. *Vita Karoli*, 11, ed. Halphen, p. 34.
2. Michel Rouche, 'Les Aquitains, ont-ils trahi avant la bataille de Poitiers?', *Le Moyen Age* 74 (1968), pp. 5–26, and Roger Collins, 'Deception and Misrepresentation in Early Eighth Century Frankish Historiography: Two Case Studies', in Jörg Jarnut, Ulrich Nonn and Michael Richter (eds), *Karl Martell in seiner Zeit* (Sigmaringen, 1993), pp. 227–47.
3. ARF s.a. 788, ed. Kurze, p. 82.
4. Walter Pohl, 'Verlaufsformen der Ethnogenese – Awaren und Bulgaren', in Herwig Wolfram and Walter Pohl (eds), *Typen der Ethnogenese unter besonderer Berücksichtigung der Bayern* (2 vols, Vienna, 1990), 1, pp. 113–24 on the creation of the Avar ethnic identity. For their material culture see Gerhard Bott and Walter Meier-Arendt (eds), *Awaren in Europa. Schätze eines asiatischen Reitervolkes 6.–8. Jh.* (Frankfurt am Main, 1985).
5. Menander Protector frags 12.1–7, ed. R. C. Blockely, *The History of Menander the Guardsman* (Liverpool, 1985), pp. 128–43; N. Christie, *The Longobards* (Oxford, 1995), pp. 58–68; Walter Pohl, *Die Awaren. Ein Steppenvolk in Mitteleuropa 567–822 n. Chr.* (Munich, 1988), pp. 58–66.
6. Wilfried Menghin *et al.* (eds), *Germanen, Hunnen und Awaren: Schätze der Völkerwanderungszeit* (Nuremburg, 1987), pp. 199–294; István Bóna, *The Dawn of the Dark Ages: the Gepids and the Lombards in the Carpathian Basin* (Engl. trans. of Hungarian original, Budapest, 1976), pp. 28–38.
7. Walter Pohl, 'Ergebnisse und Probleme der Awarenforschung', *Mitteilungen des Instituts für österreichische Geschichtsforschung*, 96 (1988), pp. 247–74.
8. For example, Albert Herrmann, *Die Gobi im Zeitalter der Hunnenherrschaft* (Stockholm, 1935).
9. For the identification of the Avars with the Jou-Jan, see A. Kollautz and M. Hisayuki, *Geschichte und Kultur eines völkerwanderungszeitlichen Nomadenvolks: die Jou-jan der Mongolei und die Awaren in Mitteleuropa*, 2 vols (Klagenfurt, 1970).
10. O. Maenchen-Helfen, 'Huns and Hsiung-nu', *Byzantion*, 17 (1944/5), pp. 222–43.

11. Following some of the analysis of nomadism in Owen Lattimore, *The Inner Asian Frontiers of China* (2nd edn, New York, 1951), pp. 53–102.

12. A. N. Stratos, *Byzantium in the Seventh Century*, I: 602–34 (Amsterdam, 1968), pp. 173–95.

13. A. N. Stratos, *Byzantium in the Seventh Century*, IV: 668–85 (Amsterdam, 1978), pp. 93–113. For the Bulgars in Charles's time see Jonathan Shepard, 'Slavs and Bulgars', in *NCMH*, pp. 228–48.

14. E. A. Thompson, *A History of Attila and the Huns* (Oxford, 1948), pp. 73–124.

15. That this was a conscious *desideratum* amongst such nomad confederacies can be seen from the inscription of the Turkish ruler Bilgä Khagan. See René Giraud, *Les règnes d'Elterich, Qapghan et Bilgä (680–734)* (Paris, 1960), pp. 7–23. On relations between pastoralists and sedentary societies see Chris Wickham, 'Pastoralism and under-development', *Settimane*, 31 (1985), pp. 401–51.

16. Pohl, *Die Awaren* (see note 5 above), pp. 94–126.

17. Istvan Bonà, 'Neue Nachbarn im Osten – Die Awaren', in Hermann Dannheimer and Heinz Dopsch (eds), *Die Bajuwaren von Severin bis Tassilo 488–788* (Munich, 1988), pp. 108–17.

18. ARF s.a. 788, ed. Kurze, p. 82; Walter Pohl, *Die Awarenkriege Karls des Großen 788–803* (Vienna, 1988), pp. 16–17.

19. Rev. s.a. 788, ed. Kurze, p. 83; for the Italian events see pp. 68–71 above.

20. P. D. King, *Charlemagne* (London, 1986), p. 21. The last recorded diplomatic exchange between the Avars and Byzantium dates to 676. Paul Lemerle, 'Invasions et migrations dans les Balkans depuis la fin de l'époque romaine jusqu' au VIIIe siécle', *Revue Historique*, 211 (1954), pp. 265–308, at p. 299 and n. 3.

21. He seems to have spent from Christmas of 789 to the Spring of 791 in or around Worms, with only an excursion by boat down the river Main to his palace at Salz in the Summer of 790. According to the Reviser, this was undertaken in order not to give the appearance of being idle! Rev. s.a. 790.

22. ARF s.a. 791, ed. Kurze, p. 88.

23. The same set of questions also applies to relations with the Vikings in the ninth century, whose attacks on wealthy and vulnerable monastic and episcopal centres could also seem and/or be intended to be overtly anti-Christian.

24. ARF and Rev. s.a. 791, ed. Kurze, pp. 88–9; *Annales Mettenses Priores* s.a. 791, ed. de Simson, p. 79; see Michael McCormick, *Eternal Victory: Triumphal Rulership in Late Antiquity, Byzantium and the Early Medieval West* (Cambridge, 1986), pp. 342–87.

25. *MGH Epp.*, IV, pp. 528–9.

26. For this campaign see Pohl, *Die Awarenkriege* (note 18 above), pp. 17–21 and 48; and in general Josef Deér, 'Karl der Große und der Untergang des Awarenreiches', in *KdG*, 1, pp. 719–91.

27. Theoderic, a relative of Charles, took a leading part in the Saxon wars in 781 and 793 (see ARF); Meginfred, a correspondent of Alcuin, was killed on campaign in Benevento (Alcuin, ep. 211, ed. Dümmler, pp. 351–2).

28. ARF and Rev. s.a. 791, ed. Kurze, pp. 88–9; *Annales Laureshamenses s.a. 791*, ed. G. Pertz, *MGH SS*,1, p. 34. The role of the Bohemians in this venture is not mentioned, though it seems as if Frankish forces could march through their territory with impunity. This is their first appearance in the sources relating to the reign.

29. Rev. s.a. 791, ed. Kurze, p. 89.
30. It may be, as Janet Nelson has suggested, that their horses had been as badly affected by the pest as those of the Franks.
31. ARF and Rev. s.a. 792, ed. Kurze, pp. 92–3.
32. Rev. s.a. 793, ed. Kurze p. 93. In characteristic fashion ARF does not mention the fate of Theoderic's army or Charles's planned expedition at all.
33. *Annales Laureshamenses* s.a. 793, ed. Pertz, p. 35; Rev. indicates the degree of success achieved by the raiders, despite the efforts of local Frankish counts.
34. ARF s.a. 795, ed. Kurze, p. 97.
35. On Eric see James Bruce Ross, 'Two Neglected Paladins of Charlemagne, Erich of Friuli and Gerold of Bavaria', *Speculum*, 20 (1945), pp. 212–35.
36. Pohl, *Die Awaren* (note 5 above), pp. 306–8.
37. ARF s.a. 796; Rev. s.a. 796, which rather plays down the role of duke Eric's expedition; ed. Kurze, pp. 98–99.
38. Rev. s.a. 795, ed. Kurze, p. 97.
39. Thomas J. Barfield, *The Perilous Frontier: Nomadic Empires and China 221 BC to AD 1757* (Oxford, 1989), pp. 132–3; see also Pohl, *Die Awaren* (note 5 above), pp. 300–1.
40. ARF s.a. 811, ed. Kurze, p. 135. (I do not follow P. D. King's translation which changes the word order to make him an Avar noble.)
41. On nomad warfare and strategies to combat it see Arthur Waldron, *The Great Wall of China. From History to Myth* (Cambridge, 1990).
42. Barfield, *The Perilous Frontier* (note 39 above), pp. 131–45.
43. For a broader perspective see Christopher L. Beckwith, *The Tibetan Empire in Central Asia* (Princeton, 1987), pp. 173–96.
44. Jenö Szücs, 'The Three Historical Regions of Europe: an outline', *Acta Historica Academiae Scientiarum Hungaricae*, 29 (1983), pp. 131–84.
45. Martin Eggers, *Das 'Großmährische Reich'. Realität oder Fiktion?* (Stuttgart, 1995), pp. 29–51.
46. For materials from the region traditionally thought to be Greater Moravia see Susan Beeby, David Buckton and Zdenek Klanica, *Great Moravia. The Archaeology of Ninth-Century Czechoslovakia* (London, 1982).
47. For the primary location south of the Danube see Charles R. Bowlus, *Franks, Moravians and Magyars. The Struggle for the Middle Danube 788–907* (Philadelphia, 1995), and for the Hungarian theory see Eggers, *Das 'Großmährische Reich'* (note 45 above).
48. ARF and Rev. s.a. 799, ed. Kurze, pp. 108–9; on Gerold see Ross, 'Two Neglected Paladins of Charlemagne' (note 35 above).
49. *Annales Mettenses Priores* s.a. 803, ed. de Simson, p. 90.
50. ARF s.a. 805, ed. Kurze, pp. 119–20.
51. Pohl, *Die Awarenkriege*, pp. 25–29 for the period 797 to 811.
52. Pohl, *Die Awaren* (note 5 above), pp. 293–304 for arguments about a possible 'double kingship' amongst the Avars.
53. ARF s.a. 805. *Annales Sancti Emmeramni* s.a. 805, ed. G. Pertz, *MGH SS* 1, p. 93; a set of annals for the years 748 to 823, associated with the monastery of St Emmeran in Regensburg (Bavaria).
54. J. M. Wallace-Hadrill, *The Frankish Church* (Oxford, 1983), pp. 416–17.
55. ARF s.a. 811, ed. Kurze, p. 135.

56. ARF s.a. 811, ed. Kurze, p. 135; see Pohl, *Die Awaren* (note 5 above), pp. 304–5 on the *Canizauci*.
57. ARF s.a. 822, ed. Kurze, p. 159; Pohl, *Die Awaren* (note 5 above), pp. 323–8.
58. M. Hellmann, 'Karl und die slawische Welt zwischen Ostsee und Böhmerwald', in *KdG*, 1, pp. 708–18.
59. ARF s.a. 805 and 806, ed. Kurze, pp. 119–21.
60. *Chronicle of Moissac* s.a. 805, ed. G. Pertz, *MGH SS*, 1, pp. 307–8.
61. Bowlus, *Franks, Moravians and Magyars* (note 47 above), pp. 57–8.
62. Warren Treadgold, *The Byzantine Revival, 780–842* (Stanford, 1988), pp. 135–74.

7 Reform and Renewal, 789–99

1. Philippe Wolff, *The Awakening of Europe* (Harmondsworth, 1968), pp. 36–108.
2. Alan Thacker, 'Bede's Ideal of Reform', in Patrick Wormald, Donald Bullough and Roger Collins (eds), *Ideal and Reality in Frankish and Anglo-Saxon Society* (Oxford, 1983), pp. 130–53.
3. Paul Fouracre and Richard A. Gerberding, *Late Merovingian France: History and Hagiography 640–720* (Manchester, 1996), pp. 133–253 for translation of and commentary on the *Vita Audoini, Acta Aunemundi* and *Passio Leudegarii*.
4. *Desiderii Episcopi Cadurcensis Epistulae*, ed. Wilhelm Arndt, *MGH Epp.*, III, pp. 191–214; reprinted in *CCSL*, 117, pp. 310–42.
5. R. McKitterick, 'The Scriptoria of Merovingian Gaul', in eadem., *Books, Scribes and Learning in the Frankish Kingdoms, 6th–9th Centuries* (Aldershot, 1994), item I. See also Ian Wood, 'Administration, Law and Culture in Merovingian Gaul', in R. McKitterick (ed.), *The Uses of Literacy in Early Medieval Europe* (Cambridge, 1990), pp. 63–81.
6. *Concilia Galliae*, ed. C. de Clercq, *CCSL*, cxlviiiA, pp. 323–6.
7. J. M. Wallace-Hadrill, *The Frankish Church* (Oxford, 1983), pp. 143–61; Timothy Reuter, ' "Kirchenreform" und "Kirchenpolitik" im Zeitalter Karls Martells: Begriffe und Wirklichkeit', in Jörg Jarnut, Ulrich Nonn and Michael Richter (eds), *Karl Martell in seiner Zeit* (Sigmaringen, 1994), pp. 35–59.
8. F. Prinz, *Frühes Monchtum im Frankenreich* (2nd edn, Darmstadt, 1988), pp. 121–51.
9. P. Riché, 'Le renouveau culturel à la cour de Pépin III', *Francia*, 2 (1974), pp. 59–70.
10. D. Bullough, 'Aula Renovata. The Carolingian Court before the Aachen Palace', *PBA*, 71 (1985), pp. 267–301, at pp. 269–70.
11. These have probably been preserved because they were capitularies *legibus addenda* 'to be added to the codes', that required special consultation both to promulgate or, it may equally be assumed, to abrogate.
12. E. A. Thompson, *The Goths in Spain* (Oxford, 1969), pp. 277–89.
13. Ed. Boretius, item 10, pp. 24–6, preserved in seventeen manuscripts: Hubert Mordek, *Bibliotheca capitularium regum Francorum manuscripta* (Munich, 1995), p. 1080. There are arguments as to whether the year was 742 or 743. The day is specified in the text, and the lack of reference to the last Merovingian king Childeric III (743–51) means that it can be no later than 743.

14. See J. Jarnut, 'Bonifatius und die fränkischen Reformkonzilien (734–748)', *Zeitung für Rechtsgeschichte. Kanonistische Abteilung.* 96 (1979), pp. 1–26; cf. C. Cubitt, *Anglo-Saxon Church Councils c. 650–c. 850* (Leicester, 1995), pp. 102–10. The phrase 'church reform' needs to be treated circumspectly: T. Reuter, '"Kirchenreform" und "Kirchenpolitik" im Zeitalter Karl Martells: Begriffe und Wirklichkeit', in J. Jarnut, U. Nonn and M. Richter (eds), *Karl Martell in seiner Zeit* (Sigmaringen, 1994), pp. 35–59.

15. Bede, *Historia Ecclesiastica,* I.29, ed. Bertram Colgrave and R. A. B. Mynors (rev. edn, Oxford, 1991), pp. 104–6.

16. For doubts that this was the universal Irish practice it has normally been thought to be, see Richard Sharpe, 'Some Problems Concerning the Organisation of the Church in Early Medieval Ireland', *Peritia,* 3 (1984), pp. 230–70.

17. Ed. Boretius, no. 28, cl. 8, p. 75. The Arles vs. Vienne dispute was an old one, going back to the fifth century and frequently revived. See Elie Griffe, *La Gaule chrétienne à l'époque romaine,* 2 (Paris and Toulouse, 1957), pp. 114–29. In 794 it was resolved on the basis of papal letters relating to the earlier difficulties.

18. On Aldebert and his heresy see Boniface, epp. 59–60, ed. M. Tangl, *MGH Epistulae Selectae,* 1, pp. 108–25, and Theodor Schieffer, *Winfrid-Bonifatius und die christliche Grundelegung Europas* (Freiburg, 1954), pp. 231–2 and 241–5.

19. Ed. Boretius, item 14, pp. 31–2.

20. Ibid., item 14, pp. 32–7; for widows and orphans in Charles's capitularies see, for example, Boretius, item 33, cl. 5, p. 93, item 34, cl. 19, p. 101, etc.

21. Confirmation in 769 of Pippin's *Aquitanian Capitulary:* ed. Boretius, item 18, clauses 1 and 2, pp. 42–3. The intensity of the Aquitanian war of the 760s may help explain the lack such legislation after about 758.

22. See the published articles from the commemorative conference: *Saint Chrodegang* (Metz, 1967).

23. J. M. Wallace-Hadrill, *The Frankish Church* (Oxford, 1983), pp. 171–6.

24. *Nomina Episcoporum* in *MGH Capit.* I, ed. Boretius, pp. 221–2. The text is found only in MS Vatican Pal. lat. 577, fol. 6.

25. In 761 Pippin held his assembly at Düren (ARF s.a. 761, ed. Kurze, p. 18), but the locations of those of 760 and 762 are not given. Attigny was the site of the 765 assembly (ARF s.a. 765, p. 22), but the names of the participants point towards a date in the early 760s.

26. Ed. Boretius, item 88, pp. 187–8.

27. Ed. Boretius, item19, pp. 44–6, published by Baluze from a now-lost manuscript. For its status as forgery see F. Lot, 'Le premier capitulaire de Charlemagne', in *Annuaire de l'Ecole pratique des Hautes-Etudes* (1924/5); on the collection of 'Benedict the Levite' see Ganshof, *Recherches sur les capitulaires* (Paris, 1958), p. 71.

28. *Capitulare Haristallense,* ed. Boretius, item 20, pp. 46–51; clauses 9, 11, 17 and 23 deal with thieves (*latrones*) and with the protection of travellers.

29. Robert Markus, 'Gregory the Great's *Rector* and his Genesis', in Jacques Fontaine, Robert Gillet and Stan Pellistrandi (eds), *Grégoire le Grand* (Paris, 1986), pp. 137–46; Robert Markus, *Gregory the Great and his World* (Cambridge, 1997), 26–33.

30. *Admonitio Generalis,* preface, ed. Boretius, item 22, tr. King, p. 209.

31. G. Martínez Díez, *La colección canónica hispana,* 1 (Madrid, 1966), pp. 257–354, including its Gallic diffusion. See Charles Munier, 'Nouvelles recherches sur

l'Hispana chronologique', *Revue des sciences religieuses*, 40 (1966), pp. 400–10, for some doubts on Isidore's role.

32. See R. McKitterick, 'Knowledge of Canon Law in the Frankish Kingdoms Before 789: the Manuscript Evidence', *Journal of Theological Studies*, n.s. 36 (1985), pp. 97–117; eadem., *The Frankish Church and the Carolingian Reforms, 789–895* (London, 1977), pp. 1–44.

33. *Admonitio Generalis*, cl. 82, ed. Boretius, item 22, trans. King, p. 219.

34. F.-K. Scheibe, 'Alcuin und die *Admonitio Generalis*', *DA*, 14 (1958), pp. 221–9. See too Bullough, '*Aula renovata* (note 10 above), pp. 293–5.

35. P. Godman (ed.), *Alcuin: the Bishops, Kings and Saints of York* (Oxford, 1982), lines 1526–35, p. 120 and Introduction, pp. xxxv–xxxix.

36. For the king's presence in Parma: *Diplomata*, no. 132 (15 March 781); for the meeting see *Vita Alcuini*, ch. 9, ed. W. Arndt, *MGH SS*, XV (Hanover, 1887), p. 198. There may have been a previous meeting in the late 770s.

37. D. Bullough, 'Aula Renovata' (note 10 above), p. 287.

38. For the letters see F.-K. Scheibe, 'Alcuin und die Briefe Karls des Grossen', *DA*, 15 (1959), pp. 181–93, and for the *De Litteris* see L. Wallach, 'Charlemagne's *De litteris colendis* and Alcuin: A Diplomatic-Historical Study', *Speculum*, 26 (1951), pp. 288–305.

39. C. J. B. Gaskoin, *Alcuin* (Cambridge, 1904), p. 94, n. 4.

40. For examples of other, much smaller 'specialist' collections of Alcuin letters see Colin Chase (ed.), *Two Alcuin Letter Books* (Toronto, 1975).

41. *Vita Karoli*, 25, ed. Halphen, p. 74.

42. Ibid.; Lewis Thorpe, trans. *Einhard and Notker the Stammerer: Two Lives of Charlemagne* (Harmondsworth, 1969), p. 79 makes the surprising decision to translate the last of these as 'astrology'!

43. Rev. s.a. 792, ed. Kurze, pp. 91 and 93.

44. D. Bullough, 'Roman Books and the Carolingian *renovatio*', *Studies in Church History*, 14 (1977); reprinted with additions and corrections in idem., *Carolingian Renewal* (Manchester, 1991), pp. 1–38.

45. Walter Ullmann, *The Carolingian Renaissance and the Idea of Kingship* (Cambridge, 1969), pp. 11–12; Bullough, 'Roman Books' (note 44 above), pp. 14 and 29, n. 46. Jean Gaudemet, *Les sources du droit de l'Eglise en occident du IIe au VIIe siécle* (Paris, 1985), pp. 130–7 for the *Dionysiana*.

46. Cyrille Vogel, 'La réforme liturgique sous Charlemagne', in B. Bischoff (ed.), *KdG*, II (Düsseldorf, 1965), pp. 217–32; see also Roger E. Reynolds, 'The Organisation, Law and Liturgy of the Western Church, 700–900', in *NCMH*, pp. 587–621, at pp. 617–21.

47. Gregory Dix, *The Shape of the Liturgy* (London, 1945), pp. 208–37, 434–526, 546–612; Louis Duchesne, *Christian Worship*, trans. M. L. McClure (5th edn, London, 1920), pp. 120–60.

48. W. S. Porter, *The Gallican Rite* (London, 1958), pp. 9–56.

49. D. M. Hope, *The Leonine Sacramentary: A Reassessment of its Nature and Purpose* (Oxford, 1971), pp. 132–44.

50. *Admonitio Generalis*, cl. 80, ed. Boretius, p. 61; *Letter to the Readers*, ed. Boretius, item 29, pp. 78–9.

51. B. Moreton, *The Eighth Century Gelasian Sacramentary* (Oxford, 1976).

52. *Codex Carolinus*, no. 89, ed. W. Gundlach, *MGH Epp.*, III, p. 626.

53. Hans Lietzmann (ed.), *Das Sacramentarium Gregorianum nach dem aachener Urexemplar* (3rd edn, reprinted Münster, 1967), pp. xv–xxv.

54. Gerald Ellard, *Master Alcuin Liturgist* (Chicago, 1956), pp. 127–44 for the older view. On Benedict's authorship see J. Deshusses, 'Le "Supplément" au sacramentaire grégorien: Alcuin ou Benoît d'Aniane?', *Archiv für Liturgiewissenschaft*, 9 (1965), pp. 48–71; see also idem. (ed.), *Le sacramentaire grégorien*, 1 (Fribourg, 1971), pp. 62–70, and idem., 'Les messes d'Alcuin', *Archiv für Liturgiewissenschaft*, 14 (1972), pp. 7–41.

55. For a survey of developments in Frankish monasticism in this period see Josef Semmler, 'Karl der Grosse und das fränkische Mönchtum', in *KdG*, II, pp. 255–89.

56. *Annales Laueshamenses* s.a. 786, ed. Georg Pertz, *MGH SS*, 1, p. 33.

57. An extant early ninth-century MS made for Reichenau (St Gallen Stiftsbibliothek 914) is very closely related to this copy that Charles received from Monte Casino. See Adalbert de Vogüé (ed.), *La Règle de Saint Benoît*, vol. 1 (Paris, 1972), pp. 320–7, and Paul Meyvaert, 'Problems Concerning the "Autograph" Manuscript of Saint Benedict's Rule', *Revue Bénédictine*, 70 (1959), pp. 1–21.

58. Canons 13, 14, 16; cf. also canon 20, which orders bishops to know 'the monastic rule'; ed. Boretius, item 28, pp. 75–6.

59. *Annales Laureshamenses* s.a. 802, ed. Pertz (note 56 above), p. 39.

60. *Concilium Remense*, ed. Albert Werminghof, *MGH Concilia*, 1, item 35, clause 9, p. 255.

61. Bonifatius Fischer, 'Bibeltext und Bibelreform unter Karl dem Grossen', in *KdG*, II, pp. 156–216.

62. Bonifatius Fischer, 'Bibelausgaben des frühen Mittelalters', *Settimane di studio del Centro italiano sull'alto medioevo*, vol. 10 (1963), pp. 519–600; for a shorter survey see Richard Marsden, *The Text of the Old Testament in Anglo-Saxon England* (Cambridge, 1995), pp. 5–24.

63. Alcuin, ep. 261, ed. Dümmler, pp. 418–19.

64. Raphael Loewe, 'The Medieval History of the Latin Vulgate', in G. W. H. Lampe (ed.), *Cambridge History of the Bible*, 2 (Cambridge, 1969), pp. 102–53, at pp. 134–7.

65. Jean Hubert, Jean Porcher and W. F. Volbach, *Carolingian Art* (Engl. trans., London, 1970), pp. 78–91. The name 'Ada', that of a putative and probably non-existent sister of Charles, is entirely misleading.

66. F. L. Ganshof, 'Observations sur la date de deux documents administratifs émanent de Charlemagne', *MIöG*, 62 (1954), pp. 83–91, believed that the revision was that of Alcuin of c. 800, but this seems unlikely.

67. Ed. Boretius, item 30, pp. 80–1.

68. On Eutropius see A. H. M. Jones *et al.* (eds), *Prosopography of the Later Roman Empire*, 1: 260–395 (Cambridge, 1971), p. 317.

69. On which see p. 63 above.

70. The surviving fragments of the original work and Paul's epitome are in W. M. Lindsay (ed.), *Sextus Pompeius Festus, de verborum significatu quae supersunt cum Pauli epitome* (Leipzig, 1913).

71. See Walter Goffart, 'Paul the Deacon's *Gesta episcoporum Mettensium* and the Early Design of Charlemagne's Succession', *Traditio*, 42 (1986), pp. 59–93.

72. Roger Wright, 'Late Latin and Early Romance: Alcuin's *De Orthographia* and the Council of Tours (813)', *Papers of the Liverpool Latin Seminar*, 3 (Liverpool, 1981), pp. 343–61.

73. David Ganz, 'The Preconditions for Caroline Minuscule', *Viator*, 18 (1987), pp. 23–44, and idem., 'Book Production in the Carolingian Empire and the Spread of Caroline Minuscule', in *NCMH*, pp. 786–808; see also Bernhard Bischoff, *Latin Palaeography*, trans. D. ó Cróinín and David Ganz (Cambridge, 1990), pp. 100–18.

74. Rosamond McKitterick, *The Carolingians and the Written Word* (Cambridge, 1989) for the fullest and most optimistic assessment of literacy in this period.

75. Einhard, *Vita Karoli*, 24–5, ed. Halphen, pp. 70–6.

76. Edited in Liutpold Wallach, 'Charlemagne's *De litteris colendis* and Alcuin', *Speculum*, 26 (1951), pp. 288–305, reprinted with brief revisions in idem., *Alcuin and Charlemagne* (2nd edn, New York, 1968), pp. 198–226. See Herrad Spilling, 'Die Entstehung der karolingischen Minuskel', in *794: Karl der Große in Frankfurt am Main* (Sigmaringen, 1994), p. 53.

77. Hariulf, ed. F. Lot, *Chronique de l'abbaye de Saint-Riquier* (Paris, 1894); Bernhard Bischoff, 'Manuscripts in the Age of Charlemagne', in idem., *Manuscripts and Libraries in the Age of Charlemagne*, trans. M. M. Gorman (Cambridge, 1994), pp. 20–55, at pp. 26–7; German original in *KdG*, 2, pp. 233–54.

78. Edmund Bishop, 'Angilbert's Ritual Order for Saint-Riquier', in his *Liturgica Historica* (Oxford, 1918), pp. 314–32; for an attempted reconstruction see Susan A. Rabe, *Faith, Art and Politics at Saint-Riquier* (Philadelphia, 1995), pp. 111–37.

79. David Ganz, *Corbie in the Carolingian Renaissance* (Sigmaringen, 1990), pp. 36–56, 132–41, 158.

80. Bischoff, *Manuscripts and Libraries* (note 77 above), pp. 36–7.

81. Wolfgang Erdmann and Alfons Zettler, 'Zur karolingischen und ottonischen Baugeschichte des Marienmünsters zu Reichenau-Mittelzell', in Helmut Maurer (ed.), *Die Abtei Reichenau* (Singmaringen, 1974), pp. 481–522.

82. On aristocratic lay literacy in the Visigothic period see Roger Collins, 'Literacy and the Laity in Early Medieval Spain', in McKitterick (ed.), *Uses of Literacy* (note 5 above), pp. 109–33.

83. Ian Wood, 'Administration, Law and Culture in Merovingian Gaul', *ibid.*, pp. 63–82; David Ganz, 'Bureaucratic Shorthand and Merovingian Learning', in Patrick Wormald, Donald Bullough and Roger Collins (eds), *Ideal and Reality in Frankish and Anglo-Saxon Society* (Oxford, 1983), pp. 58–75.

84. Michael M. Gorman, 'The Encyclopedic Commentary Prepared for Charlemagne by Wigbod', *Recherches Augustiniennes*, 17 (1982), pp. 173–201, who suggests that Wigbod was using the library of Lorsch, but contrary to his argument, Augustine's *De Genesi ad litteram* does seem to have been available there.

85. John Marenbon, *From the Circle of Alcuin to the School of Auxerre* (Cambridge, 1981), pp. 30–9 on its philosophical learning. See in general John J. Contreni, 'The Carolingian Renaissance: Education and Literary Culture', *NCMH*, pp. 709–57, especially pp. 747–57.

86. *Vita Karoli*, 32, ed. Halphen, p. 88; ARF s.a. 807, ed. Kurze, p. 123.

87. Donald Bullough, *The Age of Charlemagne* (2nd edn, London, 1973), pp. 99–130.

88. *Vita Karoli*, ch. 25, ed. Halphen, p. 74.

89. C. J. B. Gaskoin, *Alcuin* (Cambridge, 1904), pp. 128–32.
90. Bullough, '*Aula Renovata*' (note 10 above).

8 Frankfurt and Aachen, 792–4

1. Einhard, *Vita Karoli*, 20, ed. Halphen, p. 62: whether his deformity turned Charles against him or whether Einhard is making his appearance fit his crime cannot be known; *Annales Laureshamenses*, ed. Georg Pertz, *MGH SS*, 1, p. 35.
2. *Codex Carolinus*, ed. W. Gundlach, *MGH Epp.*, III, no. 45, pp. 560–3.
3. On Charles and his family see Janet Nelson, 'La famille de Charlemagne', *Byzantion*, 61 (1991), pp. 194–212.
4. Rev. s.a. 792, ed. Kurze, pp. 91, 93; Einhard, *Vita Karoli*, 20, ed. Halphen, p. 62.
5. See Matthias Becher, *Eid und Herrschaft. Untersuchungen zum Herrscherethos Karls des Großen* (Sigmaringen, 1993), pp. 78–87 and 195–201.
6. Ed. Boretius, item 23, clause 18, p. 63. Clause 24 of this text consists of the tantalisingly opaque phrase 'Concerning shoes in the Roman fashion'!
7. Ed. Boretius, item 25, clauses 1 and 2, p. 66.
8. Alf Uddholm (ed.), *Marculfi Formularum Libri Duo* (Uppsala, 1962); Becher, *Eid und Herrschaft* (note 5 above), pp. 88–144.
9. For this procedure and for the legitimate reasons for which a vassal could withdraw from his obligations to his lord see Boretius, item 104, clause 8, p. 215. F. L. Ganshof, *Feudalism*, trans. Philip Grierson (3rd edn, London, 1964), pp. 20–50; cf. Susan Reynolds, *Fiefs and Vassals* (Oxford, 1994), pp. 17–47.
10. ARF and Rev. (especially the latter) s.a. 792, ed. Kurze, pp. 90–1; the Lorsch annalist, like all of the authors of the minor annals, did not find this worthy of being recorded. For an overview of this controversy see Wilhelm Heil, 'Der Adoptionismus, Alkuin und Spanien', in Bernhard Bischoff (ed.), *KdG*, II (Düsseldorf, 1965), pp. 95–154. The best treatment of the origins and nature of the theology itself is that of John C. Cavadini, *The Last Christology of the West: Adoptionism in Spain and Gaul, 785–820* (Philadelphia, 1993), which shows how Alcuin and the Frankish bishops misunderstood it. See also David Ganz, 'Theology and the Organisation of Thought', in *NCMH*, pp. 758–85, especially pp. 762–6.
11. Philip Grierson, 'Money and Coinage under Charlemagne', in W. Braunfels (ed.), *KdG*, 1, pp. 501–36; more generally there is Mark Blackburn, 'Money and Coinage', in *NCMH*, pp. 538–59.
12. Ingeborg Huld-Zetsche, *NIDA – Eine römische Stadt in Frankfurt am Main* (Stuttgart, 1994); E. Orth, 'Frankfurt am Main im Früh- und Hochmittelalter', in *Frankfurt am Main. Die Geschichte der Stadt* (2nd edn, Sigmaringen, 1994), pp. 1–10.
13. *Ausgrabungen im Bartholomeuskirche zu Frankfurt am Main* (Frankfurt am Main, 1996).
14. *Annales Laureshamenses* s.a. 794, ed. Georg Pertz, *MGH SS*, 1, p. 36 for Paulinus and Peter; ARF and Rev. s.a. 794, ed. Kurze, pp. 94–5.

15. *Epistola Karoli Magni ad Elipandum*, ed. A Werminghoff, *MGH Concilia*, II, pt 1, p. 159. Liutpold Wallach, *Alcuin and Charlemagne*, p. 166 argues that Alcuin was the only cleric from Britain present, but this is not the sense of the text. See J. M. Wallace-Hadrill, *Early Germanic Kingship* (Oxford, 1971), p. 118.

16. Ed. Boretius, item 28, clauses 4 and 5, p. 74.

17. H. B. Meyer, 'Zur Stellung Alkuins auf dem Frankfurter Konzil', *Zeitschrift für katholische Theologie*, 81 (1959), pp. 455–60. Why Alcuin never rose up the ecclesiastical hierarchy, other than becoming lay (i.e. non-monastic) abbot of St Martin's Tours in 796, is not known.

18. P. Jaffé, *Regesta Pontificum Romanorum* (2 vols, Leipzig, 1885), no. 2479 (dated to the period 785 to 791).

19. Donald Bullough, 'Alcuin and the Kingdom of Heaven', in Uta-Renate Blumenthal (ed.), *Carolingian Essays* (Washington, DC, 1983, pp. 1–69 at p. 39; *Admonitio Generalis*, clause 82, ed. Boretius, p. 61.

20. Alcuin (ep. 208, ed. Dümmler, p. 346) subsequently referred to about 20,000 laymen and clerics, including bishops, being brought back into the fold of orthodoxy around the Spanish march, but the nature of the theological argument was such that it is hard to believe they were conscious adherents of a sect. The commission to which Alcuin referred was really sent to ensure that only orthodox Christological beliefs were being expounded.

21. H.-X. Arquillière, *L'Augustinisme politique* (2nd edn, Paris, 1972), pp. 156–69.

22. Cavadini, *Last Christology* (note 10 above), pp. 24–44.

23. Ibid., pp. 38–45.

24. Ed. Boretius, nos 21 and 25, pp. 51–2 and 66–7; for re-dating of these to 792/3 see F. L. Ganshof, 'Note sur deux capitulaires non datés de Charlemagne', in *Miscellanea historica in honorem Leonis van der Essen* (Brussels, 1947), I, pp. 123–33.

25. W. Levison, *England and the Continent in the Eighth Century* (Oxford, 1946), appendix XI, pp. 314–23. Alcuin, epp. 200–208, ed. Dümmler, pp. 330–46.

26. Gary B. Blumenshine (ed.), *Liber Alcuini contra haeresim Felicis* (Vatican City, 1980). On the manuscript, MS Paris B. N. lat. 1572 see also Bullough, 'Alcuin and the Kingdom of Heaven' (note 19 above), pp. 49–50.

27. *PL* 99, cc. 343–468; on this see Levison, *England and the Continent* (note 25 above), p. 156 and Bullough, 'Alcuin and the Kingdom of Heaven' (note 19 above), p. 51 and n. 117.

28. André Grabar, *L'Iconoclasme byzantin* (2nd edn, Paris, 1984); Ernst Kitzinger, 'The Cult of Images in the Age before Iconoclasm', in idem., *The Art of Byzantium and the Medieval West* (Bloomington and London, 1976), pp. 90–156; Robin Cormack, *Writing in Gold: Byzantine Society and its Icons* (London, 1985), chs 3 and 4.

29. Warren Treadgold, *The Byzantine Revival 780–842* (Stanford, 1988), pp. 75–89, but cf. Mark Whittow, *The Making of Orthodox Byzantium, 600–1025* (Basingstoke, 1996), pp. 149–50.

30. The ruins of the church in which the council of 787 was held may still be seen in Iznik (Nicaea) in Turkey; the site of the 325 council now lies below a lake. See N. H. Baynes, *Constantine the Great and the Christian Church* (2nd edn, London, 1972), especially p. 21.

31. *LP: Vita Hadriani*, 88, ed. Louis Duchesne, *Le 'Liber Pontificalis'* (2nd edn, 3 vols, Paris, 1955), 1, pp. 511–12; trans. Davis, p. 168.

32. On this period see Whittow, *Orthodox Byzantium* (note 29 above), pp. 150–6.
33. *Opus Caroli Regis contra synodum (Libri Carolini)*, ed. A. Freeman, *MGH Concilia 2, supplementum I*, replacing the older edition by Hubert Bastgen, *MGH Concilia 2, supplementum* of 1924.
34. *Opus Inlustrissimi et Excellentissimi seu Spectabilis Viri Caroli ... contra synodum que in partibus Graetiae pro adorandis imaginibus stolide sive arroganter gesta est.* Walter Berschin, *Greek Letters and the Latin Middle Ages*, trans. Jerold C. Frakes (Washington, DC, 1988), pp. 111–13.
35. Ann Freeman, 'Theodulf of Orleans and the *Libri Carolini*', *Speculum*, 32 (1957), pp. 663–705; 'Further Studies in the *Libri Carolini*', *Speculum*, 40 (1965), pp. 203–89; 'Further Studies in the *Libri Carolini*, III: the Marginal Notes in Vaticanus Latinus 7207', *Speculum*, 46 (1971), pp. 597–612 on Theodulf's authorship; Luitpold Wallach, *Diplomatic Studies in Latin and Greek Documents from the Carolingian Age* (Ithaca and London, 1977), pp. 161–294 argues for Alcuinian authorship; Paul J. Meyvaert, 'The Authorship of the "Libri Carolini". Observations prompted by a recent book', *Revue Bénédictine*, 89 (1979), pp. 29–57, reviewing the entire controversy and favouring the case for Theodulf.
36. J. M. Wallace-Hadrill, *The Frankish Church* (Oxford, 1983), pp. 217–25.
37. For arguments based on this presupposition see Ann Freeman, 'Theodulf of Orleans: a Visigoth at Charlemagne's Court', in J. Fontaine and C. Pellistrandi (eds), *L'Europe héritière de l'Espagne wisigothique* (Madrid, 1992), pp. 185–94.
38. Council of Frankfurt: item 28, cl. 2, ed. Boretius, p. 73; trans. King, *Charlemagne*, p. 224.
39. Ann Freeman, 'Carolingian Orthodoxy and the Fate of the Libri Carolini', *Viator*, 16 (1985), pp. 65–108.
40. E. Ewig, 'Résidence et capitale pendant le haut môyen age', *Revue Historique*, 230 (1963), pp. 25–72; cf. Carlrichard Brühl, 'Remarques sur les notions de "capitale" et de "résidence" pendant le haut môyen age', *Journal des Savants* (1967), pp. 193–215.
41. Adolf Gauert, 'Zur Struktur und Topographie der Königspfalzen', in *Deutsche Königspfalzen. Beiträge zu ihrer historischen und archäologischen Erforschung*, 2 (Göttingen, 1965), pp. 1–60; and the articles in Franz Staab (ed.), *Die Pfalz* (Speyer, 1990).
42. ARF and Rev. s.a. 787, ed. Kurze, pp. 80–1. Charles was also resident there in 774 (ibid., p. 40), and it was the site of his 807 assembly (*Chronicle of Moissac*, ed. Pertz, *MGH SS*, 1. p. 309).
43. K. J. Conant, *Carolingian and Romanesque Architecture* (2nd edn, Harmondsworth, 1966), pp. 51–3; R. Krautheimer, *Rome. Profile of a City, 312–1308* (Princeton, 1980), pp. 33–58.
44. C. Rauch and H. J. Jacobi, *Ausgrabungen in der Königspflaz Ingelheim 1909–1914* (Mainz, 1976). New excavations are currently being undertaken on this site.
45. See Ernst Günther Grimme, *Der Dom zu Aachen. Arkitektur und Ausstattung* (Aachen, 1994) for the history of the building and its contents.
46. Leo Hugot, *Aachen Cathedral* (English trans. Aachen, 1988), p. 29; Grimme, *Der Dom zu Aachen* (note 45 above), pp. 52–5.
47. Ludwig Falkenstein, *Der 'Lateran' der karolingischen Pfalz zu Aachen* (Cologne-Graz, 1962), pp. 32–91.

48. L. Hugot, 'Die Pfalz Karls des Grossen in Aachen', in W. Braunfels and H. Schnitzler (eds), *KdG*, 2 (Düsseldorf, 1965), pp. 534–72; also Conant, *Carolingian Architecture*, pp. 46–51.

49. J. Hubert, J. Porcher and W. F. Volbach, *Carolingian Art* (London, 1970), pp. 45–7, which also mentions a presumed palace site at Geneva, discovered in 1953, of similar plan if on a smaller scale to that of Ingelheim.

50. On this building and excavations around it see *Trier. Kaiserresidenz und Bischofssitz* (Mainz, 1984), pp. 139–61.

51. On Late Roman ceremonial see Otto Treitinger, *Die oströmische Kaiser- und Reichsidee nach ihrer Gestaltung im höfischen Zeremoniell* (Jena, 1938; reprinted Darmstadt, 1956).

52. *Vita Karoli* 23, ed. Halphen, p. 70.

53. Janet L. Nelson, 'The Lord's Anointed and the People's Choice: Carolingian Royal Ritual' in David Cannadine and Simon Price (eds), *Rituals of Royalty* (Cambridge, 1987), pp. 137–80; reprinted in eadem., *The Frankish World 750–900* (London, 1996), pp. 99–131.

54. Jörg Jarnut, 'Die frühmittelalterliche Jagd unter rechts- und sozialgeschichtlichen Aspekten', *Settimane*, 31 (1985), pp. 765–808.

55. M. Balzer, 'Paderborn als karolingischer Pfalzort', *Deutsche Königspfalzen*, 3 (1979), pp. 9–85.

56. M. Balzer, *Die karolingische und die ottonisch-salische Königspfalz in Paderborn. Ein Kurzführer durch das Museum in der Kaiserpfalz* (3rd edn, 1984).

57. *Annales Petaviani* and *Annales Mosellani* s.a. 776 and 777, ed. Georg Pertz, *MGH SS*, 1, pp. 16 and 496; cf. ARF and Rev s.a. 777, ed. Kurze, pp. 48–9. See Karl Hauck, 'Paderborn, das Zentrum von Karls Sachsen-Mission 777' in J. Fleckenstein and K. Schmid (eds), *Adel und Kirche* (Freiburg, Basel, Vienna, 1968), pp. 92–140.

58. Karl Hauck, 'Karl als neuer Konstantin 777. Die archäologischen Entdeckungen in Paderborn in historischer Sicht', *FS*, 20 (1986), pp. 513–40.

9   The Imperial Coronation of 800, and its Aftermath

1. ARF and Rev, ed. Kurze, pp. 98–9, enter this in the annal for 796; *LP: Hadrian I* 97, ed. Louis Duchesne, *Le 'Liber Pontificalis'* (2nd edn, 3 vols, Paris, 1955), 1, p. 514, dates his burial to 26 December (795).

2. *Vita Karoli*, 19, ed. Halphen, p. 60.

3. See T. F. X. Noble, *The Republic of St. Peter: the Birth of the Papal State, 680–825* (Philadelphia, 1984), pp. 138–83.

4. *LP: Leo III*, 1, ed. Duchesne (note 1 above), 2, p. 1; Noble, *Republic of St. Peter*, pp. 198–9.

5. Noble, *Republic of St. Peter*, p. 226; L. Duchesne, *The Beginnings of the Temporal Sovereignty of the Popes* (London, 1908), p. 63.

6. Alcuin, ep. 159, ed. Dümmler p. 258. In this letter Alcuin also referred to Arn's previous description of the new pope's 'religious way of life' and his justice.

7. *LP: Leo III*, 12, ed. Duchesne (note 1 above), 2, pp. 4–5; trans. R. Davis, *Lives of the Eighth-Century Popes* (Liverpool, 1992), pp. 184–6.

8. Rev. s.a. 799, ed. Kurze, p. 107, which adds that he was lowered from the walls of the city by night, implying that Rome was in the hands of Leo's opponents.

9. *LP: Leo III*, 14–15, ed. Duchesne (note 1 above), 2, p. 5.

10. On the Laurentian schism see Jeffrey Richards, *The Popes and the Papacy in the Early Middle Ages, 476–752* (London, 1979), pp. 69–99; John Moorhead, *Theoderic in Italy* (Oxford, 1992), pp. 114–39.

11. Alcuin, ep. 174, ed. Dümmler, pp. 287–89.

12. Alcuin, epp. 177 and 178, ed. Dümmler, pp. 292–5, seem to suggest that Charles was contemplating an expedition to Rome himself in July 799.

13. R.-J. Loenertz, '*Actus Silvestri*. Genèse d'une légende', *Revue d'Histoire Ecclesiastique*, 70 (1975), pp. 426–39. The only extant manuscript of these Symmachan forgeries is Paris BN lat. 3836 (C.L.A., vol. 5, no. 554), written in late 8th century 'Corbie' a-b script, which may well be the very one that Alcuin had read.

14. Alcuin, epp. 179 and 184, ed. Dümmler, pp. 296–7 and 308–10.

15. Rev. s.a. 799, ed. Kurze, p. 107; *LP: Leo III* 16, ed. Duchesne (note 1 above), 2, pp. 5–6.

16. *LP: Leo III*, 17, ibid., 2, p. 6.

17. Alcuin, ep. 184, ed. Dümmler, p. 309.

18. See H. Beumann, 'Nomen Imperatoris. Studien zur Kaiseridee Karls des Grossen', *Historische Zeitschrift*, 185 (1958), pp. 515–49.

19. Ammianus Marcellinus, XX.iv. 14–18; Julian of Toledo, *Historia Wambae*, 2, ed. Wilhelm Levison, *MGH SRM*, 5, pp. 501–2.

20. F. Homes Dudden, *Gregory the Great. His Place in History and Thought* (2 vols, London, 1905), 1, p. 221 and n. 3.

21. ARF and Rev. s.a. 801, ed. Kurze, pp. 112–13; *Annales Laureshamenses* s.a. 800, ed. Georg Pertz, *MGH SS*, 1, p. 38.

22. Diploma no. 191, ed. Tangl, p. 191; ARF s.a. 800, ed. Kurze, p. 110.

23. ARF s.a. 792 and 796; Rev. s.a. 796, ed. Kurze, pp. 90 and 98–9.

24. Diploma no. 192, ed. Tangl, p. 192, was issued at Tours on 2 June; ARF s.a. 800, ed. Kurze, p. 110.

25. ARF s.a. 800, ed. Kurze, p. 110; on the significance of the twelfth milestone see J. Déer, 'Die Vorrechte der Kaisers in Rom', *Schweizer Beiträge für allgemeinen Geschichte*, 15 (1957), pp. 5–63; also Robert Folz, *Le Couronnement impérial de Charlemagne* (Paris, 1964); English trans. *The Coronation of Charlemagne* (London, 1974), pp. 135–6.

26. Sabine MacCormack, *Art and Ceremony in Late Antiquity* (Berkeley, 1981), pp. 17–89.

27. ARF s.a. 800, ed. Kurze, pp. 110, 112.

28. For arguments over the text of the oath see H. Adelson and R. Baker, 'The Oath of Purgation of Pope Leo III in 800', *Traditio*, 8 (1952), pp. 35–80, and L. Wallach, 'The Genuine and Forged Oath of Pope Leo III', *Traditio*, 11 (1955), pp. 37–63.

29. ARF s.a. 801, ed. Kurze, p. 114; *LP: Leo III*, 26, ed. Duchesne (note 1 above), 2, p. 8.

30. This is most fully argued in A. Grabois, 'Charlemagne, Rome and Jerusalem', *Revue belge de philologie et d'histoire*, 59 (1981), pp. 792–809.

31. *Annales Laureshamenses* s.a. 800, ed. Pertz, p. 38.

32. Lawrence Nees, *A Tainted Mantle: Hercules and the Classical Tradition in the Carolingian Court* (Philadelphia, 1991), pp. 3–17.

33. Ibid., pp. 110–43.

34. Peter Godman (ed.), *Alcuin: the Bishops, Kings and Saints of York* (Oxford, 1982), pp. lxxii–iii.

35. Henry Mayr-Harting, 'Charlemagne, the Saxons and the Imperial Coronation of 800', *English Historical Review*, 111 (1996), pp. 1113–33.

36. Warren Treadgold, *The Byzantine Revival 780–842* (Stanford, 1988), pp. 60–126; S. Runciman, 'The Empress Irene the Athenian', in Derek Baker (ed.), *Medieval Women (Studies in Church History, Subsidia*, 1, 1978), pp. 101–18.

37. P. E. Schramm, 'Die Anerkennung Karls des Grossen als Kaiser', *Historische Zeitschrift*, 172 (1951), pp. 449–515.

38. Peter Classen, *Karl der Grosse, das Papsttum und Byzanz* (Sigmaringen, 1988), pp. 62–80. The dubious text is W. Kurze (ed.), *Codex Diplomaticus Amiatinus* (Rome, 1874), item 49.

39. ARF s.a. 813, ed. Kurze, p. 138; Thegan, *Vita Hludowici Imperatoris*, 6, ed. Ernst Tremp, *MGH SRG*, 64, pp. 180–4. This probably took place on 11 September.

40. F. L. Ganshof, 'Some Observations on the *Ordinatio Imperii* of 817', in idem., *The Carolingians and the Frankish Monarchy* (London, 1971), pp. 273–88.

41. Herwig Wolfram, *Intitulatio I: Lateinische Königs- und Fürstentitel bis zum Ende des 8. Jahrhunderts, MIöG*, Ergänzungsband 21 (1967), pp. 217–24.

42. ARF s.a. 801, ed. Kurze, pp. 114, 116.

43. Helmut Beumann, 'Nomen imperatoris: Studien zur Kaiseridee Karls des Großen', *Historische Zeitschrift*, 185 (1958), pp. 515–49; Herwig Wolfram, *Intitulatio 2: Lateinische Herrscher- und Fürstentitel im neunten und zehnten Jahrhundert (MIöG*, Ergänzungsband 24, 1973), pp. 19–58.

44. Peter Classen, '*Romanum gubernans Imperium*. Zur Vorgeschichte der Kaisertitular Karls des Großen', *DA*, 9 (1951), pp. 103–21.

45. For example, the preface to the *Divisio Regni* of 806, ed. Boretius, item 45, p. 126. In such contexts he also used his title of *Rex Langobardorum*.

46. Charles's letter to Michael I, ed. Ernst Dümmler, *MGH Epp. IV*, p. 556; Folz, *Couronnment impérial* (note 25 above), pp. 193–208 = *Coronation of Charlemagne*, pp. 164–74 for Charles's imperial status and Byzantium.

47. For the Visigothic equivalent, expressed in the 'Laus Spaniae' prologue to Isidore of Seville's *Historia Gothorum* (625/6), ed. Cristobal Rodríguez Alonso, *Las Historias de los Godos, Vándalos y Suevos de Isidoro de Sevilla* (León, 1975), pp. 168–70; see Suzanne Teillet, *Des Goths à la nation gothique* (Paris, 1984), pp. 463–502.

48. K. A. Eckhardt (ed.), *Lex Salica: 100 Titel-Text* (Weimar, 1953), prologue, pp. 88–90.

49. Alcuin, letters 177, 185, 200, 234, 245, ed. Dümmler, *MGH Epp.*, IV, pp. 292, 310, 331, 379, 397.

50. Judith McClure, 'Bede's Old Testament Kings', in Patrick Wormald, Donald Bullough and Roger Collins (eds), *Ideal and Reality in Frankish and Anglo-Saxon Society* (Oxford, 1983), pp. 76–98.

51. Otto Treitinger, *Die oströmische Kaiser und Reichsidee* (Jena, 1938).

52. On these diplomatic exchanges see M. Borgolte, *Der Gesandtenaustausch der Karolinger mit den Abbasiden und mit den Patriarchen von Jerusalem* (Munich, 1976).

53. It is very well reproduced as the *Amir al Mumminin* of ARF s.a. 801, ed. Kurze, p. 114.

54. It has been suggested that the unusually realistic depiction of elephants in such ninth-century manuscripts as the Physiologus, MS Bern Burgerbibliothek 318, ff. 7r-22v, derived from the presence at the Carolingian court for nearly a decade of this living example.

55. Grabois, 'Charlemagne, Rome and Jerusalem' (note 30 above), pp. 805–6.

56. ARF s.a. 812, ed. Kurze, p. 136; Theophanes, *Chronographia* s.a. 6304, ed. de Boor, p. 494.

57. Sabine G. MacCormack, *Art and Ceremony in Late Antiquity* (Berkeley, 1981), pp. 222–66.

58. Einhard, *Vita Karoli* 29, ed. Holder-Egger, p. 33.

59. They relate to what Einhard read in Suetonius's *Vita Augusti*, 84–9, describing Augustus's literary and philological interests and quirks.

60. Ed. Boretius, item 33, pp. 91–9. This only survives in one manuscript: MS Paris BN lat. 4613, and the text is partly corrupt.

61. Boretius, item 34, pp. 99–102, printing texts from four manuscripts; also W. A. Eckhardt, 'Die Capitularia missorum specialia von 802', *DA*, 12 (1956), pp. 498–516, which prints another text, thought to be that for the *missi* sent to Aquitaine.

62. F. L. Ganshof, *Recherches sur les Capitulaires* (Paris, 1958), pp. 55–65 and 76–85; Hubert Mordek, 'Karolingische Kapitularien', in Raymund Kottje and Hubert Mordek (eds), *Überlieferung und Geltung normativer Texte des frühen und hohen Mittelalters* (Sigmaringen, 1986), pp. 25–50.

63. Boretius, item 34, pp. 101–2.

64. Boretius, item 33, clauses 3 to 9, pp. 92–3; trans. King, p. 234.

65. J. M. Wallace-Hadrill, 'The Bloodfeud of the Franks', *Bulletin of the John Rylands Library*, 41 (1959), reprinted in idem., *The Long-haired Kings* (London, 1962), pp. 121–47.

66. Capitularies nos 35 clause 47, 44 clause 9, 46 clause 2 etc., ed. Boretius, pp. 104, 124, 131.

67. F. L. Ganshof, 'Charlemagne's Programme of Imperial Government', in idem., *The Carolingians and the Frankish Monarchy* (London, 1971), pp. 55–85.

68. Alcuin, letter 217, ed. Dümmler, pp. 360–1.

69. *Liber Pontificalis: Leo III*, ch. 24, ed. Duchesne, 2, pp. 7–8.

70. *Annales Sancti Amandi* s.a. 790, ed. Georg Pertz, *MGH SS*, 1, p. 12; *Annales Mettenses Priores* s.a. 789, ed. B. de Simson, *MGH SRG*, 10, p. 77; the silence on this of ARF/Rev. is noteworthy, and indicative of later dates of composition, perhaps following the death of the younger Charles in 811.

71. Ed. Boretius, item 45, pp. 126–30.

72. Peter Classen, 'Karl der Grosse und die Thronfolge im Frankenreich', in *Festschrift für Hermann Heimpel* (Göttingen, 1972), 2, pp. 109–34.

73. ARF s.a. 812 and 813, ed. Kurze, pp. 136–8; Bernard's kingdom did not include Bavaria.

74. Folz, *Couronnement impérial* (note 25 above), pp. 211–42 = *Coronation of Charlemagne*, pp. 181–208; idem., *L'idée d'empire en Occident du Ve au XIVe siècle* (Paris, 1953), pp. 25–46.

75. *Vita Karoli*, 33, ed. Halphen, pp. 92–102; cf. Suetonius, *De Vita Caeasarum*, ed. J. C. Rolfe (2 vols, London and Cambridge, Mass., 1913): *Divus Augustus*, 101, vol. 1, pp. 284–6.

76. Cf. Antoni Udina I Abelló, *La successió testada a la Catalunya altomedieval* (Barcelona, 1984).
77. Ulrich Nonn, 'Merowingische Testamente', in *Die Franken. Wegbereiter Europas* 1 (Mainz, 1996), pp. 505–8, and p. 9 above.
78. Thus, on the supposed dispersal of his library, see Bernhard Bischoff, 'The Court Library under Louis the Pious', in idem., *Manuscripts and Libraries in the Age of Charlemagne* (Cambridge, 1994), pp. 76–92.

10 Frontiers and Wars, 793–813

1. *Vita Lebuini Antiqua* 4, in H. Wolfram *et al.*, *Quellen zur Geschichte des 7. und 8. Jahrhunderts* (Darmstadt, 1982), p. 386.
2. *Annales Laureshamenses* s.a. 795, ed. Georg Pertz, *MGH SS*, 1, p. 36.
3. Rev. s.a. 793; cf. ARF s.a. 793 (ed. Kurze, pp. 93–4), which says they had broken faith. Other annals make no mention of this at all.
4. ARF and Rev. s.a. 794, ed. Kurze, pp. 94–7; *Annales Laureshamenses* s.a. 794, ed. Pertz (note 2 above), p. 36, adds that Charles gave priests to the Saxons following their submission, suggesting an intensification of the presence of the Frankish church in Saxony.
5. ARF s.a. 795, ed. Kurze, p. 96.
6. ARF and Rev. s.a. 789, ed. Kurze, pp. 84–7. This campaign may have been necessitated by raids by the Wiltzi on the upper Elbe and Ohre valleys. They were said by the Reviser to be 'always hostile to the Franks and towards their neighbours'.
7. *Annales Laureshamenses* s.a. 795, ed. Pertz, p. 36.
8. Rev. s.a. 795, trans. King, p. 126.
9. Rev. s.a. 795, ed. Kurze, p. 97; cf. ARF.
10. *Annales Laureshamenses* s.a. 796, ed. Pertz, p. 37; ARF and Rev. s.a. 796, ed. Kurze, pp. 98–100.
11. ARF and Rev. s.a. 797, ed. Kurze, pp. 100–3; *Annales Laureshamenses* s.a. 797, ed. Pertz, p. 37.
12. Ibid.
13. ARF and Rev. s.a. 798, ed. Kurze, pp. 102–5.
14. *Helmoldi Presbyteri Bozoviensis Cronica Slavorum*, ed. J. M. Lappenberg, *MGH SRG*, pp. 112, 120, 134, etc.
15. *Annales Laureshamenses* s.a. 798, ed. Pertz, p. 37.
16. On the other hand, Henry Mayr-Harting, 'Charlemagne, the Saxons and the Imperial Coronation of 800', *English Historical Review*, 111 (1996), pp. 1113–33, argues that it was the need to 'validate and make acceptable his rule of the Saxon aristocracy' (p. 1113) that led Charles into seeking an imperial title.
17. ARF and Rev. s.a. 799, ed. Kurze, pp. 106–7: the Franks in 799 seem to have been involved in negotiations between their allies the Abodrites and the latter's traditional enemies the Wiltzi.
18. ARF s.a. 802, ed. Kurze, p. 117.
19. *Annales Laureshamenses* s.a. 799, ed. Pertz, p. 38. While this source does not specify the legal status of these Saxons, only those rendered servile could have been thus treated.

20. *Chron. Moissac*, s.a. 802, ed. Georg Pertz, *MGH SS*, 1, pp. 306–7; trans. King, p. 146. Wihmodia, with its two sub-divisions, was Saxon land: see *ARF* s.a. 804, ed. Kurze, p. 118.

21. For example, ARF s.a. 808, 809, ed. Kurze, pp. 125, 128–9, etc.

22. *Annales Mettenses Priores* s.a. 804, ed. B. de Simson, *MGH SRG*, p. 91.

23. Raimund Ernst, *Die Nordwestslaven und das fränkische Reich* (Berlin, 1976), pp. 138–54.

24. Alcuin, ep. 6, ed. Dümmler, p. 31.

25. ARF s.a. 798, ed. Kurze, p. 104.

26. ARF s.a. 805 and 806, ed. Kurze, pp. 120, 122; *Chronicle of Moissac*, s.a. 805, ed. Pertz, pp. 307–8. On these campaigns see Charles R. Bowlus, *Franks, Moravians and Magyars. The Struggle for the Middle Danube, 788–907* (Philadelphia, 1995), pp. 58–60.

27. H. H. Andersen, 'Kongegrave', *Skalk* (1985); L. Hedeager, *Iron-Age Societies* (Oxford, 1992), pp. 242–55.

28. David M. Wilson, *Civil and Military Engineering in Viking Age Scandinavia* (Paul Johnstone Lecture: 1978).

29. Henrik M. Jensen, 'The Archaeology of Danish Commercial Centres', in Calvin B. Kendall and Peter S. Wells (eds), *Voyage to the Other World: The Legacy of Sutton Hoo* (Minneapolis, 1992), pp. 171–82; Lotte Hedeager, 'Kingdoms, Ethnicity and Material Culture: Denmark in a European Perspective', in Martin Carver (ed.), *The Age of Sutton Hoo* (Woodbridge, 1992), pp. 279–300. See in general Niels Lund, 'Scandinavia, c. 700–1066', in *NCMH*, pp. 202–27.

30. J. Hines, 'The Scandinavian Character of Anglian England: An Update', in Carver (ed.), *Age of Sutton Hoo* (note 29 above), pp. 315–29; cf. James Campbell, 'The Impact of the Sutton Hoo Discovery on the Study of Anglo-Saxon History', in Kendall and Wells (note 29 above), pp. 79–101.

31. Gregory of Tours, *Libri Historiarum*, III.3, ed. Bruno Krusch and Wilhelm Levison, *MGH SRM* 1 (rev. edn), p. 99.

32. Rev. s.a. 782 and 777, ed. Kurze, pp. 61 and 49.

33. W. Levison, *England and the Continent in the Eighth Century* (Oxford, 1946), p. 110.

34. Anskar's *Miracula Willehadi*, ed. G. Pertz, *MGH SS*, 2, pp. 379–84; anon., *Vita Willehadi*, pp. 384–90. See Ian Wood, 'Christians and Pagans in Ninth-century Scandinavia', in B. Sawyer *et al.* (eds), *The Christianisation of Scandinavia* (Alingsås, 1987), pp. 36–67.

35. Alcuin, ep. 6, ed. Dümmler, p. 31.

36. Alcuin, epp. 107 and 111, ed. Dümmler, pp. 153–4, 159–62; see also Peter Cramer, *Baptism and Change in the Early Middle Ages c. 200–c. 1150* (Cambridge, 1993), pp. 185–7.

37. *Magistri Adam Bremensis Gesta Hammaburgensis Ecclesiae Pontificum*, ed. B. Schmeidler, *MGH SRG* (Hanover and Leipzig, 1917), pp. 17–18. Adam notes that Willeric was also known as Willeharius; two different bishops may be being conflated into one.

38. Rimbert, *Vita Anskari*, ed. G. Waitz, *MGH SRG*, 55, pp. 30–7.

39. Adam of Bremen, ed. Schmeidler (note 37 above), p. 18.

40. Rev. s.a. 800, ed. Kurze, p. 111.

41. ARF s.a. 804, ed. Kurze, pp. 118–19.

42. *ARF* s.a. 808, ed. Kurze, p. 125.

43. *Chronicle of Moissac* s.a. 808, ed. Pertz, p. 308; ARF s.a. 808, ed. Kurze, p. 125.

44. ARF s.a. 808, ed. Kurze, p. 126.

45. See the Orkhon inscriptions: Thomas J. Barfield, *The Perilous Frontier* (Oxford, 1989), pp. 146–50.

46. ARF s.a. 809, ed. Kurze, p. 129.

47. *Chronicle of Moissac* s.a. 809, ed. Pertz, pp. 308–9; for the rest see ARF s.a. 809, ed. Kurze, p. 129.

48. ARF s.a. 809, ed. Kurze, pp. 129–30.

49. Raimund Ernst, *Die Norwestslaven und das fränkische Reich* (Berlin, 1976), pp. 154–74.

50. ARF s.a. 810, ed. Kurze, pp. 131–2.

51. ARF s.a. 811, ed. Kurze, p. 134, where the names of the envoys from both sides are recorded.

52. ARF s.a. 810, ed. Kurze, pp. 131–2; for its recovery see ARF s.a. 811, ed. Kurze, p. 135.

53. Ibid., s.a. 810, pp. 132–3.

54. ARF s.a. 811, ed. Kurze, p. 135.

55. *Annales Bertiniani* s.a. 834, ed. Félix Grat, Jeanne Vielliard and Suzanne Clémencet, *Annales de Saint-Bertin* (Paris, 1964), p. 14.

56. F. L. Ganshof, 'La fin du règne de Charlemagne, une décomposition', *Zeitschrift für schweizerische Geschichte*, 28 (1948), pp. 533–52; translated (by Janet Sondheimer) as 'The Last Period of Charlemagne's Reign; a Study in Decomposition', in F. L. Ganshof, *The Carolingians and the Frankish Monarchy* (London, 1971), pp. 240–55.

57. F. L. Ganshof, 'L'échec de Charlemagne', *Comptes rendues des séances de l'Académie des Inscriptions et Belles Lettres* (Paris, 1947), pp. 248–54; idem., *The Carolingians and the Frankish Monarchy* (London, 1971), pp. 256–60.

58. H. Fichtenau, *Das Karolingische Imperium* (Zurich, 1949); trans. by P. Munz as *The Carolingian Empire* (Oxford, 1957).

59. The 'SS Reichsführer' Heinrich Himmler, who saw himself as a reincarnation of the Saxon king Henry I the Fowler (919–36), was particularly incensed by Charles's slaughter of the Saxons at Werden, and set up a monument to commemorate them. Hitler, on the other hand, saw it as a necessary precondition to the unification of the German people and its acquisition of 'Western culture'. See Albert Speer, *Inside the Third Reich* (London and New York, 1970), pp. 147–48.

60. In part such a view inevitably depends upon the author's perceptions of the ensuing reign of Louis. For this see his 'Louis the Pious Reconsidered', *History*, 42 (1957), pp. 171–80; reprinted in idem., *The Carolingians and the Frankish Monarchy* (London, 1971), pp. 261–72.

61. P. D. King, *Charlemagne* (London, 1986), pp. 45–7.

62. T. Reuter, 'Plunder and Tribute in the Carolingian Empire', *Transactions of the Royal Historical Society*, 5th series, 35 (1985), pp. 75–94.

63. T. Reuter, 'The End of Carolingian Military Expansion', in Godman and Collins, pp. 391–405.

64. Donald Bullough, *The Age of Charlemagne* (2nd edn, London, 1973), p. 195, and P. D. King, *Charlemagne* (London, 1986), p. 46.

65. ARF s.a. 806, 807, 809, 810, 812, 813, ed. Kurze, pp. 120–39. King, *Charlemagne* (note 61 above), pp. 45–6.

66. ARF s.a. 828, ed. Kurze, p. 176.

67. Geoffrey Barraclough, *The Crucible of Europe* (London, 1976), pp. 62–8.

68. Warren Treadgold, *Byzantium and its Army 284–1081* (Stanford, 1995), pp. 44–64, 72–6, 101–5.

69. Warren Treadgold, *The Byzantine Revival 780–842* (Stanford, 1988), pp. 267–327; Mark Whittow, *The Making of Orthodox Byzantium 600–1025* (London, 1996), pp. 165–93.

SELECT BIBLIOGRAPHY

1 Sources

Alcuin, *Epistolae*, ed. Ernst Dümmler, *MGH Epp.*, vol. 4 (1895); see also Colin Chase (ed.), *Two Alcuin Letter-Books* (Toronto, 1975).

Annales Guelfybertani, ed. Georg Heinrich Pertz, *MGH SS*, vol. 1 (1826).

Annales Laureshamenses, ibid.

Annales Mettenses Priores, ed. Bernhard von Simson, *MGH SRG*, vol. 10 (1905).

Annales Mosellani, ed. Georg Heinrich Pertz, *MGH SS*, vol. 1 (1826).

Annales Petaviani, ibid.

Annales Regni Francorum, ed. Friederich Krauze, *MGH SRG*, vol. 6 (1895).

Annales Sancti Amandi, ed. Georg Heinrich Pertz, *MGH SS*, vol. 1 (1826).

Boniface, *Epistolae*, ed. M. Tangl, *MGH Epistolae Selectae*, vol. 1 (1916).

Capitularia Regum Francorum, vol. 1, ed. Alfred Boretius, *MGH Capit.* (1883).

Chartae Latini antiquiores, vols 13–19, ed. Hartmut Atsma *et al.* (Zurich, 1981–7).

Chronicon Moissacense, ed. Georg Heinrich Pertz, *MGH SS*, vol. 1 (1826).

Codex Carolinus, ed. Wilhelm Gundlach, *MGH Epp.*, vol. 3 (1892).

Concilia aevi Karolini (742–842), ed. Albert Werminghoff, *MGH Conc.*, 2 (1906).

Epistolae Karolini aevi, vols 1 and 2, ed. Ernst Dümmler and Wilhelm Gundlach, *MGH Epp.*, vols 3 and 4 (1892 and 1895).

Einhard, *Vita Karoli*, ed. Louis Halphen (Paris, 1938); see also ed. Oswald Holder-Egger, *MGH SRG*, vol. 25 (1911).

Ermoldus Nigellus, *In Honorem Hludowici ... Augusti*, ed. Edmond Faral, *Ermold le Noir: Poème sur Louis le Pieux* (Paris, 1932).

Fredegar: *The Fourth Book of the Chronicle of Fredegar*, ed. J. M. Wallace-Hadrill (London, 1960).

Gesta Sanctorum Patrum Fontanellensis Coenobii, ed. F. Lohier and J. Laporte (Rouen, 1936).

Gesta Episcoporum Mettensium of Paul the Deacon, ed. Georg Heinrich Pertz, *MGH SS*, vol. 2 (1829).

Gregory of Tours, *Historiarum Libri Decem*, ed. Bruno Krusch and Wilhelm Levison, *MGH SRM*, vol. 1 (new edn, 1951).

P. Lauer and C. Samaran (eds), *Les diplômes originaux des Mérovingiennes* (Paris, 1908).

Liber Historiae Francorum, ed. Bruno Krusch, *MGH SRM*, vol. 2 (1888).

Liber Pontificalis, ed. Louis Duchesne (2nd edn, 3 vols, Paris, 1955).

Libri Carolini, ed. Ann Freeman, *MGH Concilia*, vol. 2, *Supplementum* (1996).

J. M. Pardessus (ed.), *Diplomata, Chartae, Epistolae, Leges ad res gallo-francicas spectantia* (2 vols, Paris, 1843).

Poeta Saxo, ed. Paul von Winterfeld, *MGH Poetae*, vol. 4 (1899).

Thegan, *Vita Hludowici Imperatoris*, ed. Ernst Tremp, *MGH SRG*, vol. 64 (1995).
Theodulf of Orléans, *Opera poetica*, ed. Ernst Dümmler, *MGH Poetae*, vol. 1 (1881).
Vita Adalhardi or *Epitaphium Arsenii* of Pascasius Radbertus, *PL*, vol. 120.
Vita Walae of Paschasius Radbertus, *PL*, vol. 120.
Walahfrid Strabo, *Visio Wettini*, ed. Hermann Knittel (Sigmaringen, 1986).

2   English Translations of Sources

Allott Stephen, *Alcuin of York* (York, 1974) – a selection of his letters.
Bachrach, Bernard S., *Liber Historiae Francorum* (Lawrence, KS, 1973).
Cabaniss Allen, *Charlemagne's Cousins: Contemporary Lives of Adalard and Wala* (New York, 1967).
Davis, Raymond, *The Lives of the Eighth-Century Popes (Liber Pontificalis)* (Liverpool, 1992) – extends up to Stephen IV (816–17).
Dutton, Paul Edward, *Carolingian Civilization: A Reader* (Ontario, 1993).
Loyn, H. R. and Percival, John, *The Reign of Charlemagne* (London, 1975).
King, P. D., *Charlemagne: Translated Sources* (Lancaster, 1987).
Scholz, Bernard Walter, *Carolingian Chronicles* (Ann Arbor, MI, 1970) – ARF and Nithard
Thorpe, Lewis, *Einhard and Notker the Stammerer: Two Lives of Charlemagne* (Harmondsworth, 1969).

3   Selected Secondary Literature

Adelson, H. and Baker, R., 'The Oath of Purgation of Pope Leo III in 800', *Traditio*, 8 (1952), pp. 35–80.
Angenendt, Arnold, 'Rex et Sacerdos. Zur Genese der Königssalbung', in Norbert Kamp and Joachim Wollasch (eds), *Tradition als historische Kraft* (Berlin/New York, 1982), pp. 100–18.
Balzaretti, Ross, 'Charlemagne in Italy', *History Today*, 46 (1996), pp. 28–34.
Bachrach, Bernard S., *Armies and Politics in the Early Medieval West* (Aldershot, 1993).
Banniard, Michel, *Viva Voce. Communication écrite et communication orale du IVe au IXe siècle en Occident latin* (Paris, 1992), pp. 305–422.
Becher, Matthias, 'Drogo und die Königserhebung Pippins', *FS*, 23 (1989), pp. 131–53.
Becher, Matthias, 'Neue Uberlieferung zum Geburtsdatum Karls des Grossen', *Francia*, vol. 19 (1992), pp. 37–60.
Becher, Matthias, *Eid und Herrschaft. Untersuchungen zum Herrscherethos Karls des Großen* (Sigmaringen, 1993).
Bertolini, Ottorino, 'Carlomagno e Benevento', *KdG*, vol. 1, pp. 609–701.
Beumann, Helmut, '*Nomen imperatoris. Studien zur Kaiseridee Karls des Großen; Historische Zeitschrift*, vol. 185 (1958), pp. 515–49; reprinted in idem.,

Ideengeschichtliche Studien zu Einhard und anderen Geschichtsschreibern des frühen Mittelalters (Darmstadt, 1962), pp. 80–114.

Beumann, Helmut, Franz Brunhölzl and Wilhelm Winkelmann (eds), *Karolus Magnus et Leo Papa. Ein paderborner Epos vom Jahre 799* (Paderborn, 1966).

Bonnell, Heinrich, Eduard, *Die Anfänge kes karolingischen Hauses* (Munich, 1866).

Borgolte, Michael, *Geschichte der Grafschaften Alemanniens in fränkischer Zeit* (Sigmaringen, 1984).

Bosl, Karl, *Bayerische Geschichte* (Munich, 1976), pp. 30–50.

Boussard, Jacques, *Charlemagne et son temps* (Paris, 1968).

Brown, T. S., *Gentlemen and Officers: Imperial Administration and Aristocratic Power in Byzantine Italy, 554–800 AD* (London, 1984).

Brunhölzl, Franz, *Geschichte der lateinischen Literatur des Mittelalters*, vol. 1 (Munich, 1975).

Buchner, Rudolf, 'Das merowingische Königtum', *Vorträge und Forschungen*, vol. 3: *Das Königtum* (1956), pp. 143–54.

Buckler, F. W., *Harunu'l-Rashid and Charles the Great* (Cambridge, Mass., 1931).

Bullough, Donald, 'The Counties of the *Regnum Italiae* in the Carolingian Period (774–888): a topographical study – I', *Papers of the British School at Rome*, vol. 23 (1955), pp. 148–68.

Bullough, Donald, 'The Dating of Codex Carolinus Nos. 95, 96, 97, Wilchar, and the Beginnings of the Archbishopric of Sens', *DA*, vol. 18 (1962), pp. 223–30.

Bullough, Donald, 'I vescovi di Pavia nei secoli ottavo e nono: fonti e cronologia', in the *Atti del 40 Congresso internazionale di studi sull'alto medioevo* (Spoleto, 1969), pp. 317–28.

Bullough, Donald, '*Europae Pater*: Charlemagne and his Achievement in the Light of Recent Scholarship', *English Historical Review*, vol. 85 (1970), pp. 59–105.

Bullough, Donald, *The Age of Charlemagne* (2nd edn, London, 1973).

Bullough, Donald, 'Alcuin and the Kingdom of Heaven', in Uta-Renate Blumenthal (ed.), *Carolingian Essays* (Washington, DC, 1983), pp. 1–69.

Bullough, Donald, 'Albuinus deliciosus Karoli regis. Alcuin of York and the Shaping of the Early Carolingian Court', in Lutz Fenske *et al.* (eds), *Institutionen, Kultur und Gesellschaft im Mittelalter. Festschrift für Josef Fleckenstein zu seinem 65. Geburtstag* (Sigmaringen, 1984), pp. 73–92.

Bullough, Donald, '*Aula Renovata*. The Carolingian Court before the Aachen Palace', *Proceedings of the British Academy*, vol. 71 (1985), pp. 267–301.

Bullough, Donald, 'Ethnic History and the Carolingians: an Alternative Reading of Paul the Deacon's *Historia Langobardorum*', in C. Holdsworth and T. P. Wiseman (eds), *The Inheritance of Historiography* (Exeter, 1986), pp. 85–105.

Bullough, Donald, *Carolingian Renewal* (Manchester, 1991).

Classen, Peter, 'Romanum gubernans imperium: zur Vorgechichte der Kaisertitular Karls des Großen', *DA*, vol. 9 (1951), pp. 103–21.

Classen, Peter, 'Karl der Grosse und die Thronfolge im Frankenreich', in *Festschrift für Hermann Heimpel*, vol. 2 (Göttingen, 1972), pp. 109–34.

Classen, Peter, 'Der erste Römerzug in der Weltgeschichte', in Helmut Beumann (ed.), *Historische Forschungen für Walter Schlesinger* (Cologne/Vienna, 1974), pp. 325–47.

Classen, Peter, 'Bayern und die politische Mächte im Zeitalter Karls des Grossen und Tassilos III', in Siegfried Haider (ed.), *Die Anfänge des Klosters Kremsmünster* (Linz, 1978), pp. 169–87.

Classen, Peter, *Karl der Große, das Papsttum und Byzanz* (2nd edn, Sigmaringen, 1988).

Collins, Roger, *The Arab Conquest of Spain, 710–797* (Oxford, 1989).

Collins, Roger, 'Pippin I and the Kingdom of Aquitaine', in Peter Godman and Roger Collins (eds), *Charlemagne's Heir: New Approaches to the Reign of Louis the Pious* (Oxford, 1990).

Collins, Roger, *Early Medieval Europe 300–1000* (London, 1991), pp. 260–86.

Collins, Roger, 'Deception and Misrepresentation in Early Eighth-Century Frankish Historiography: Two Case Studies', in Jörg Jarnut *et al.* (eds), *Karl Martell in seiner Zeit* (Sigmaringen, 1994), pp. 227–47.

Collins, Roger, 'The Carolingians and the Ottonians in an Anglophone World', *Journal of Medieval History*, vol. 22 (1996), pp. 97–114.

Collins, Roger, *Fredegar* (Historical and Religious Writers of the Latin West, vol. 13: Aldershot, 1996).

Collins, Roger, 'The Reviser Revisited. Another Look at the Alternative Version of the *Annales Regni Francorum*', in A. C. Murray (ed.), *After Rome's Fall: Narrators and Sources of Early Medieval History* (Toronto, forthcoming).

Constable, Giles, '*Nona et decima*: an Aspect of the Carolingian Economy', *Speculum*, vol. 35 (1960), pp. 224–50.

Constantinescu, Radu, 'Mélanges d'histoire littéraire carolingienne', *Revue Roumaine d'Histoire*, vol. 2 (1970), pp. 221–35.

Cubitt, Catherine, *Anglo-Saxon Church Councils c. 650–c. 850* (Leicester, 1995).

Dannheimer, Hermann, *Auf den Spuren der Bajuwaren. Archäologie des frühen Mittelalters in Altbayern* (Pfaffenhofen, 1987).

Dannheimer, Hermann and Dopsch, Heinz (eds), *Die Bajuwaren von Severin bis Tassilo 488–788* (Munich, 1988).

Déer, Josef, 'Karl der Große und der Untergang des Awarenreiches', *KdG*, vol. 1, pp. 719–89.

Delaruelle, E., 'Charlemagne, Carloman, Didier et la politique du mariage franco-lombard (770–771)', *Revue d'histoire et de l'église de France*, vol. 170 (1932), pp. 213–24.

Depreux, Philippe, *Prosopographie de l'entourage de Louis le Pieux (781–840)* (Sigmaringen, 1997).

Desmulliez, Janine, and Milis, Ludo, *Histoire des provinces françaises du Nord*, vol. 1 (Dunkerque, 1988), pp. 187–244.

Dorr, Robert, 'Beiträge zur Einhardsfrage', *NA*, vol. 10 (1884/5), pp. 241–307.

Duft, Johannes, *Die Abtei St. Gallen. 1: Beiträge zur Erforschung ihrer Manuskripte* (Sigmaringen, 1990).

Dutton, Paul Edward, *The Politics of Dreaming in the Carolingian Empire* (Lincoln, Nebraska, 1994).

Eckhardt, Karl August, *Die Kapitulariensammlung Bischof Ghaerbalds von Lüttich* (Göttingen, 1955).

Ernst, Raimund, *Die Nordwestslaven und das fränkische Reich* (Berlin, 1976).

Falkenstein, Ludwig, *Der'Lateran'der karolingischen Pfalz zu Aachen* (Cologne, 1966).

Fichtenau, Heinrich, *Das karolingische Imperium* (Zurich, 1949); English trans. *The Carolingian Empire* (Oxford, 1968).

Fleckenstein, Josef, *Die Hofkapelle der deutschen Könige*, vol. 1: *Die karolingische Hofkapelle* (Stuttgart, 1959).

Fleckenstein, Josef, 'Karl der Große und sein Hof', *KdG*, vol. 1, pp. 24–50.

Folz, Robert, *Le Souvenir et la Légende de Charlemagne dans l'Empire germanique médiéval* (Paris, 1950).

Folz, Robert, *L'Idée d'Empire en Occident du Ve au XVe siècle* (Paris, 1953).

Folz, Robert, *Le couronnement impérial de Charlemagne* (Paris, 1964); revised English translation: *The Coronation of Charlemagne* (London, 1974).

Fouracre, Paul, 'Observations on the Outgrowth of Pippinid Influence in the *Regnum Francorum* after the Battle of Tertry (687–715)', *Medieval Prosopography*, vol. 5 (1984), pp. 1–31.

Fouracre, Paul, 'Merovingian History and Merovingian Hagiography', *Past and Present*, vol. 127 (1990), pp. 3–38.

Fouracre, Paul and Gerberding, Richard A., *Late Merovingian France: History and Hagiography 640–720* (Manchester, 1996).

Freeman, Ann, 'Theodulf of Orléans and the *Libri Carolini*', *Speculum*, vol. 32 (1957), pp. 663–705.

Freeman, Ann, 'Further Studies in the *Libri Carolini*', *Speculum*, vol. 40 (1965), pp. 203–89.

Freeman, Ann, 'Further Studies in the *Libri Carolini*, III: the Marginal Notes in *Vaticanus Latinus* 7207', *Speculum*, vol. 46 (1971), pp. 597–612.

Fried, Johannes *et al.* (eds), *794: Karl der Große in Frankfurt am Main* (Sigmaringen, 1994).

Ganshof, François-Louis, *Recherches sur les capitulaires* (Paris, 1958).

Ganshof, François-Louis, 'Charlemagne et les institutions de la monarchie franque', *KdG*, vol. 1, pp. 349–93.

Ganshof. François-Louis, 'Charlemagne et l'administration de la justice dans la monarchie franque', *KdG*, vol. 1, pp. 394–419; both of the above are translated in idem., *Frankish Institutions under Charlemagne* (New York, 1970).

Ganshof, François-Louis, 'Note sur les "Capitula de Causis cum Episcopis et Abbatibus tractandis" de 811', *Studia Gratiana*, vol. 13 (1967), pp. 1–26.

Ganshof, François-Louis, 'Karl der Grosse', *Rheinische Lebensbilder*, vol. 3 (1968), pp. 7–19.

Ganshof, François-Louis, 'L'armée sous les Carolingiens', *Settimane di studio del Centro italiano di studi sull'alto medioevo*, vol. 15 (1968), pp. 109–30.

Ganshof, François-Louis, 'L'historiographie dans la monarchie franque sous les Mérovingiens et les Carolingiens', *Settimane*, vol. 17 (1970), pp. 631–85.

Ganz, David, 'The Preconditions for Caroline Minuscule', *Viator*, vol. 18 (1987), pp. 23–44.

Ganz, David, 'Corbie and Neustrian Monastic Culture', in Hartmut Atsma (ed.), *La Neustrie*, 2 vols (Sigmaringen, 1989), vol. 2, pp. 339–48.

Ganz, David, and Goffart, Walter, 'Charters Earlier than 800 from French Collections', *Speculum*, vol. 65 (1990), pp. 906–32.

Ganz, David, *Corbie in the Carolingian Renaissance* (Sigmaringen, 1990).

Gaskoin, C. J. B., *Alcuin* (Cambridge, 1904).

Gasparri, Stefano, *I Duchi Longobardi* (Rome, 1978).

Gauert, Adolf, 'Noch einmal Einhard und die letzen Merowinger', in Lutz Fenske *et al.* (eds), *Institutionen, Kultur und Gesellschaft im Mittelalter: Festschrift für Josef Fleckenstein zu seinem 65. Geburtstag* (Sigmaringen, 1984), pp. 59–72.

Geary, Patrick J., *Aristocracy in Provence: The Rhône Basin at the Dawn of the Carolingian Age* (Stuttgart/Philadelphia, 1985).

Genrich, Albert, *Die Altsachsen* (Hildesheim, 1981).

Gerberding, Richard A., *The Rise of the Carolingians and the 'Liber Historiae Francorum'* (Oxford, 1987).

Godman, Peter, *Poetry of the Carolingian Renaissance* (London, 1985).

Godman, Peter, *Poets and Emperors: Frankish Politics and Carolingian Poetry* (Oxford, 1986).

Godman, Peter, and Collins, Roger (eds), *Charlemagne's Heir: New Aspects of the Reign of Louis the Pious* (Oxford, 1991).

Gorman, Michael M., 'The Encyclopedic Commentary on Genesis Prepared for Charlemagne by Wigbod', *Recherches Augustiniennes*, vol. 17 (1982), pp. 173–201.

Gorman, Michael M., 'A Carolingian Epitome of St Augustine's *De Genesi ad Litteram'*, *Revue des Etudes Augustiniennes*, vol. 29 (1983), pp. 137–44.

Grabois, Aryeh, 'Charlemagne, Rome and Jerusalem', *Revue belge de philologie et d'histoire*, vol. 59 (1981), pp. 792–809.

Grierson, Philip, *Dark Age Numismatics* (London, 1979).

Grimme, Ernst, Günther, *Der Dom zu Aachen* (Aachen, 1994).

Hallenbeck, Jan T., *Pavia and Rome: The Lombard Monarchy and the Papacy in the Eighth Century* (Philadelphia, 1982).

Halphen, Louis, *Etudes critiques sur l'histoire de Charlemagne* (Paris, 1921).

Halphen, Louis, *Charlemagne et l'empire carolingien* (Paris, 1947); the 1995 Paris reprint contains a bibliographical essay by Pierre Riché on recent work on the period: pp. 513–45.

Hlawitschka, Eduard, 'Die Vorfahren Karls des Großen', *KdG*, vol. 1, pp. 51–82.

Hauck, Karl, 'Paderborn, das Zentrum von Karls Sachsen-Mission 777', in Josef Fleckenstein and Karl Schmid (eds), *Adel und Kirche. Gerd Tellenbach zum 65. Geburtstag dargebracht von Freunden und Schülern* (Freiburg/Basel/Vienna, 1968), pp. 92–140.

Hauck, Karl, 'Karl als neuer Konstantin 777. Die archäologischen Entdeckungen in Paderborn in historischer Sicht', *FS*, vol. 20 (1986), pp. 513–40.

Hauck, Karl, 'Apostolischer Geist im *genus sacerdotale* der Liudigeriden', in K. Hauck *et al.* (eds), *Sprache und Recht: Festschrift für Ruth Schmidt-Wiegand zum 60. Geburtstag* (Berlin/New York, 1986), pp. 191–219.

Heidrich, Ingrid, 'Les maires du palais neustriens du milieu du *VIIe* au milieu du *VIIIe* siècle', in Hartmut Atsma (ed.), *La Neustrie*, 2 vols (Sigmaringen, 1989), vol. 1, pp. 217–30.

Hoffmann, H., *Untersuchungen zur karolingischen Annalistik* (Bonn, 1958).

Hofmann, Hanns, Hubert, 'Fossa Carolina', *KdG*, vol. 1, pp. 437–53.

Jahn, Joachim, *Ducatus Baiuvariorum: Das bairische Herzogtum der Agilolfinger* (Stuttgart, 1991).

Jarnut, Jörg, 'Untersuchungen zu den fränkisch-alemannischen Beziehungen in der ersten Hälfte des 8. Jahrhunderts', *Schweizerische Zeitschrift für Geschichte*, vol. 30 (1980), pp. 7–28.

Jarnut, Jörg, *Geschichte der Langobarden* (Stuttgart, 1982).

Jarnut, Jörg, 'Wer hat Pippin 751 zum König gesalbt?', *FS*, vol. 16 (1982), pp. 45–57.

Jarnut, Jörg, 'Die fruuhmittelalterliche Jagd unter rechts- und sozialgeschichtlichen Aspekten', *Settimane di studio del Centro italiano di studi sull'alto medioevo*, vol. 31 (1985), pp. 765–98.

Jarnut, Jörg, *Agilolfingerstudien* (Stuttgart, 1986).

Jarnut, Jörg, 'Alemannien zur Zeit der Doppelherrschaft der Hausmeier Karlmann und Pippin', in Rudolf Schieffer (ed.), *Beiträge zur Geschichte des Regnum Francorum* (Sigmaringen, 1990), pp. 57–66.

Jarnut, Jörg, 'Genealogie und politische Bedeutung der agilolfingischen Herzöge', *MIöG*, vol. 99 (1991), pp. 1–22.

Jarnut, Jörg, 'Ein Bruderkampf und seine Folgen: Die Krise des Frankenreiches (768–771)', in Georg Jenal (ed.), *Herrschaft, Kirche, Kultur: Beiträge zur Geschichte des Mittelalters* (Stuttgart, 1993), pp. 165–76.

Johannek, Peter, 'Der fränkische Handel der Karolingerzeit im Spiegel der Schriftquellen', in Klaus Düwel *et al.* (eds), *Untersuchungen zu Handel und Verkehr der vor- und frühgeschichtlichen Zeit in Mittel- und Nordeuropa*, vol. IV (Göttingen, 1987), pp. 7–68.

Kaemmerer, Walter, 'Die Aachener Pfalz Karls des Großen in Anlage und Uberlieferung', *KdG*, vol. 1, pp. 322–47.

Kahl, H.-D., 'Karl der Große und die Sachsen: Stufen und Motive einer historischen Eskalation', in H. Ludat and R. Schwinges (ed.), *Politik, Gesellschaft, Geschichtsschreibung. Gießener Festgabe Franticek Graus* (Cologne/Vienna, 1982), pp. 49–130.

Karl der Große: Werk und Wirkung – exhibition catalogue (Aachen, 1965).

Kasten, B., *Adalhard von Corbie. Die Biographie eines karolingischen Politikers und Klostervorstehrs* (Düsseldorf, 1985).

King, P. D., *Charlemagne* (London, 1986).

Kleinklausz, Arthur, *Eginhard* (Paris, 1942).

Krah, Adelheid, 'Zur Kapitulariengesetzgebung in und für Neustrien', in Hartmut Atsma (ed.), *La Neustrie*, 2 vols (Sigmaringen, 1989), vol. 1, pp. 565–82.

Krüger, Karl Heinrich, 'Zur beneventanischen Konzeption der Langobardengeschichte des Paulus Diaconus', *FS*, vol. 15 (1981), pp. 18–35.

Le Jan, Régine, *Famille et pouvoir dans le monde franc (viie-xe siècle)* (Paris, 1995).

Lehmann, Paul, *Erforchung des Mittelalters*, 4 vols (Stuttgart, 1959/60).

Levillain, Léon, *Examen critique des chartes mérovingiennes et carolingiennes de l'Abbaye de Corbie* (Paris, 1902), pp. 77–96.

Levison, Wilhelm, *England and the Continent in the Eighth Century* (Oxford, 1946).

Levison, Wilhelm, 'Zu den Annales Mettenses', in idem., *Aus rheinischer und fränkischer Frühzeit* (Düsseldorf, 1948), pp. 474–83.

Lewis, Suzanne, 'A Byzantine "Virgo Militans" at Charlemagne's Court', *Viator*, vol. 11 (1980), pp. 71–93.

Löwe, Heinz, 'Bonifatius und die bayerisch-fränkische Spannung', *Jahrbuch für fränkische Landesforschung*, vol. 15 (1955), pp. 85–127.

Lot, Ferdinand, 'Le concepte d'empire à l'époque carolingienne', *Mercure de France*, vol. 330 (1947), pp. 413–27.

McKitterick, Rosamond, *The Frankish Church and the Carolingian Reforms, 789–895* (London, 1977).

McKitterick, Rosamond, *The Frankish Kingdoms under the Carolingians* (London, 1983).

McKitterick, Rosamond, *The Carolingians and the Written Word* (Cambridge, 1989).

McKitterick, Rosamond (ed.), *Carolingian Culture: Emulation and Innovation* (Cambridge, 1994).

McKitterick, Rosamond (ed.), *The New Cambridge Medieval History,* vol. II: *c. 700– c. 900* (Cambridge, 1995).

McKitterick, Rosamond, *The Frankish Kings and Culture in the Early Middle Ages* (Aldershot, 1995).

Manacorda, F., *Richerche sugli inizi della dominazione dei Carolingi in Italia* (Rome, 1968).

Manitius, Max, 'Einharts Werke und ihr Stil', *NA*, vol. 7 (1881/2), pp. 517–68.

Marenbon, John, *From the Circle of Alcuin to the School of Auxerre: Logic, Theology and Philosophy in the Early Middle Ages* (Cambridge, 1981).

Maurer, Helmut (ed.), *Die Abtei Reichenau. Neue Beiträge zur Geschichte und Kultur des Inselklosters* (Sigmaringen, 1974).

Mayr-Harting, Henry, 'Charlemagne as Patron of Art', *Studies in Church History*, vol. 28 (1992), pp. 43–77.

Mayr-Harting, Henry, 'Charlemagne, the Saxons and the Imperial Coronation of 800', *English Historical Review*, vol. 111 (1996), pp. 1113–33.

Metz, Wolfgang, *Das karolingische Reichsgut* (Berlin, 1960).

Meyvaert, Paul, 'The Authorship of the *Libri Carolini*; Observations Prompted by a Recent Book', *Revue Bénédictine*, vol. 89 (1979), pp. 29–57.

Mildenberger, Gerhard, *Germanische Burgen* (Münster, 1978).

Monod, G., *Etudes critiques sur les sources de l'histoire carolingienne*, pt 1 (Paris, 1898).

Mordek, Hubert, 'Karolingische Kapitularien', in H. Mordek (ed.), *Überlieferung und Geltung normativer Texte des frühen und hohen Mittelalters* (Sigmaringen, 1986), pp. 25–50.

Mordek, Hubert, *Biblioteca capitularium regum Francorum manuscripta: Überlieferung und Traditionszusammenhang der fränkischen Herrschererlasse* (Munich, 1995).

Müllejans Hans, (ed.), *Karl der Große und sein Schrein in Aachen* (Aachen, 1988).

Mütterich Florentine, and Weiner, Andreas, *Illuminierte Handschriften der Agilolfinger- und frühen Karolingerzeit* (Munich, 1989).

Nees, Lawrence, *The Tainted Mantle: Hercules and the Classical Tradition at the Carolingian Court* (Philadelphia, 1991).

Nelson, Janet, 'On the Limits of the Carolingian Renaissance', *Studies in Church History*, vol. 14 (1977), pp. 51–69.

Nelson, Janet, 'The Lord's Anointed and the People's Choice: Carolingian Royal Ritual', in David Cannadine and Simon Price (eds), *Rituals of Royalty: Power and Ceremonial in Traditional Societies* (Cambridge, 1987), pp. 137–80.

Nelson, Janet, 'Literacy in Carolingian Government', in Rosamond McKitterick (ed.), *The Uses of Literacy in Early Medieval Europe* (Cambridge, 1990), pp. 258–96.

Nelson, Janet, 'La famille de Charlemagne', *Byzantian*, vol. 61 (1991), pp. 194–212.

Nelson, Janet, 'Gender and Genre in Women Historians of the Early Middle Ages', in J.-P. Genet (ed.), *L'historiographie médiévale en Europe* (Paris, 1991), pp. 149–63.

Nelson, Janet, *The Frankish World 750–900* (London, 1996).

Nelson, Janet, 'Making a Difference in Eighth-Century Politics: the Daughters of Desiderius', in Alexander C. Murray (ed.), *After Rome's Fall: Narrators and Sources of Early Medieval History*.

Nicoll, W. S. M., 'Some Passages in Einhard's *Vita Karoli* in Relation to Suetonius', *Medium Ævum*, vol. 44 (1975), pp. 117–20.

Pohl, Walter, *Die Awaren. Ein Steppenvolk in Mitteleuropa 567–822 n. Chr.* (Munich, 1988).

Pohl, Walter, *Die Awarenkriege Karls des Großen 788–803* (Vienna, 1988).

Pohl, Walter, 'Ergebnisse und Probleme der Awarenforschung', *MIöG*, vol. 96 (1988), pp. 247–74.

Rabe, Susan A., *Faith, Art and Politics at Saint-Riquier* (Philadelphia, 1995).

Rauch Chr, and Jacobi, H. J., *Ausgrabungen in der Königspfalz Ingelheim 1909–1914* (Mainz, 1976).

Reuter, Timothy, 'Plunder and Tribute in the Carolingian Empire', *Transactions of the Royal Historical Society*, 4th series, vol. 35 (1985), pp. 75–94.

Reindel, Kurt, 'Bayern im Karolingerreich', *KdG*, vol. 1, pp. 220–46.

Riché, Pierre, 'De la Haute Epoque à l'expansion du réseau monastique', in André Vernet (ed.), *Histoire des bibliothèques françaises* (Paris, 1989), pp. 15–27.

Rouche, Michel, 'Les Aquitains ont-ils trahi avant la bataille de Poitiers?', *Le Môyen Age*, vol. 1 (1968), pp. 5–26.

Salrach, Josep M., *El procés de formació nacional de Catalunya (segles VIII–IX)*, 2 vols (Barcelona, 1978).

Saurma-Jeltsch, Lieselotte E. (ed.), *Karl der Große als vielberufener Vorfahr* (Sigmaringen, 1994).

Schieffer, Rudolf, *Die Karolinger* (Stuttgart, 1992).

Schieffer, Theodor, *Winfrid-Bonifatius und die christliche Grundlegung Europas* (Freiburg, 1954).

Schrimpf, Gangolf (ed.), *Kloster Fulda in der Welt der Karolinger und Ottonen* (Frankfurt am Main, 1996).

Semmler, Josef, 'Zur pippinidisch-karolingischen Sukzessionkrise 714–723', *DA*, vol. 33 (1977), pp. 1–36.

Smith, Julia M. H., *Province and Empire: Brittany and the Carolingians* (Cambridge, 1992).

Staab, Franz (ed.), 'Die Pfalz. *Probleme einer Begriffsgeschichte vom Kaiserpalast auf dem Palatin bis zum heutigen Regierungsbezirk* (Speyer, 1990).

Stoclet, Alain, 'Gisèle, Kisyla, Chelles, Benediktbeuron et Kochel. Scriptoria, bibliothèques et politique à l'époque carolingienne', *Revue Bénédictine*, vol. 96 (1986), pp. 250–70.

Stoclet, Alain, *Autour de Fulrad de Saint-Denis (v. 710–784)* (Geneva, 1993).

Sullivan, Richard E., 'The Carolingian Age: Reflections on its Place in the History of the Middle Ages', *Journal of Medieval and Renaissance Studies*, vol. 18 (1988), pp. 267–306.

Sullivan, Richard E., *Christian Missionary Activity in the Early Middle Ages* (Aldershot, 1994).

Tellenbach, Gerd, 'Vom karolingischen Reichsadel zum deutschen Reichsfürstand', in Theodor Mayer (ed.), *Adel und Bauern im deutschen Staat des Mittelalters* (Leipzig, 1943), pp. 22–73.

Treadgold, Warren, *The Byzantine Revival 780–842* (Stanford, 1988).

Treffort, Cécile, *L'église carolingienne et la mort* (Lyon, 1996).

Ullmann, Walter, *The Carolingian Renaissance and the Idea of Kingship* (Cambridge, 1969).

Verbruggen, Jean François, 'L'armée et la strategie de Charlemagne', *KdG*, vol. 1, pp. 420–36.

Wallace-Hadrill, J. M., *The Long-haired Kings and Other Studies in Frankish History* (London, 1962).

Wallace-Hadrill, J. M., *Early Germanic Kingship in England and on the Continent* (Oxford, 1971).

Wallace-Hadrill, J. M., *Early Medieval History* (collected articles) (Oxford, 1975).

Wallace-Hadrill, J. M., *The Frankish Church* (Oxford, 1983).

Wallace-Hadrill, J. M., *The Barbarian West 400–1000* (rev. edn, Oxford, 1996).

Wallach, Luitpold, *Alcuin and Charlemagne* (2nd edn, Ithaca, 1968).

Wallach, Luitpold, *Diplomatic Studies in Latin and Greek Documents from the Carolingian Age* (Ithaca/London, 1977).

Wattenbach-Levison, *Deutschlands Geschichtsquellen im Mittelalter*, vol. 2: *Die Karolinger vom Anfang des 8. Jahrhunderts bis zum Tode Karls des Großen* (Weimar, 1953).

Weinrich, L., *Wala, Graf, Mönch und Rebell* (Berlin, 1963).

Werner, Karl Ferdinand, 'Bedeutende Adelsfamilien im Reich Karls des Großen', *KdG*, vol. 1, pp. 83–143; English trans. in Timothy Reuter, 'Important Noble Families in the Kingdom of Charlemagne', pp. 137–201.

Werner, Karl Ferdinand, '*Missus-Marchio-Comes.* entre l'administration centrale et l'administration locale de l'empire carolingien', in Werner Paravicini and K. F. Werner (eds), *Histoire comparée de l'administration (IVe–XVIIIe siècles)* (Sigmaringen, 1980), pp. 191–239.

Werner, Matthias, *Adelsfamilien im Umkreis der frühen Karolinger* (Sigmaringen, 1982).

Whittow, Mark, *The Making of Orthodox Byzantium, 600–1025* (London, 1996).

Wieczorek, Alfred, *et al.* (eds), *Die Franken. Wegbereiter Europas*, 2 vols (Mainz, 1996).

Winkelmann, Wilhelm, *Beiträge zur Frühgeschichte Westfalens* (Münster, 1984).

Wolfram, Herwig, *Intitulatio 1: lateinische Königs- und Fürstentitel bis zum Ende des 8 Jahrhunderts* (Vienna, 1967).

Wolfram Herwig (ed.), *Intitulatio 2: lateinische Herrscher- und Fürstentitel im neunten und zehnten Jahrhundert* (Vienna, 1973).

Wolfram Herwig, and Schwarcz, Andreas (eds), *Die Bayern und ihre Nachbarn* (2 vols, Vienna, 1985).

Wolfram, Herwig, *Die Geburt Mitteleuropas. Geschichte Österreichs vor seiner Entstehung* (Berlin, 1987).

Wolfram, Herwig and Pohl, Walter (eds), *Typen der Ethnogenese unter besonderer Berücksichtigung* (2 vols, Vienna, 1990).

Wood, Ian, *The Merovingian Kingdoms, 450–751* (London, 1994).

Wormald, Patrick, '*Lex Scripta* and *Verbum Regis*: Legislation and Germanic Kingship from Euric to Cnut', in P. H. Sawyer and I. N. Wood (eds), *Early Medieval Kingship* (Leeds, 1977), pp. 105–38.

INDEX